COMPETENCY-BASED PERFORMANCE IMPROVEMENT:
A Strategy for Organizational Change

David D. Dubois, Ph.D.

TABLE OF CONTENTS

FIGURES

CHAPTER 5

CHAPTER 7

CHAPTER 8

CHAPTER 9

CHAPTER 10

FOREWORD

Many books have been written about competency and performance improvement. Indeed, these topics seem to be the elusive goals sought by many organizations.

We had the opportunity to meet Dr. Dubois and to speak with him about the work he had been doing in this area. We were impressed by his experience and insight, and actively encouraged him to write this book. We think it will prove to be an outstanding contribution to the literature in the field of Human Resource Development (HRD).

From our conversations with Dr. Dubois, we obtained an important insight which is reflected in this book: the need for a systematic approach to improving performance. We also learned that although individual performance improvement is essential, it must be reinforced by the organization and whatever organizational changes are necessary to ensure its success.

Systems thinking is now more than thirty years old. Unfortunately, it appears that many members of our current generation of HRD practitioners are not familiar with systems theory and how it can be applied to the HRD field. In this book, systems theory is discussed and then applied to performance improvement.

Dr. Dubois also shares with us his research into various models for developing competency-based learning on the job—recent and future. Models are always important and helpful, and we can never have too many of them. It becomes the responsibility of the HRD practitioner to differentiate among those that are useful and those that are not. We are sure that you will find the models presented in this book very useful.

Competency is another area about which much has been written, but with too little of the depth found in this book. To present helpful ideas on competency, Dubois has drawn important materials from a variety of sources and woven it into the model.

The book is not only based on theory and research, but on actual practice and application. It is all too easy to overlook the material at the end of a book, particularly when it merely looks like a compilation of case studies. We suggest you take a lengthy pause after reading the first seven chapters. There is a good deal of provocative material there that you should take time to think about and perhaps even test out. Then, go back to this book and read the last three chapters, which show how the model in the book was applied in three different specific situations.

There is a great deal packed into this book, and you should not be discouraged or overwhelmed by the wealth of material. It is not the kind of book that one can read through easily. There are many challenges to HRD practitioners that will arise from these pages. Take the time to examine them. It will be well worth the effort.

Leonard Nadler   Zeace Nadler

ACKNOWLEDGEMENTS

Completing the work that made this book possible required the generosity, assistance, and goodwill of many persons.

The graphics and the cover design for this book were created and produced by Bernard Lasen. His expertise and effort contributed in many other significant ways to this project. His advice and patience during the revision stages were a tremendous asset.

The preparation of numerous draft versions of the manuscript for this book required able word processing and handling. Robert Reed completed a substantial number of those tasks through the preparation of the final manuscript, and at times under very difficult circumstances, and in an admirable manner.

Several persons reviewed (without compensation) my materials during their various stages of development. Their contributions of time, expertise, suggestions, and patience significantly contributed to the final results. These persons included Alex Douds, Richard Fischer, William Foster, James Howell, Karin Kolodziejski, Peggy Linden, Patricia McLagan, Leonard Nadler, Zeace Nadler, and Patricia Sweeney.

The job of researching and writing about organization practices was an important part of my work for this project. Many opportunities and obstacles were continuously encountered. My coauthors for the final three chapters of this book, the organizations they represent, and those employed by those organizations, helped make those chapters a reality. These coauthors include Alex Douds (Human Technology, Inc.), Edmund Karoly (Defense Mapping Agency, U.S. Department of Defense), Karin Kolodziejski (Tektronix, Inc.), and Martin Smith (New England Telephone Company).

Obtaining primary information for the topics included in this book was essential to its successful completion. Several individuals made special efforts to help me in this regard. Those persons included Richard Boyatzis, Barry Brown, Martha Cantwell, Nancy Dixon, William Foster, George O. Klemp, Jr., Karin Kolodziejski, Genie LaBorde, Bernard Lasen, John Lawson, Patricia McLagan, Michael O'Brien, Nancy Olson, and Chief Petty Officer W. Posey (USN).

Words of appreciation for my editor, Mary George, are certainly deserved. Her contributions to this project are visibly evident, as you will soon recognize. She gave me sensitive, insightful, and constructive criticism that *significantly* changed the course of the work.

My publisher, Robert W. Carkhuff, provided support in many ways when I needed it. I especially thank him for his "low alpha-wave" way of working with me; he did a lot of listening and a lot more intelligent responding. He and his staff at

HRD Press have been resourceful and reliable "colleagues" throughout the completion of this project.

Although extensive effort was expended to acknowledge the sources of my material, any attempt I might make to thank, by name, all those persons who contributed their ideas and experiences to the contents of this book will be incomplete. Certain ideas and opinions expressed in this book were influenced, reworked, and enhanced many times over by the information I read or heard from literally dozens of practitioners and theorists. Your contributions made this a better product, and for them I thank each of you.

Finally, I want to thank my mother, Edith Dubois, for her many unselfish deeds and kind words during the completion of this project. Her contributions improved the quality of the journey.

ABOUT THE AUTHOR

Dr. Dubois brings more than thirty years of training and experience in the practice of human resource development (HRD) to this book.

He received his bachelor's degree in mathematics and education at Indiana University of Pennsylvania (Indiana, PA), and holds a master's degree in mathematics and education as well as an interdisciplinary Ph.D. in science education (earth sciences) from The American University (Washington, DC). He earned a postgraduate master's degree in counseling from Virginia Polytechnic Institute and State University (Blacksburg, VA). In recognition of his academic and professional achievements, he has been elected to membership in the Honor Society of Phi Kappa Phi, Sigma Xi, and Phi Delta Kappa.

Dubois has very diverse work experience in HRD, including full-time employment by the Montgomery County (MD) Public Schools, The George Washington University (Institute for Educational Leadership), and Headquarters of the U.S. Postal Service. He has served in numerous leadership capacities in HRD with those organizations.

Dr. Dubois was selected to be a National Education Policy Fellow (1979-1980) with the Institute for Educational Leadership (at that time associated with The George Washington University) through national competition. In that capacity, he was a senior education policy fellow with the U.S. Department of Education at the National Center for Education Statistics, where he was responsible for work with national bilingual and vocational education research issues.

His professional HRD experience also includes several years as an Adjunct Professor and Research Assistant Professor at The American University. He has numerous published articles in internationally recognized, professional journals, on topics that range from human resources to oral and maxillofacial medicine and surgery.

Dubois is presently a consultant to individuals and organizations in the public, private, academic, and nonprofit sectors. He has been an invited presenter and workshop leader on HRD topics for organizations. Among them are the National Society for Performance and Instruction, the Executive Study Conference, University of Michigan, Ford Motor Company (World Headquarters), State University of New York at Albany, American Society for Training and Development (national conference), the American Counseling Association (national conference), and the Institute for Educational Leadership, Inc.

David Dubois holds active memberships in the American Society for Training and Development, the National Society for Performance and Instruction, the American Counseling Association, the National Career Development Association, the District of Columbia Mental Health Counselors Association, and the Maryland Association for Counseling and Development. He is both a member of the Professional Standards Committee of the National Career Development Association and a member of the Publishing Review Committee for the American Society for Training and Development.

INTRODUCTION TO COMPETENCY-BASED PERFORMANCE IMPROVEMENT

PROLOGUE

Is it easy for you to identify with one or more aspects of the vignettes described below? If you answer "Yes" and if you also have a role in helping an organization create, implement, or manage human resource development (HRD) opportunities, then you will find this book helpful.

Vignette 1

You are the chief executive officer (CEO) or the president of an organization. Your HRD department offers an impressive array of courses and other HRD opportunities. HRD serves clients representing a large number of organization occupations and work units which collectively contribute to the success of the organization.

You are now reviewing the HRD budget for the coming year, along with other department proposals. Several questions about the HRD function come to mind as you deliberate on the commitment of resources to HRD. How is HRD linked to helping the organization meet its business objectives? Each year the HRD budget increases and the additional resources are largely invested in doing more training. How will more training influence employee competence and the achievement of corporate objectives? You question whether HRD programs (and training in particular) are conceptually integrated, systematic, and efficient—i.e., are they as cost-effective as they could be? Are the HRD training and education curricula integrated within and across work units and levels of occupations? Are content areas of the curricula over or under emphasized? Are there gaps or duplications in the curricula?

In other words, are training and education opportunities targeted to produce optimally competent workers at the lowest possible cost? Would it be financially advantageous for the organization to commit additional resources to HRD, especially to the training and education functions? How can the effectiveness and efficiency of the organization's training and education programs be improved, thereby reducing their cost and improving the probability of enhanced employee competence?

Vignette 2

As the Vice President (or the training/education manager) for HRD in your organization, you respond to "dual client" relationships. First, you must satisfy your firm's department managers, who are the leaders in policy and organization operations for the organization. Second, you must concurrently satisfy field operations managers and their subordinates, located over a wide geographic area. As its major responsibility, the HRD department designs and delivers formal training and some education for field operations. Your department also creates and maintains responsibility for other HRD opportunities related to corporate training and education. Accordingly, HRD has two dimensions in your organization. First, it is a policy support "arm" for "corporate." Second, it has a pivotal role in facilitating employee performance improvement. The two clients usually do not agree on what should or will be accomplished through HRD. Demands from both clients for new, additional, or modifications to existing training are constant. The types and forms of training needed are changing in response to perceived and real employee competence *needs*, and these are driven by business competition.

It's somewhat a paradox that despite the demands for training and education, organization support for HRD is less than desired. It is not unusual to hear concerns that employees consistently do not understand how the training they receive can be used to improve their job performance. One explanation might be that the HRD program content is driven by the results of limited front-end analyses. "Wants" and "needs" tend to become one and the same. Resources are seldom available to do the work the way you know it should be done. Brief front-end analysis reports are drafted following hurriedly completed performance analyses, job reviews, and the collection of limited information on the trainees. HRD staff have a limited view of the meaning of "competence." For them, competence means that employees "know" certain things about their job, and "skill development" activities are generally reserved for training technical employees in the psychomotor domain of their job. The critical "mindsets" which employees need to perform their jobs in an exemplary rather than a mediocre manner tend to be ignored or are given minimal attention in the department curricula. The department's training and education curricula also lack conceptual cohesiveness. Students express their annoyance about content repetition across courses. It appears that the content is not located in the curriculum when employees most need it, and the content is repeated again and again in other curriculum elements.

Paradoxically, each year the training and education budgets increase. About 80 percent of the budget increase that you plan to request next year will be committed to additional training activities. Your request will probably cause the CEO to ask some difficult questions: How does training contribute to getting competent employee performance at minimum cost? Are we overtraining and/or undertraining? Is the overall HRD curriculum effective and cost-effective, and does the HRD function significantly help the organization meet its business goals? You do not look forward to this year's budget defense session!

Vignette 3

As a professional trainer, you deliver training and education in your position as an employee (or consultant) to the HRD department of a medium-sized international organization. For the courses you teach, you are given an instructor's guide, the student materials, and all other instructional media. You've had neither a role in conducting the front-end needs assessment nor a role in designing the curriculum plan or the instructional strategies prescribed to convey the content.

Students remark that you are doing a great job, but that the courses are too "theory-based." Translated, this means that they do not understand how to apply the course content to improve their job performance. Most students report that it will be next to impossible for them to implement what they experience in training while on the job because they are unable to make the transition from "theory to practice." Opportunities for the learners to receive training performance feedback are very limited by the instructional designs. The courses you teach are largely centered on developing trainees' job knowledge. The instructional activities do not include opportunities for the employees to demonstrate that they have acquired critical job competencies while in the classroom. In summary, formal training does not appear to help employees become competent in critical areas of their job while they are in training.

Elements of these vignettes were taken from three levels of a composite of organizations, including for-profit and nonprofit businesses, and government agencies. They describe situations in HRD practice that are typical (to one degree or another) of most organizations which sponsor HRD opportunities. They suggest numerous issues of effectiveness and efficiency in the HRD function. Even limited, small-scale HRD programs in organizations can be adversely impacted by effectiveness and efficiency issues of the type depicted in the vignettes.

Several factors, some of which are not under the control of HRD managers and staff, influence the potential effectiveness and efficiency of organization-based HRD. However, if its managers care enough, the HRD function can gain and maintain firm control of its performance improvement curricula, of how those curricula are translated into instructional programs, and of how its clients perceive the contributions of HRD to organization effectiveness or profitability. This book will help you learn how to design and deliver effective and efficient performance improvement programs that enhance employees' job competence in ways that contribute to the achievement of an organization's strategic goals or objectives.

DEVELOPING A COMPETENCE PERSPECTIVE

In order to provide you with a context for the concepts and processes that you will encounter throughout this book, some basic definitions, concepts, and an overall "competence perspective" are presented in this section.

Human resource development (HRD) is an organized set of learning experiences provided by an employer within a specified period of time to bring about the possibility of performance improvement and/or personal growth. Within HRD there are three activity areas: training, education, and development. As defined by Nadler and Nadler (1989):

- *Training* results in learning that is focused on the present job of the learner.

- *Education* is learning focused on a future job for the learner.

- *Development* is learning that is not focused or referenced to any particular job.

In the context of this book, only the *training* or *education* components of HRD, using competency-based processes and procedures, will be emphasized. When the word "development" is used, it is usually because reference is being made to an exemplary practices program that included the word "development" in its title or that included a development component. The exemplary case reports described in chapters 8, 9, and 10 include examples of "training" and "education." In chapters 8 and 10, a combination of both of these dimensions of performance improvement can be observed.

The words "competence," "competency," and "competency model" are problematic. Many definitions and conceptual frameworks have been advanced over the past several years in an attempt to reduce the confusion and, consequently, to improve the state-of-the-practice regarding their use (Folley, 1980; Blank, 1982; Boyatzis, 1982; Zemke, 1982; Marlowe & Weinberg, 1985; McLagan, 1990; and Kolodziejski, 1991).

As a first step toward developing a "competence perspective," let's review Ron Zemke's research findings in this difficult area, and then try to get clear on what a "competency" is, relative to the term's use in this book. (All of the above terms will be formally defined later in this chapter.)

Zemke (1982) interviewed several experts in the field to determine "precisely what makes a competency" (p. 28). He concluded that there was no unified agreement about what makes a competency and what does not:

> Competency, competencies, competency models, and competency-based training are Humpty Dumpty words meaning only what the definer wants them to mean. The problem comes not from malice, stupidity or marketing avarice, but instead from some basic procedural and philosophical differences among those racing to define and develop the concept and to set the model for the way the rest of us will use competencies in our day-to-day training efforts. (p. 28)

It is easiest to think of a "competency" in its most generic form as any underlying characteristic an individual possesses and uses which leads to successful performance in a life role (adapted from Boyatzis, 1982). Variations in this definition are influenced or determined by its application context and procedural and philosophical differences. You can further develop your "competence perspective" by becoming familiar with three major approaches that have been used to identify competencies:

- Modified Task Analysis Approach (MTAA)

- Critical Trait Approach (CTA)

- Situational Approach (SA)

Modified Task Analysis Approach

The MTAA is a slight variation of the task analysis methods that most HRD persons are already familiar with. States Zemke (1982), "This approach is basically the task listing task analysis technique most trainers know, but with some minor niceties added" (pp. 28-29). This approach was explained and exemplified by William Blank (1982). Task-analytic approaches to job or work analysis find their most useful and frequent applications in the concrete, less abstract jobs. The MTAA, therefore, is probably the most appealing approach to use for technical and vocational training or education. These types of training or education are generally laden with cognitive knowledge and skills, as well as with psychomotor competencies. These types of competencies are easily identified by a skilled task analyst.

Since extensive information on this topic already exists in the literature (e.g., Blank, 1982), attention will not be given to MTAA in this book beyond the introduction given here.

Critical Trait Approach

The next approach for competency identification, the Critical Trait Approach (CTA), supports the building of competency models. To use this approach, a practitioner must be able to identify the critical personal traits, behaviors, and other characteristics of employees that distinguish exemplary from average job performance. Unlike task-analytic approaches, the CTA places its emphasis on the underlying personal traits and other characteristics required for successful job performance.

The Job Competence Assessment Method (JCAM) is a critical trait research process which has been developed for determining critical job competencies. JCAM has been modified several times since it was first created by David C. McClelland and his associates at McBer and Company. Chapter 3 includes a detailed explanation of the most recent version of JCAM available at the time of publication.

The use of JCAM to determine and differentiate competencies requires two conditions: that the job already exists within an organization, and that selected job performers are available, with whom specialists can conduct employee interviews. The JCAM was not created to deal with the design of future jobs. The primary data on job performance, which is used to determine the competencies for the job, comes from those who perform the work in an exemplary or average manner. Other information sources are tapped and used, however, in order to complete the JCAM. A major research task in executing JCAM is to determine what competencies the exemplary performers possess and use that distinguish their performance from that of the average performers.

The CTA raises certain problematic issues.

First, the definition of a trait is at issue. The use of the word "trait" (or "traits") is often misinterpreted. States Zemke (1982), "Most psychology texts define a trait as 'a relatively permanent and enduring quality that a person shows in most situations'" (p. 29). For those who generally align themselves with the CTA school of thought, traits are only a part of the competence picture. Zemke (1982) quotes

James A. Burruss on this point as follows: "A finished competency description contains more than traits. It usually includes skills and abilities as well as motivation patterns and traits. But is our [McBer and Company's] view that even traits can be modified and developed" (p. 29).

Second, there is also a misperception among at least some practitioners that the CTA ignores or altogether dismisses paying analytic attention to the job tasks and activities an employee performs. For persons who hold this misperception, either a "task-analytic" approach or a "competencies" approach is elected; to them, the situation is reduced to an "either-or," rather than to a "both-and," situation. Yet even just a cursory review of the limited literature available on the details of CTA makes it abundantly clear that there is a relationship between one's personal competencies and the performance of job tasks and activities. Simplistically stated, employees' acquired competencies drive their capability to perform job tasks and activities.

CTA and other approaches related to CTA embrace and emphasize focusing attention on the long-term endurance and value of human competencies rather than placing an emphasis on, and confidence in, an individual's ability to perform a set of job tasks and activities in the present. The contemporary *and growing* trend toward instability in employees' job tasks and activities, and the requirement that employees acquire and apply transferrable job competencies, could account for the recent increase in interest in competency-based performance improvement applications in organizations. It is becoming a strategic way of life for some HRD practitioners who must deal with increasing amounts of job chaos in their organizations!

CTA can be applied to concrete jobs (e.g., assembly-line work) as well as to abstract jobs (e.g., management). However, CTA is especially useful for defining the competencies for professional, managerial, and executive roles—in general, jobs of a more abstract, rather than a concrete, nature.

Situational Approach

The third technique for identifying competencies and creating competency models is Patricia McLagan's Situational Approach (SA). As with other approaches, it has been refined since it was reported by Zemke in 1982. Her experiences with job competency modeling recently appeared in an article on a flexible approach to job design and competency modeling (McLagan, 1990).

If any of the three approaches brings an element of unity and eclecticism to the competency modeling process, it would probably be the SA. The exact methods and techniques used during a SA application largely depend upon how concrete or abstract the job is, whether the job already exists in the organization, and whether a set of related jobs are under analysis for their component competencies. Zemke (1982) quotes McLagan as follows: "You can't prescribe one look for a competency model or one method for developing them . . . . High-level jobs are very abstract and require special approaches. Lower level jobs are much more concrete and the competency models for them look like task analyses" (p. 30).

McLagan's ongoing work with the SA has led her to refine her initial concept of a competency. In 1982, she used the following definition: "[A competency] is a capability of an individual which relates to superior performance in a role or job. It may be a knowledge, skill, intellectual strategy or a cluster of all three that may apply to one or many work units. The level of generality (scope) of a competency statement depends on its intended uses" (Zemke, 1982, p. 30). In 1990, McLagan defined a competency as "a personal capability that is critical to the production of a quality [job] output or outputs . . . . We have found five categories of competencies to be useful . . . . Three are skill or capability categories: physical, inter- and intrapersonal, and cognitive process. Two are knowledge categories: broad business/industry knowledge and specialist knowledge" (McLagan, 1990, p. 374).

One of the distinguishing features of the SA is its flexibility. McLagan, quoted by Zemke (1982), sums it up in this way:

> Our approach is somewhat anthropological in nature. We use a number of data-gathering methods and try to triangulate on the critical competencies . . . . Our associates work with the people who determine the parameters of the job and who can tell us what the job produces that is of value to the organization . . . . We are trying to communicate the key themes that explain excellence in behavior in the organization . . . . So the terms we use create a language about performance for people to use in the organization. That language has to be acceptable and comfortable to users. The competency model has to be written within the users' scope of thinking. (pp. 30, 31)

The SA is described in detail in chapter 3. In this chapter, you will also find a generic set of steps for taking McLagan's current approach to flexible job design and competency modeling (see McLagan, 1990).

Up to this point, certain key words and phrases have been used, whose general meanings were sufficient for a brief introduction to the competence scenario. The section which follows formally defines how these words and phrases, as well as others, will be used in the main body of this book.

DEFINITIONS

In light of the information provided thus far, it will be useful and advantageous to use the following definitions for the key terms and phrases in this book:

- **Job competence.** Job competence is an employee's *capacity to meet (or exceed) a job's requirements by producing the job outputs* at an expected level of quality within the constraints of the organization's internal and external environments.

- **Job competency.** A job competency is an *underlying characteristic of an employee (i.e., motive, trait, skill, aspects of one's self-image, social role, or a body of knowledge)* which results in effective and/or superior performance in a job (Boyatzis, 1982, pp. 20-21).

- **Competency model.** A competency model includes *those competencies that are required for satisfactory or exemplary job performance* within the context of a person's job roles, responsibilities and relationships in an organization and its internal and external environments (adapted from Boyatzis, 1982).

- **Job competency menu.** A job competency menu *lists all the competencies that are important* for the successful production and delivery of the entire range of an organization's job outputs (McLagan, 1990, p. 374).

- **Curriculum.** A curriculum consists of *a system of performance improvement opportunities* (such as courses, programs, learning intervention, or other forms of performance improvement opportunities), the *content specifications* for them, and a *conceptual framework* for linking the opportunities in a sequential manner which will provide efficient and effective learning opportunities for employees.

- **Competency-based curriculum.** A competency-based curriculum is one whose *content specifications are defined in competence terms*, consistent with the definitions above.

THE HRD CHALLENGE IN ORGANIZATIONS

The collective experience of many persons in organization HRD, reflected by the vignettes that opened this introduction, lead to the following conclusions:

- HRD is not always perceived as being linked to developing the employee competencies most needed to help an organization meet its strategic business or organization goals and objectives.

- HRD does not consistently receive the level of senior management visibility, endorsement, and support which is required in order for it to have optimal impact on improving employees' job competence and, subsequently, their job performance.

- HRD curricula (if one exists) and the instructional programs or learning opportunities that result from them often lack conceptual and cohesive integration. They are oftentimes not developed in a systematic manner. This deficit of curriculum integration results in reduced cost-effectiveness and carries with it a potential for lost opportunities to achieve competent employee performance. An expenditure of employees' time away from their jobs to participate in training or education that might result in only minimal (or no) value-added contribution to organization objectives is hardly defensible at any level of an organization.

- HRD does not consistently and explicitly acknowledge, include, and integrate a "total corporate" or strategic organization perspective into its curricula, learning activities, and instructional implementation processes. Oftentimes, HRD is not explicitly linked to the guiding principles and norms of the organization. This can result in training or education which is viewed by employees and their managers as unrealistic, esoteric, or unnecessary.

- Curriculum planning—if it is done at all—is often hampered by not having a set of guiding principles for the design, delivery, evaluation, and management of an organization's performance improvement programs.

- HRD curricula and the instruction which results from them frequently focus on only the knowledge or skills that employees require to complete job tasks and activities. This is not a composite picture of *competent* performance by any means. Job competence is a complex phenomenon. Other underlying personal characteristics that employees need for successful job performance are often only minimally addressed or are altogether ignored as key components of the performance improvement process. Consequently, employees return to the workplace with competency gaps that should have been closed during the performance improvement experience.

• Upon their return to the workplace, employees do not always recognize ways to apply to their jobs the training or education content they have received. This is partially due to the fact that classroom and other types of training or education activities do not always reflect the complete requirements for competent job performance. Classroom experiences are frequently too heavily invested in "learning about" the job (Boyatzis, 1982). In fact, what the HRD professional actually intends to do is to provide these employees with experiences in thinking, feeling, and acting competently through their acquisition of global job competence. However, the overall approach was created with a limited view of the performance improvement requirements.

Many HRD professionals are concerned about these issues and are looking for ways to solve these problems, or at least to minimize their negative, nonproductive effects within their organizations. One way they can begin to address these problems is by ensuring that their performance improvement opportunities are competency-based *and* that the strategic relationship of those opportunities are clear organization-wise. This book was written with the primary purpose of helping HRD practitioners solve these problems.

THE GOALS OF THIS BOOK

An objective of the HRD systems described in this book is to achieve competent employee performance that contributes to meeting an organization's strategic goals and objectives in effective and efficient ways. The competency-based performance improvement systems which result from the application of the Strategic Systems Model are consistent with a model of human performance which recognizes and incorporates the complex relationships among individual, work-group, and organization performance. Curriculum planning and learning opportunities which result from those plans are created, implemented, evaluated, and maintained in a systematic manner. They are based upon systems theory, and they are committed to locating and utilizing the most cost-effective solutions to human performance problems (Rothwell & Kazanas, 1992, p. 3).

The professional literature provides little help to those who need to understand, plan, create, implement, and evaluate effective and efficient *competency-based* performance improvement systems. Zemke (1982) put it this way: "For all the rhetoric about the benefits of competencies and competency-based training, few working trainers are exactly sure what the experts mean when they start praising and promoting competencies" (p. 28). The situation does not appear to have significantly improved over the past ten years, despite a growing interest in competency-based programs. Given this serious shortfall, this book was written to

1. State and explain key concepts for competency-based performance improvement in organizations;

2. Describe the application and implementation of the concepts, using a systems approach to performance improvement in organizations; and

3. Illustrate the implementation of the concepts and techniques in three very different organization settings, including a Fortune 500 company, a large regional public utility, and a Federal high-tech agency.

Quite early in this project, I decided to focus on examples and illustrations of the concepts in the area of competency-based management and executive performance improvement. There were several reasons for this decision.

First, descriptions and examples of competency-based training designs for concrete or less abstract jobs abound in human resource development books and other literature. In light of this, it hardly seemed necessary to illustrate those ideas once again.

Second, by comparison, little *in-depth* information has been published on the application methods and experiences of those who have used the CTA and the SA methods. Managerial, executive, and professional jobs are rich application areas where some HRD professionals have truly struggled with the issues found in this book—and in many cases, with successful outcomes. What has been published on these successful outcomes stops short of providing the types of information, guidance, and direction which practitioners need in order to utilize the information in their own work.

Third, management occupations, in particular, are undergoing a massive revolution, consistent with business conditions in a global marketplace and economy. Bolt

(1985) cites several reasons for this, including dramatic increases in external competition, greater demands for productivity, the directions of top management, changing business strategies, worldwide economic conditions, advances in information technology, the changing nature of the workplace, and legislative requirements. Consequently, management training is a very rich application of a competency-based approach. The techniques for a competency-based approach to management training and education included in this book have been successfully applied to other subject-matter areas. Due, however, to the complexities which affect management training and education curricula and program designs in most organizations, and the intense current interest in developing managers for new job roles and requirements, I have emphasized those applications.

In the following chapters, you will be invited to:

- "Think systems" by learning some basic principles of systems theory and observing how they are applied to organization training or education

- Learn how to apply a Strategic Systems Model to create, implement, and maintain effective and efficient competency-based training or education systems in organizations

- Learn how to gain broad-based support within an organization for the training and/or education function(s) by taking a competency-based, systems approach to performance improvement

- Learn how to construct custom competency or performance models or menus for employee job performance

- Learn how to create a competency-based training or education curriculum system

- Learn how to create and implement organization or work unit-based curriculum systems which support the provision and maintenance of continuous-progress, competency-based training or education opportunities for employees

- Learn how to create the raw materials needed for competency-based instruction

- Learn how to monitor, evaluate, and maintain the performance of competency-based training and education systems

- Learn about the experiences and the results achieved by three large organizations (a Fortune 500 company, a large regional public utility, and a technical federal agency) which have created and implemented exemplary competency-based performance improvement systems

HOW TO USE THIS BOOK

The ideas, concepts, and methods found in this book are presented consistent with a Strategic Systems Model for creating and implementing competency-based performance improvement systems. Each key step in the Strategic Systems Model is the focus of a subsequent chapter.

Each chapter builds on the concepts and meanings which preceded it. However, this does not necessarily prevent you from using certain chapters as an individual reference or guide for developing an aspect of a specific application. If you decide to do this, your project must meet the subsystems' conditions and requirements as they are described within the context of the Strategic Systems Model.

This book deals with training and education *systems* as they exist in an organization context. Chapter 1 includes a discussion of systems theory and its application to organization HRD. As you read and apply the concepts found in this book, you must remember that what occurs in one part of an organization's performance improvement system—although initially it might seem insignificant—will impact other parts of the system, and even the larger organization's subsystems and system. Therefore, you must think of the ramifications of any action in a *holistic* rather than *isolated* sense. Beyond paying attention to the need to be comprehensive and precise in carrying out the details of the work, you must also be *systematic* in what you do.

SUMMARY

Several vignettes that illustrate many of the HRD challenges found in organizations today opened this introduction to competency-based performance improvement systems. A "competence perspective" was presented, and several key terms were defined as they will be used throughout this book. The goals of this book and the benefits it offers were presented. Suggestions for its use were included.

REFERENCES

Blank, W. F. (1982). *Handbook for developing competency-based training programs.* Englewood Cliffs, NJ: Prentice-Hall.

Bolt, J. F. (1985, January). A revolution in management training and development. *Training and Development Journal, 39*(1), pp. 11-12.

Boyatzis, R. E. (1982). *The competent manager: A model for effective performance.* New York: John Wiley and Sons.

Elkin, G. (1990). Competency-based human resource development: Making sense of the ideas. *Industrial and Commercial Training, 22*(4), pp. 20-25.

Folley, J. D., Jr. (1980). Identifying competencies. In J. W. Springer (Ed.), *Job performance standards and measures* (ASTD Research Series, Paper No. 4). Madison, WI: American Society for Training and Development.

Kolodziejski, K. (1991). *Competency model? Task analysis? What do I do?* Presentation at the 1991 ASTD National Conference, San Francisco, CA (AudioTape No. 91AST-M10). Alexandria, VA: American Society for Training and Development.

Marlowe, H. A., Jr., & Weinberg, R. B. (1985). *Competence development: Theory and practice in special populations.* Springfield, IL: Charles C. Thomas Publishers.

McLagan, P. A. (1990). Flexible job models: A productivity strategy for the Information Age. In J. P. Campbell and R. J. Campbell & Associates, *Productivity in organizations.* San Francisco, CA: Jossey-Bass.

Nadler, L., & Nadler, Z. (1989). *Human resource development: Concepts and a model.* San Francisco: Jossey-Bass.

Rothwell, W. J., & Sredl, H. J. (1992). *The ASTD guide to professional human resource development roles and competencies, Volume I* (2nd ed.). Amherst, MA: HRD Press.

Zemke, R. (1982, May). Job competencies: Can they help you design better training? *Training, 19*(5), pp. 28-31.

Chapter 1

A MODEL FOR CREATING COMPETENCY-BASED PERFORMANCE IMPROVEMENT IN ORGANIZATIONS

The objective of this chapter is to provide you with a Strategic Systems Model (or plan) for creating competency-based performance improvement programs or interventions in organizations. In order to fully understand the attributes of the Strategic Systems Model, you must first understand basic principles of systems theory in the context of organization HRD. The next section of this chapter includes highlights of those systems principles. The use of systems principles in HRD is illustrated with an application to a hypothetical organization management training and education system. The chapter concludes with a presentation and explanation of the Strategic Systems Model.

SYSTEMS PRINCIPLES AND HRD

The application of the principles of systems theory to the practice of HRD is one area of the profession where leading HRD professionals believe that we are "doing things right." A significant trend in HRD has been the application of systems principles to solving problems in the practice of HRD (e.g., Gradous, 1989; Rothwell

& Kazanas, 1992). A systems approach is a powerful problem-solving mechanism. Consequently, in this book a systems approach has been linked with a competency-based approach to performance improvement as a partial, yet significant, remedy for some of the performance improvement inefficiencies that organizations experience. A competency-based approach coupled with a total organization systems approach to creating and managing performance improvement programs impacts overall efficiencies. Subsequent chapters in this book illustrate ways these efficiencies are achieved. For the present, however, it is important for you to understand key systems principles which are useful in organization HRD practices.

Systems Principles for HRD Practice

Several definitions and explanations of systems and their attributes have recently been offered by HRD practitioners.

Patricia McLagan (in Gradous, 1989) defined a system as "a collection of interdependent, organized parts that work together in an environment to achieve the purpose of the whole" (p. 66).

William Rothwell and H. C. Kazanas (1992) explained that a system is a mechanism which accepts a set of raw materials (e.g., people, capital, information, ingredients), applies activities to those materials in order to increase their value, and results in one or more outputs (e.g., services, finished goods, products) that are released to the environment. Systems are dependent upon their external environment for both their inputs and the reception of their outputs. There is a flow pattern for the inputs and outputs. Most systems include subsystems, which interact with environmental suprasystems—which are systems within a system (pp. 9-11).

Ronald Jacobs (1989) wrote:

> Systems function independently, carrying on interdependent exchanges of information with other systems across boundaries. Systems use information to reform themselves, to respond to change, and to maintain themselves under pressure . . . . Man-made systems are distinguishable from natural systems in that they are goal-oriented and must be intentionally designed and managed to achieve those goals . . . . Systems theory suggests that although problems may differ in the specific content, they are essentially the same in their basic structures. Further, problems within systems have definable causes. The causes may have multiple sources which in turn can be linked to actions that

could be taken to remove the indicators and thus solve the problems . . . . problems are not isolated or random events, but are the result of a set of antecedent conditions that cannot be predicted or controlled. (p. 30)

Patricia McLagan (in Gradous, 1989, pp. 69-76) cited and discussed eight systems processes that are useful to HRD. They are summarized below.

1. Systems tend to move toward balance with their environment and parts of the system tend to work together in particular relationships.

2. Systems require feedback to tell them how the environment is responding to them. Systems also require feedforward, which is information they use for creating goals.

3. Growth is the process of increasing the size of a system by obtaining resources from the environment. If net value is not returned to the environment, then a system becomes limited.

4. All systems have a conversion process. That is, within its environment, there are inputs which are acted upon by the system processes; also, there are outputs which result from the inputs and processes that act upon them.

5. Knowledge exchange is typical of higher-order systems; they have an ability to find and to recognize appropriate information. Information is moved from one part of a system to another.

6. Human and organization systems make executive decisions about what they will become and how. These decisions can change a system's purposes, goals, structures, and processes.

7. Development is the creation of a new capacity in a system, and this increases the cost-benefit ratio of the system outputs.

8. Interventions are deliberate, temporary actions intended to help a system make major changes in its goals, structures, or processes.

For more in-depth coverage of systems theory, see Senge, 1987; vonBertalanffy, 1968; or Gradous, 1987.

Implications

A systems approach to creating performance improvement opportunities has clear implications for instructional professionals for two reasons:

> First, instructional designers recognize the critical importance of adapting to changes in the environment and even anticipating them. Organizational and individual effectiveness depends on how well work results match environmental demands. Hence, one question that should be asked in any performance improvement effort is this: *How much will this project contribute to the organization's ability to adapt to changing environmental conditions?* If the answer is "not much" or "we don't know," then it could well be that performance improvement activities should be directed to other projects. Second, instructional designers recognize that any *corrective* action taken to change one subsystem will affect others. The parts of any organization (system) are as interdependent as strands of a spiderweb.... For example, if a change is made in the kinds of people selected into a job category, it will affect the kind of training they should receive. Large system changes in organizations will have effects that are partially predictable—and partially unpredictable. (Rothwell & Kazanas, 1992, p. 11)

An Illustration of Systems Principles Applied to HRD

Large organizations, in particular, are beginning to adopt (with various degrees of sophistication and success) HRD performance improvement systems that systematically track employees' job performance and progress, identify their needs for professional or other types of growth, and provide them with HRD opportunities from entry level through senior or advanced levels of a job or occupation. As the organization's systems (e.g., recruitment, manufacturing, marketing, operations) change, so must the performance improvement systems also change. Performance improvement systems are created and implemented when they will be the most beneficial for achieving an organization's strategic objectives. A systems approach supports flexibility in both job structuring and the performance improvement opportunities required to maintain and improve employees' competencies. Corrective actions in a subsystem's components are easily recognized and identified for correction. Restructuring is more easily accommodated because the actions that are required are immediately evident.

Management and leadership training and education systems are a useful illustration of the application of systems principles to HRD. In a systems-based management performance improvement scenario, employees are systematically educated or trained for professional roles as managers. An illustration of this follows.

Organizations that have implemented a management training or education system often begin by selecting those employees who are individual contributors and *educating* their employees on the attributes, advantages, and disadvantages of a management career in the organization. This education intervention might include providing aspiring managers with an overview of the organization's management needs and the potential opportunities for growth, advancement, or individual achievement within the strategic context of the organization.

Also, with increasing frequency, organizations are providing their candidates with an assessment of their personal characteristics in the form of factor-analytic scales, which compare the candidates' characteristics with those of others who have been judged as successful managers. This assessment is usually accompanied by an overview of management as it is practiced within the context of the organization's strategic goals and culture. Structured activities or alternative assignments are often provided following formal learning programs that help the management candidate develop job knowledge, managerial skills, and the mindsets required for exemplary managers within the larger organization system.

From a systems perspective, there is a constant information exchange between the organization systems and the competence acquisition and development systems in a program of this sort. The feedback and feedforward of information are critically important aspects of this process. As professional growth occurs, the candidate moves into increasingly larger areas of managerial (or other) responsibility and performance. Knowledge exchange is a major component of the management competency development system.

High-performing or high-promise individual contributors are identified and selected for promotion to initial-level management positions as a result of their successful participation in the pre-management education opportunities described above, and of their willingness to become managers. Next they are formally *trained* as initial-level managers. This process might include an assessment of current supervisory or managerial competence, an analysis of their job performance gaps, and the completion of formal training, on-the-job application exercises, and so forth.

If promoted to a mid-level (or some other) management position, their managerial (rather than supervisory) competence in the new position is assessed, a diagnosis of performance gaps is completed, and one or more training interventions designed to close those gaps are completed. Each subsequent movement among the management occupations could result in the completion of similar activities, each of which constitutes a performance improvement subsystem of a larger HRD system. This systems approach brings subject-matter continuity and efficiency to the performance improvement process. The correct content is presented to the correct employees at the correct or most appropriate time in their career and development cycle.

When the Strategic Systems Model is used to create a competency-based management training system, each level or type of management will usually have its own training subsystem. When an integrated systems approach is used, the management performance improvement system is perceived by organization leaders to be a strategic and an integral business component of the larger organization system it was designed to support. Managers in the organization system must have the competence required to manage in ways that directly contribute to achieving strategic organization goals. The training subsystems, each with its own themes and objectives, are conceptually integrated with one other and with the organization's larger training or education system. Ideally, horizontally and vertically integrated training or education systems which are competency-based should help employees grow in competent performance from where they are at any point in time to where they must be, in an organized, systematic manner.

Management performance improvement systems need to be sufficiently flexible in order to accommodate the training or education of persons who become part of the organization's management cadre at other than entry-level positions. Given the extensive mobility evident in the contemporary business world, management training and education systems must be content-integrated to the degree that they can meet a wide variety of employee performance demands. Current trends in business and other organizations of using "team leadership" roles rather than the more traditional roles of "supervisor" or "manager" further complicate this scenario. A systems approach helps HRD track and solve problems that help them maintain currency in their performance improvement systems, where changing roles are a way of life.

In conclusion, efficient and effective results will be realized by the application of a systems approach to an organization's management performance improvement opportunities. Several of the ideas noted above are well illustrated in a case report by H. Wayne Smith (1985) wherein he describes how a systematic, competency-based approach was taken to design and implement a management development program at Phillips Petroleum Company. Smith's article also includes a discussion of the roadblocks that were encountered and how they were managed.

THE STRATEGIC SYSTEMS MODEL

There has been a slow but steady movement to implement integrated, continuous-progress, and competency-based performance improvement systems in organizations. To date, relatively few organizations have totally invested their energies at this level. My experience in this area indicates that many HRD practitioners do not have the technical competencies that are needed to create, implement, and maintain competency-based training and education systems of the type described here. Those who do embark on this work quickly tend to become entangled in an endless and unproductive web of disagreement on philosophies, definitions, methodologies, and so forth. This book was written to help those who want to create and maintain responsive competency-based performance improvement systems within their organization without getting caught in any (or at least fewer) of those unproductive webs. Very little space is allotted in this book to academic discourse or arguments about the purity of the practices. The methods which are included have been demonstrated to be useful and practical in organization settings. They produce results. (The final three chapters of this book support this assertion.)

A five-step Strategic Systems Model for creating and maintaining competency-based employee performance improvement systems in an organization context is presented in Figure 1.1 on the following page. Because each key step in the model is the focus of a later chapter (chapters 2, 3, 4, 5, and 7), only a brief synopsis of each step is presented here.

Step 1. Front-end Needs Analysis, Assessment, and Planning

In this first step of the application of the Strategic Systems Model, an organization is confronted by a problem or some needs-oriented situation. This need could have been a *reactive* approach to a situation or a set of circumstances either external or internal to the organization, or it might represent a *proactive* initiative that is motivated by a predicted or anticipated situation. In practice, however, an organization's many performance improvement needs tend to be identified in a reactive way, rather than from a proactive posture.

Numerous questions are usually asked and answered at this stage of the application of the Strategic Systems Model. A fairly typical sample includes the following:

- How critical is the perceived need (or needs) to the organization's strategic success?

- What level of investment in performance improvement interventions is warranted in order to achieve the desired job outputs or results?

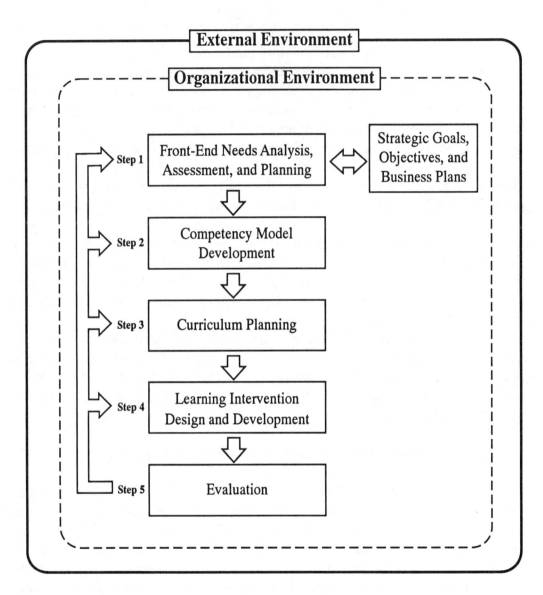

Figure 1.1: Strategic Systems Model for Competency-Based Performance Improvement in Organizations

- Will the ultimate return on the cost of a competency-based performance improvement process be sufficient to warrant the required investment?

- Are there alternatives to HRD-sponsored performance improvement opportunities which could be recommended in order to meet the perceived need(s) or to correct the identified problems?

In the final item above, the analyst asks whether a training or an education solution is the most advantageous solution to the performance problem. Other solutions might be more appropriate and less costly; for example, feedback methods, job performance aids, reward systems, employee selection practices, or organizational redesign (Rothwell & Kazanas, 1992, p. 13). Or analyses might reveal that a combination of training and non-training solutions are needed to correct the observed performance gap or gaps. Each situation must be judged on its own merits.

"Pseudo-needs" are differentiated from "real needs" through information collection, analyses, and assessments. To accomplish this, a strategic management analysis of the situation within the organization context is completed. You will notice from Figure 1.1 that there will always be a two-way information exchange between the planning partners and the organization's strategic goals and objectives. The needs are reviewed, and a broad-based plan is developed to determine how meeting those needs will contribute to the achievement of the organization's strategic management goals.

The work completed at this step of the Strategic Systems Model is a *macro-level* needs analysis. The knowledge, skills, and other underlying characteristics (i.e., competencies) that employees need for successful job performance are not identified in detail at this time. Once a competency model or menu for a job is available, it can be used—with other data—to conduct a *micro-needs* analysis of individual employees' specific needs for performance improvement.

A plan for creating and implementing competency-based training or education opportunities that will address "real" needs is created and agreed to by the planning partners. The client or client group is briefed and appropriate revisions are made. Following any revisions and endorsement, action is taken to implement the plan. In most cases, this will mean researching the job competency requirements for the performance needs for which HRD solutions have been identified as an appropriate performance improvement alternative.

In chapter 2, a detailed discussion of this step is presented.

Step 2. Competency Model Development

The second step of the Strategic Systems Model is to plan and conduct the research needed to identify the job competence requirements and to construct one (or more) competency models for the target population. At this stage, the competencies employees need to successfully achieve the job results are researched and documented. The results of this step must be consistent with the terms of the front-end plan which resulted from Step 1. Recall that a competency model includes, at a minimum, those competencies required for satisfactory and exemplary job performance within the context of an employee's roles, responsibilities, and relationships as they contribute to the achievement of the job results.

A detailed and comprehensive micro-level assessment of the competency needs of the target population can be conducted by using the components of a competency model. These data and their analyses then become the foundation for curriculum planning and the design of performance improvement programs and interventions.

Regardless of the research and design approach that is selected, the resulting competency model must be endorsed by the client (or client group) and senior management. The front-end plans and the results of the competency model research effort become the system inputs to the curriculum planning stage of the Strategic Systems Model.

Competency model technology and its application in an organization are discussed in detail in chapter 3.

Step 3. Curriculum Planning

In this step of the Strategic Systems Model, the job competency requirements and the macro- and micro- level needs analyses are combined and translated into a curriculum plan. Recall the definition of a "curriculum" from the Introduction. A curriculum consists of a system of performance improvement opportunities, the content specifications for them, and a conceptual framework for linking the opportunities in a sequential manner that will provide efficient and effective learning opportunities for employees.

A curriculum can be designed and planned for a single job, for a related class or category of jobs, or for an entire HRD program, encompassing numerous jobs or work roles. If numerous jobs, organization units, or a wide span of control is represented by the competencies, then a sizable system of performance improvement opportunities could result. Consistent with the definition of a curriculum, the performance improvement opportunities must be outlined in relation to the competencies associated with each of them, a conceptual framework must link them, and a sequence for presenting them must be clearly specified.

The types of performance improvement opportunities that will be used to implement the training or education at the next stage of the Strategic Systems Model are included in the curriculum plan. The types of opportunities that are to be made available to employees have resource implications for the HRD department, the client, or the client group, depending on the source(s) of funding for the project. The HRD department must have considerable resources available to them if they intend to design and develop certain types of learning opportunities, such as those that use electronic technologies. In some cases, the HRD department might have only limited resources that can be committed to design and development work. In this case, they might need to rely on purchasing vendor materials or using external vendors to present learning opportunities, or they might arrange for employees to use the services of higher education agencies, such as colleges and universities, as vendors for their performance improvement programs or interventions.

Chapter 4 includes a presentation and discussion of the methods needed for competency-based curriculum planning.

Step 4. Learning Intervention Design and Development

In this step, the competencies and the elements of the curriculum plan are translated into specific, detailed competency-based performance improvement interventions. The learning interventions used to implement the curriculum plan could include, for example, formal courses, seminars, workshops, on-the-job performance improvement opportunities, independent study or reading, correspondence programs, computer-based instruction, or others—either singularly or in combination with one other.

The learning or instructional designs that result from this stage of the work should heavily rely upon the use of learner-centered, rather than teacher-centered, activities; these are activities that require active participation by employees. In a learner-centered environment, employees are responsible for the learning that takes place.

Learning interventions should always be pilot tested before full implementation. The use of a pilot test process is recommended to ensure that the content addresses the competency requirements and the needs of the learners, and that appropriate learning and implementation strategies have been used for the intervention.

Chapter 5 includes guidelines and a discussion of topics related to the design and implementation of competency-based performance improvement interventions or opportunities.

Chapter 6 supports the application of the design and development processes presented in chapter 5 by including the description of a variety of learner-centered strategies that have been found useful for implementing competency-based performance improvement interventions. Traditional approaches to employee training and education rely upon instructor-centered rather than learner-centered activities. The learning strategies that are suggested for use throughout this book rely on the use of learner-centered activities. In a learner-centered activity, the employee is an actively engaged student of the learning process rather than a passive observer of it.

Step 5. Evaluation

In this step of the Strategic Systems Model, you will create, implement, and use the findings of one or more evaluation subsystems to monitor the responsiveness of the performance improvement system to employees' job performance needs and the strategic needs of the organization. All elements of the performance improvement system are likely candidates for evaluation.

Two levels of planning and development are required at the evaluation stage of the Strategic Systems Model. First, it is necessary to create a broad-scope evaluation plan. Chapter 7 includes a model that will help you organize the various components of the plan into a cohesive, systems-driven evaluation mechanism. Once the conceptual plan is completed, evaluation projects are designed and completed in accordance with the details of the plan. An additional evaluation model, describing four types of evaluation studies that can be used for any training or education system, is presented and explained. Case examples that illustrate its application are either discussed or referenced.

A wide variety of potential assessment outcomes is possible, depending upon how the evaluation subsystem is designed and implemented. The strengths of, and the needs for, improvement in the practices under investigation should result from an analysis of the information that is collected.

Finally, it is essential to feed back the findings from the evaluation subsystem(s) to *all* of the other subsystems included in the Strategic Systems Model. A review of Figure 1.1 reveals an important relationship among the evaluation subsystem and the other subsystems of the Strategic Systems Model. Notice that the evaluation subsystem outputs become inputs to all of the remaining subsystems of the model. If an evaluation subsystem is comprehensively and carefully designed, it will be capable of revealing numerous changes associated with the organization systems and the performance improvement systems that were created to support the organization systems. These could include, for example, changes in the competency requirements for a job, an instructional intervention that is not effective, shifts in strategic emphases of the organization since the intervention was researched or designed, and so forth.

Tracking, analyzing, and evaluating the reasons for, and the impacts of, a shift in system performance can be very difficult and laborious work in the absence of systematically planned and obtained evaluation results. This is especially true for training or education systems in very large and/or geographically diverse organizations, or where decentralized delivery of the system intervention(s) is required. The breadth and depth of the evaluation subsystem will oftentimes be determined by the resources that the organization makes available to HRD for evaluation, as well as by the organization's degree of interest and commitment to evaluation as a strategy for constant and continuous improvement.

The evaluation of competency-based performance improvement systems is explained in chapter 7.

Improved Efficiency and Effectiveness

Overall gains in the efficiency and effectiveness of an organization's performance improvement efforts can be realized through the application of the Strategic Systems Model. Specifically:

- A rationale underlying the Strategic Systems Model is that all employee training or education that is sponsored by an organization is committed to improving employees' job performance in ways that will help the organization achieve its strategic objectives.

- The performance improvement interventions are research-based and emphasize the job competencies that exemplary performers use for successful job performance. The underlying high pay-off attributes of employees are identified and performance improvement is focused on helping employees acquire those attributes. Consequently, time is not wasted having employees develop attributes that do not contribute to exemplary performance.

- Competency-based training or education systems of the type described in this book are "self-marketing" because the key stakeholders and clients are involved at every stage of development. This enhances the transfer of learning potential between the HRD function and employees' managers.

- The definitions of the job competency models or menus are an outgrowth of the organization culture, norms, standards, and expectations. This improves the probability of their acceptance within the organization.

- The Strategic Systems Model can be applied in a flexible manner so that a variety of organization needs can be addressed and met.

• It ensures the creation of learning experiences that are highly specific to employees' job performance requirements and that are available at the time when they are most critically needed; thus, the probability of training transfer is improved.

• The approach supports the application and use of a wide variety of learning strategies, techniques, materials, media, and technologies.

• The approach is especially useful for creating training or education systems for developing employees' "soft" competencies—which are typical of jobs with a high percentage of affective performance requirements.

• The approach fully supports the use of a wide variety of evaluation procedures and practices.

• The approach can be used to create training or education systems in organizations of any size or breadth.

SUMMARY

Organizations are facing declining HRD budgets and constant or increasing requirements for performance improvement programs targeted at helping employees achieve strategic organization objectives. The application of the Strategic Systems Model is one way an organization can improve on both the efficiency and effectiveness of its expenditures for performance improvement. Application of the Strategic Systems Model gently forces organization players who have a stake in its performance improvement systems to acknowledge, confront, and attempt to resolve the issues or factors that impact the design and delivery of job performance improvement learning opportunities.

REFERENCES

Gradous, D. B. (Ed.). (1989). *Systems theory applied to human resource development: Theory-to-practice monograph*. Alexandria, VA: American Society for Training and Development.

Jacobs, R. L. (1989). Systems theory applied to human resource development. In D. B. Gradous (Ed.), *Systems theory applied to human resource development: Theory-to-practice monograph*. Alexandria, VA: American Society for Training and Development.

Rothwell, W. J., & Kazanas, H. C. (1992). *Mastering the instructional design process: A systematic approach*. San Francisco: Jossey-Bass.

Senge, P. (1987). Catalyzing systems thinking within organizations. In F. Masarik (Ed.), *Advances in organization development*. Norwood, NJ: Ablex.

Smith, H. W. (1985, July). Implementing a management development program. *Personnel Administrator, 30* (7), pp. 75-86.

vonBertalanffy, L. (1968). *General systems theory: Foundations, development, applications*. New York: Braziller.

Chapter 2

NEEDS ANALYSIS, ASSESSMENT, AND PLANNING IN A COMPETENCY-BASED FORMAT

The context for, and the use of, front-end needs analysis, assessment, and planning via a collective organization approach are explained in this chapter. Next, the steps for completing a front-end needs analysis, assessment, and planning project are presented and explained. Finally, suggestions are provided for doing strategic management analyses using a "total organization" approach.

IN RELATION TO THE STRATEGIC SYSTEMS MODEL

Needs are identified, analyzed and assessed, and plans for employee performance improvement are made as an outgrowth of an organization's business plans and strategic objectives. This relationship is highlighted in Figure 2.1, on the following page. In most cases, the elements of the plan that evolve from an application of Step 1 of the Strategic Systems Model impacts the development and implementation of virtually all of the products that evolve from the remaining steps and subsystems of the model.

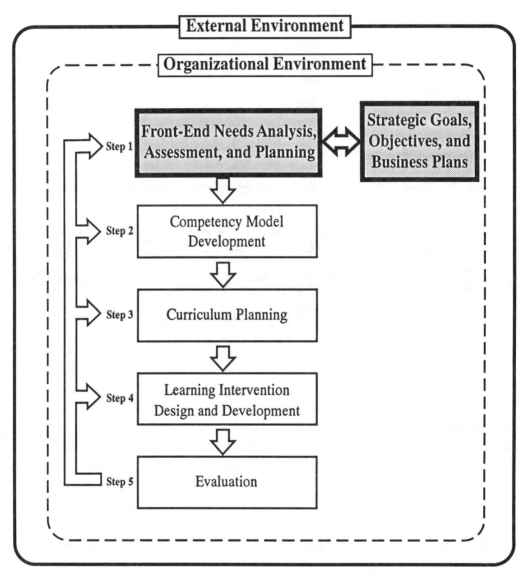

Figure 2.1: The Front-End Needs Analysis, Assessment, and Planning Subsystem
of the Strategic Systems Model

A COMPETENCE CONTEXT FOR NEEDS ANALYSIS, ASSESSMENT, AND PLANNING

Your first steps in creating competency-based training or education that will contribute to the achievement of an organization's strategies and goals are to:

- Determine the organization's goals and its strategic management initiatives for achieving those goals

- Determine the extent to which training or education can meet needs for employee competence relative to the achievement of those goals

- Construct a broadly stated but detailed plan that outlines the needs that could and should be met by training or education, the cost of meeting those needs, and budget allocations

- Determine the next steps that should be taken

When you tackle large curriculum and instruction projects, front-end organization and performance analysis, assessment, and planning are essential. It is not unusual to revisit the results of this initial planning project many times during the subsequent development and implementation of the subsystems that follow later.

Value must be added to the *total organization* when resources are committed to performance improvement interventions. Resources must be accounted for in terms of how those expenditures contribute to meeting the organization's strategic management initiatives. This linkage of employees' competence and a collective, total organization approach to the realization of an organization's strategic goals is an essential factor in developing competency-based performance improvement systems. The following is a contemporary example of this concept.

The Collective Approach: A Nation's Example

Columnist Robert J. Samuelson illustrates this relationship quite well in a 1991 article published by the *Washington Post*, entitled "The Culture of Competence (and Incompetence)." The columnist refers to the competence which was shown by Americans at all levels of the United States' role in the Persian Gulf war. He notes that "there was something about this war that demands our attention—the competence shown by Americans at all levels—precisely because competence is often conspicuously absent in government and business" (p. A19).

Samuelson later adds, "It's this culture of competence—a set of attitudes, expectations and demands—that's often missing in America today" (p. A19). Not only were our leaders competent, but they demanded this same level of competence in their troops. Our national sense of pride in the Persian Gulf victory emanates, says Samuelson, "from a sense that the 'can do' spirit is once again alive and well" (p. A19).

Samuelson is on target: Competence consists of an employee having those underlying characteristics that go beyond simply acquiring and applying knowledge and skills. Other underlying characteristics are essential for competent performance: These are the thoughts, feelings, mindsets, thought patterns, self-image, and other attributes which, *in conjunction with an individual's knowledge and skills*, make the critical differences in performance. It was that "can do spirit" or *mindset* which contributed to success.

This is not the entire story, however. Samuelson (1991) also observes that our leaders were ultimately no better than their troops: "You cannot have such a successful operation unless people all along the line perform . . . . The complexity of what occurred [in the Persian Gulf] was enormous and so, therefore, were the opportunities for failure" (p. A19). Samuelson quotes a U.S. officer after the capture of Kuwait City, who said, "Once we got rolling it was like a training exercise with live people running about. *Our training exercises are a lot harder* [emphasis added]" (p. A19). This quote implies the concept of "collective training" in organizations, which was an outgrowth of the U.S. Army's concern some years ago about ensuring the achievement of a sense of "collective competence" among its troops.

Collective Performance Improvement

In a recent article, Vernon Humphrey (1990) explains the concepts associated with this collective approach to "training the total organization," which he (and others) refers to as *collective training*. "Collective training," says Humphrey, "may revolutionize the way we analyze industrial and business performance" (p. 57). Collective performance improvement is based on the premise that the individual is part of the organizational whole. When you start with this in mind, then all training or education is provided with the intent of achieving strategic organization goals and objectives through collective employee competence.

Collective training developed as an outgrowth of the U.S. Army's concern in the 1970s that in spite of the application of an Instructional Systems Design approach to training, certain operating units inadequately performed *as units* in training exercises. This led the Army to seriously question its purposes for training. Those who studied the problem concluded that "the Army was trying to produce *organizations* that could respond rapidly under pressure, adapt quickly to changing conditions, and capitalize on opportunities. No wonder training approaches that focused entirely on individuals produced less than satisfactory results" (Humphrey, 1990, p. 57). And, according to Humphrey, " The new approach, called 'collective training,' has matured to the point where it can now serve as a model for looking at industry and business" (p. 57).

To use this approach, you must start out with the assumption that you cannot effectively understand the job until you understand the total or collective organization in which the job exists. As Humphrey (1990) notes, "No organization, no job!" (p. 58). Jobs are part of collective organization missions or operations, which themselves contribute in unique ways to achieving an organization's strategic goals. Therefore, the organization context in which a job exists and the assumptions about that context influence the competencies that employees need (including the minimum proficiency levels required) to sustain performance that contributes to achieving organization missions. Competence needs are intimately related to the context assumptions of the organization implementation environment, a subject we will return to in chapter 3.

Collective Analysis

To do a collective analysis, you need to ask and answer two questions:

> 1. What was the subject organization created to do—i.e., what are its strategic management goals?

> 2. How does the organization do it?

When you have fully answered these questions, you have then defined the context in which competency-based performance improvement opportunities should be created and implemented. From an "organization systems" point of view, jobs or occupation families are nothing more than subsystems of the larger organization system and its subsystems. Therefore, changes in any part of the organization system will have effects in the occupation families or jobs within the system. Training or education systems or interventions that result from this analysis process will have improved probabilities of producing optimal effects on the achievement of the organization's strategic goals.

A COLLECTIVE APPROACH TO NEEDS ASSESSMENT AND PLANNING

Needs analysis, assessment, and planning activities, whether focused on solving problems associated with societal, for-profit, or nonprofit organizations, have three outcomes:

- The first outcome, the needs analysis, is a statement and explanation of the gap which exists between an existing condition and a desired condition.

- The second outcome, the needs assessment, is a determination of how critical an obstacle the gap is to the pursuit of the desired condition; in other words, how important is it to close the gap?

- The third outcome, the plan, is a statement of the alternatives for closing the gaps and their relative costs.

The gaps and solution alternatives are frequently arranged in priority order, and the priorities are reconciled against a budget or other plans.

It is axiomatic that not all performance gaps can, or necessarily should, be remedied by using a training or education solution. Other factors limit the achievement of organizational goals. It is customary for HRD needs assessment and planning recommendations to include suggestions for using non-HRD alternatives or strategies for closing individual or organization performance gaps. Some of the more common strategies include the use of job redesign, modifications to operations in the job or organization environment, or modifications to employee selection or appraisal procedures.

In the balance of this chapter, only gaps that can be closed or problems that can be solved by using training or education programs or interventions will be included in the plan that results from an application of the needs analysis, assessment, and planning activities. The material included in the remainder of this book is focused on fulfilling performance improvement needs or solving problems that are most effectively and efficiently addressed by training or education solutions.

Note: Over the past few years, there has been an infusion of information in the literature on the concepts of, and the procedures for doing, front-end needs analyses and assessments in HRD. Since information on the micro-details of needs analysis and assessment are widely available in the literature and in the marketplace, those details will not be repeated here. Some useful materials on front-end needs analysis and assessment procedures are included in the chapter references.

Likewise, numerous details of strategic planning and management in organizations are available in the literature. That information will not be repeated here. Instead, suggestions and specific guidelines are included for analyzing the strategic management attributes of organizations and the relationship of those strategic management initiatives to training or education. References on this topic are also included later in the chapter.

"Needs" and "Problems"

In its most general form, a "need" actually represents a "problem" (or a set of problems). "Needs assessments," according to Roger Kaufman (1987), "provide the direction for useful problem resolution through identifying, documenting, and selecting appropriate problems" (p. 78). When problems with the most critical impact on an organization and its achievement of its most important goals are chosen for attention, clear and specific objectives can be established for pursuing the solutions. Training or education solutions which result from carefully executed needs assessments render effective and efficient interventions that, in turn, contribute to effective and efficient achievement of an organization's strategic goals.

Before launching the development and implementation of a competency-based training or education curriculum, you must ascertain whether or not your program results will solve or meaningfully contribute to the solution of the problem(s) that the organization and its clients, customers, or constituents consider important. You must also determine whether an HRD solution is the most advantageous solution. Therefore, the application of a needs analysis and assessment process is essential at some level (or levels) of the organization.

How much of an organization's operations are included in the analysis, assessment, and planning processes depends upon the depth and breadth of the problem situation. Although the problems under consideration might exist deep within the organization, their solutions must always be aligned with the achievement of the total organization's strategic management initiatives and objectives. Therefore, you must always reference your training, education, or other solutions to the larger or "total organization" context, as Humphrey recommends. The Strategic Systems Model found in Figure 3.1, chapter 3, is based entirely on that principle.

Kaufman's Model

An adaptation of a ten-step model presented in the literature by Roger Kaufman (1987, pp. 78-83) provides a framework for completing needs analysis, assessment, and planning projects within the context of the Strategic Systems Model. In his article, Kaufman portrays his model as an "approach to help even beginners with this necessary, yet often dreaded task" (p. 78). Kaufman's model is particularly attractive for use here because it:

- Is consistent with a philosophy of a collective training or education approach in organizations

- Helps the user focus on the correct elements of the operational world in relation to the organization environment and its strategic management directions

- Uses a systems approach to problem definition and the generation of solutions

- Demands the active involvement of the training or education client (or clients) and other key organization stakeholders at every stage of analysis, assessment, and planning. This is important since these persons will be called upon later at the implementation stage to make significant contributions to the success of the performance improvement solutions that might result.

You might find it helpful to review Kaufman's article. He includes some enlightening examples and illustrations which appropriately supplement the basic material presented here. Additional in-depth information on this process and on strategic planning were recently published (see Kaufman, 1991) and will also be of use to you.

The ten steps of Kaufman's model are presented in summary form below, and this is followed by an explanation of each step, framed in the context of the concepts and contents of the remaining chapters of this book. To conduct successful needs analysis, assessment, and planning projects, Kaufman (1987) recommends taking the following steps:

1. Decide to plan using data from a needs analysis and assessment.

2. Select the needs analysis, assessment and planning level: middle,comprehensive, or strategic.

3. Identify the needs analysis, assessment, and planning partners.

4. Obtain the planning partners' participation.

5. Hold the initial organization meeting, and obtain acceptance of the needs analysis, assessment, and planning level.

6. Collect needs data.

7. List the identified and documented needs.

8. Place the needs in primary order.

9. Reconcile remaining disagreements.

10. List the specific problems to be resolved and obtain final agreement among the partners.

Step 1. **Decide to plan using data from a needs analysis and assessment.**

Regardless of the organization constraints you must face, some level of needs analysis, assessment, and planning are required before launching the development and implementation of competency-based performance improvement systems. Never make assumptions about needs or how to fulfill perceived needs. A very high price is always paid, at some point, for making assumptions of this sort.

The organization must be willing to commit to the completion of this first step for creating competency-based training or education. When only limited formal needs analysis, assessment, and planning can be conducted due to organization limitations, the HRD function can complete most (if not all) of the steps outlined earlier. This will require considerably more time and the results will not be as effective. The reason for this is that the products will be viewed (by default) as HRD products rather than as client-products. Client involvement, in partnership with HRD, is absolutely critical to success. Responsibility for project products should be a shared responsibility. One way to accomplish this is to have co-facilitators or leaders for the project, including the client (or client group) and HRD. The working arrangements *must* be agreed upon *before* work begins.

Organizations without the discipline of needs analysis, assessment, and planning are a challenge to an HRD professional. Depending upon the circumstances within an organization, and its size and complexity, implementing a strategy to institution-alize a needs assessment and planning discipline has payoff. Full implementation of the steps below could require several repetitions of the process itself before that happens within the organization. You will learn how to tailor and structure the process in ways that the organization culture will support. The payoffs are well worth the effort involved to institutionalize the process.

Step 2. **Select the needs analysis, assessment, and planning level: middle, comprehensive, or strategic.**

In this step, you determine just how extensive or pervasive the problem is and how broad a focus is required for probing the organization environment for potential solutions. Three levels of analysis, assessment, and planning are available:

- The *"middle" level* focuses on the *inputs, processes,* and *products* (or results) for the situation. Notice the familiar elements of systems thinking: inputs, processes, and products or results.

- The *"comprehensive" level* combines the middle level priorities with the *organization outputs* as either products or services. When this level of analysis is used, the total organization is considered for problem identification and the development of solutions. In other words, what an organization uses, does, and delivers—whether to itself or to its external customers—is considered.

- The *"strategic" level* combines the issues of the comprehensive level with the added consideration of the degree to which the organization's contributions are useful to its customers and to the "world" in which the contributions must function. This includes what an organization uses, does, and delivers. It also examines the impacts not only upon its immediate customers, but also upon society in general. It includes the total organization *and more* as the analysis unit.

When planning and creating "total organization" competency-based programs or opportunities in organizations by using the Strategic Systems Model in this book, you will almost always—with *very few* exceptions—conduct analyses at the *strategic* level of the organization. However, as a general rule, how critical the HRD solution is to the achievement of strategic organization objectives as set forth by the organization's strategic management initiatives should dictate your decision regarding the analysis level you should use.

Kaufman (1987) recommends "the strategic level of needs assessment" and points out that "choosing the middle or comprehensive level [of needs assessment] . . . assumes that the contributions of those results will be responsive to client and societal requirements and realities" (p. 78). This assumption is oftentimes a dangerous one to make.

Recall that the objective in the context here is to create "collective" or holistic competency-based training or education interventions and systems. That is, the analyst must determine how performance will contribute to meeting the organization's goals in ways that are consistent with its strategic direction and emphases. Employees are trained or educated to perform as part of the larger organization "team," rather than as individuals, when performance improvement activities are designed according to the Strategic Systems Model in this book. Strategic analyses, therefore, are essential for ensuring the correct application of a systems approach to creating collective training or education which dovetails with the larger organization systems. (The final section of this chapter is devoted to the techniques for doing a strategic management analysis in an organization context.)

Once your "problem" is analyzed, it is possible that only one training or education intervention, that several interventions, or that a major system of interventions will result. Only after you have completed the entire ten-step process for each problem will you know how to proceed in the design and implementation of the performance improvement opportunities.

Step 3. Identify the needs analysis, assessment, and planning partners.

This is the first level of buy-in for a competency-based training or education intervention, or system of interventions, in an organization. Many of the partners you select at this stage of the project most likely will remain with the project throughout its life span. You should select certain partners who, at a later time, will be the champions for the project outcomes and any training or education programs that might result. A note of caution, however: Don't choose only friends or consistently strong supporters of the HRD function for your team of partners. You want broad-based organization endorsement of the final performance improvement program. Diversity will lend a greater degree of strength to the credibility of your results.

Every project has unique characteristics that will drive certain selection decisions about who should be on the team. Specifically, at a minimum you should include representatives from the following:

(1) those who will be most affected by the project results;
(2) those who will be responsible for implementing the plan;
(3) the clients and internal customers or other beneficiaries of the project; and
(4) the host organization's external customers or end-users of the products or services the organization renders.

You must ensure that "representativeness" is the backbone of your team member selection plan. To accomplish this, you must identify the factors that accurately represent the population and subpopulations of interest from the four types of partners described above. Some typical factors that might be observed in a particular project include socioeconomic status, literacy levels, gender, race, sexual preference, a set of family units with certain characteristics, an occupation family, a specific job, or a specifically identified collection of work units who share a common strategic organization goal. Other factors could have also been included as examples.

The following is a not-uncommon example of the requirement for diversity. A community nonprofit organization has a number of mental health therapists who serve clients from the community on a walk-in basis. Community demographics have rapidly changed over the past three years. The historical base of clients' problems has been domestic violence. With changing demographics, therapists have suddenly encountered clients with a vastly different set of problems, including HIV-seropositive issues, sexual preference and orientation issues, and alcohol abuse. There is clear evidence from a preliminary discussion with the therapists that they require some form of HRD intervention or other support to meet the new counseling demands they face on a daily basis. It is understandable why the leader for such a needs activity will want to select a diverse team of planning partners to ensure that a variety of community members and professional specialists are represented.

The precise number of persons in each group is not as important as how representative the group is with regard to the project constituencies. I suggest that you use a focus group approach to collect the information needed at this stage of the project. Those who are experienced in the use of focus groups have discovered that the size of a group should be limited to 12 or fewer persons. The project mandates and dimensions will dictate the number of focus groups you will need and, if there are several focus groups, how you will combine the information from the groups and then communicate the comprehensive findings across the groups. Reporting must be objective and timely.

The members of the focus groups will provide their opinions regarding perceived needs, some of which (but not all) will be based upon their observations or feelings. Kaufman (1987) notes that "sensed needs often provide perceived reality and sensitivity to issues of values and preferences about current problems and consequences. They also may reveal observations concerning the methods and procedures that led to the currently undesired results" (p. 80). These tend to be "soft" data, which will lead you to sources of "hard" data. The hard data are needed to support fully, to support with reservations (which implies you will probably need more or different data), or to refute the assertion(s) of need.

You must also collect hard data for the needs assessment and planning process in order to document the perceived or observed gaps in human and/or organization performance. Hard data includes such information as productivity measures, content from anecdotal records, methods or operational procedures, organization climate data, market share data, customer satisfaction survey data, defect rates, morbidity or mortality rates, divorce rates, discharge data, or employee performance observation data. The perceptions of the focus group members *and* the hard data collectively constitute the needs assessment and planning partners.

Caution: The data you use to support an assertion of need must be reliable and valid, and therefore, defensible to the focus group and others who have a stake in the outcomes of these and any future activities that might result. Without this level of confidence, you will find it difficult to gain and maintain the support you need for designing a competency-based performance improvement system which will address these problems, since stakeholders might charge that it was created from a weak or, worse yet, totally absent foundation. Many lay persons may not be professionally trained or experienced analysts who routinely judge the quality of data; however, they spot deceptive or erroneous outcomes quite easily! Don't jeopardize your chances for a total buy-in of your team's results at a later time by using faulty data or information to base early decisions or recommendations on.

Step 4. Obtain the planning partners' participation.

Notify the partners of their role and describe the objectives of the project and your expectations of their contributions to meeting those objectives. Define the partners' time commitments, contributions, the work procedures, the results expected, the support you will provide (e.g., funding, travel, supplies, clerical support, and so forth), and how the results will be used. Once commitment is gained, you should schedule the first meeting and prepare an agenda for this meeting.

Although face-to-face meetings are preferred, you could use written surveys (time-consuming to prepare, administer, analyze, and report), a computer or other electronic communications system, delphi methods, or some combination thereof. My experience suggests that the initial team meeting and other meetings where "critical path" decisions will be made should be held face to face. Other activities (transmitting data, documents for analysis, updates to project activities, routine information) can be done most efficiently and effectively by mail or electronic transmission.

As Kaufman suggests, you should sensitively and graciously remove partners who do not attend or contribute to the project and replace them with active, contributing members.

Step 5. **Hold the initial organization meeting and obtain acceptance of the needs analysis, assessment, and planning level.**

Your role is to facilitate and guide the progress of the planning team. You will provide whatever training the partners might require on technical HRD topics. You will also provide any other guidance or instructions regarding the successful execution and completion of the project.

At the initial organization meeting, you will introduce yourself and your role in the project. The planning partners are introduced and are given an opportunity to describe their anticipated contributions to the project. It is important that the partners understand the perspectives they each bring to the project. An adequate amount of time, appropriate to the situation, should be allocated to establish group cohesion and a team focus. This investment will have considerable payoff in terms of project results.

Unless you have a work group with a history of doing this type of project with you, you will need to explain the basic concepts and steps for doing a needs analysis, assessment, and planning project. You will need to explain the meaning of a performance "gap" and the procedures used for identifying and documenting them. A one-page synopsis of the process that includes an elementary example will be helpful. Taking the time to do this now will save time at later stages of the project.

The partners also need a performance improvement context in which to frame any project results that have training or education solutions. Explain the Strategic Systems Model for competency-based training or education from this book, and provide details of its application in the context of the current project. To do this, you must first define the terms that give meaning to the model. At a minimum, you should define and discuss the importance and use to be made of the following terms:

- Strategic organization or management objectives

- Job competence

- Job competency model

- Curriculum

- Any other HRD-oriented definitions you need for the project

I also suggest you choose a hypothetical employee performance gap whose problem solution can be addressed by a training intervention or a simple series of interventions. Try to select a problem whose solution requires horizontal and vertical integration with other organization systems and also with other performance improvement systems. You need not do a detailed, in-depth discussion of the application of the Strategic Systems Model for competency-based training or education. An overview in the form of a discussion, with key points referenced to a diagram of the model written on a flip chart, will serve the purpose quite well. The performance gap you use should be one with which the project team members are familiar. If they are not familiar with the problem, take the time required to give them a common group context for your example.

Once the team has assimilated the project goals and the HRD topics noted above, explain the three needs assessment and planning levels. They *must* understand the importance of completing their analyses at the strategic level. The selection of the strategic level of analysis (products, outputs, outcomes) is the *only* choice that is consistent with the strategic approach taken in this book.

Finally, task assignments are made and are agreed to by the team members. The time, place, and agenda for the next meeting are established. You should outline, with input and suggestions from the team, the specific tasks that you and they believe are critical for long-term project success. My suggestion is to have face-to-face meetings of the team when major issues and results are expected to be an outcome of the meeting. It is important that you be able to read the verbal and nonverbal communications of the team members as the project is being completed.

Note: I cannot emphasize too strongly that needs analysis, assessment, and planning *must always* be done at the strategic level of an organization. The relationships between even the most concrete or remote occupation family in an organization and the collective strategic directions of the organization must be analyzed and assessed in a strategic manner.

Included later in this chapter is a separate section on the concepts and suggestions needed to do an analysis of strategic management initiatives and objectives relative to the total organization. This later section also includes lists of research questions whose answers will provide your project team with the data required for completing the strategic analysis portion of the project.

Step 6. **Collect needs data.**

Internal data can help identify performance discrepancies internal to the organization. *External data* suggest performance discrepancies of the organization's clients and their environment.

The internal data sources and methods for collecting those data are your first consideration. The partners provide "needs sensing" data on perceived performance discrepancies. You can collect this data in face-to-face meetings or through means such as questionnaires, rating scales, or telephone interviews. Be careful to focus your questions on results, but without biasing the potential answers to the questions in any way. Any data collection instruments you use must be valid—i.e., they must measure what you want them to measure. They must also be reliable, measuring the same things consistently. You can test the reliability and validity of your questions by conducting a pilot test of them with a group of persons who are roughly equivalent to your focus group partners. Responses to the pilot test will suggest ways your questions or other forms of data collection must be revised to focus the respondents' thoughts and their responses on precisely what data you want from them.

You must also have valid and reliable information networks from which to collect the data. Otherwise, your results will be subject to discrediting rather than constructive forms of criticism. The data you receive will reveal what performance issues are important to the partners. If you have selected "representative" partners, they will reflect the issues associated with the constituencies they represent.

The second type of internal data you need is organization performance data. You will undoubtedly know some key sources of organization performance data, and you should begin collecting those data as early in the project as possible. The partners will also suggest key data sources or other data sources early in the project. Be certain to ascertain, when possible, rough estimates of the reliability and validity of any organization performance data you plan to use. Certain data will be considered "sensitive," "confidential," or "proprietary" by the provider. Obtaining and using these forms of data will probably mean that you will need to negotiate the terms and forms of their use before they will be made available to you. It is *critical* that confidentiality or privileged access agreements be maintained to their precise letter of the agreement with the provider.

External performance data are required when the analysis and planning activities are at the strategic level. Some of this data might be available within the organization. From internal organization sources, you can determine the information you need on where to best collect external performance data. These internal sources might include department heads, management information systems staff and managers, financial directors and their staff, marketing and sales professionals, a director of volunteer services, and so forth.

Remember: *Always* focus on *results* rather than on methods, means, processes, techniques, procedures, resources, or personnel. Says Kaufman (1987) on this point, "Targeting results in needs assessment is essential in relating means and ends . . . . 'Needs' for the purpose of a needs assessment are defined as gaps in results—products, outputs, and outcomes—not gaps in organizational efforts—inputs and processes" (p. 81).

Step 7. List the identified and documented needs.

The partners must agree on a set of needs—stated as results. Try to steer discussions away from any particular performance improvement methodologies. Keep the group focused on producing statements of results.

A competent needs analyst will demonstrate highly refined facilitator competence in the resolution of disputes among the partners regarding the needs. The facilitator must *listen* in order to help individuals and the group reframe fuzzy statements of needs as results. Patience, openness, and encouragement by the facilitator will usually obtain the results required to proceed to a successful set of project outcomes.

If possible, at this stage, the performance gaps that training or education can address should be stated as competencies. Even rough or broadly stated competencies (e.g., "computer programming skill using *xyz* software") are helpful for communicating the needs to others. Some might say this is inappropriate at this stage of the work, but my experience suggests otherwise.

Step 8. Place the needs in priority order.

The needs list should be organized in clear terms and then be presented to the partners for their review. You will ask the partners to reconcile the needs list with the hard and soft data provided earlier. In this step, the partners derive a common set of needs which are supported by both the hard and soft data. Next, they arrange the needs in priority order.

One useful way to set priorities is to have the partners estimate what it will cost to reduce or eliminate the need and what it will cost to ignore the need. "Cost" can be viewed very narrowly or broadly as, for example, in terms of dollars, lost resources, opportunities, time, and so forth.

Step 9. Reconcile remaining disagreements.

When disagreements or misunderstandings occur at any stage of the process, it is frequently a result of missing or inaccurate data, gaps in the partners' mutual understanding of the data, and/or the circumstances or events surrounding the problem. Kaufman (1987) states: "When disagreement still lingers, you often will have to revisit the historical context and the futures data to provide a frame of reference concerning 'what was,' 'what is,' 'what will be,' and 'what could be,' and finally selecting 'what should be'" (p. 83). This form of clarification should help you achieve the reconciliation that is needed.

Step 10. **List the specific problems to be resolved and obtain final agreement among the partners.**

In this step, you will compare the needs to the resources budgeted to meet the needs until the resources have been exhausted. Alternatives or options for meeting the needs are drawn. Additional budget or other resources required to fully meet the needs are stated. Finally, a broadly stated yet detailed plan is constructed.

The Final Plan

At a *minimum,* your final plan should include the following elements:

- The strategic context for the needs

- A statement of the needs that can be met, wholly or in part, by competency-based performance improvement interventions; a statement of needs that should be met in alternative ways

- Estimated cost(s) of meeting (or not meeting) the needs, consistent with their strategic implications

- Budget amount *allocated* versus budget amount *required* to meet the needs (just in case these do not agree!)

- Options for meeting the needs with respect to the budgeted amounts

- Time required for the procurement or development of the performance improvement opportunities

- Life-cycle estimates for the performance improvement opportunities

- An implementation timeline, consistent with the life-cycle estimates for the performance improvement activities

- A schedule for updating the performance improvement opportunities in order to guarantee consistency with changes in the organization's strategic directions, and consistent with the intervention life-cycle estimates

The level of detail and the scope of the plan that results from your investigations will be determined by how narrowly or broadly the needs investigations were defined. For example, you should expect that your plan will be relatively brief if your work centers on potential training for a single job including twenty employees in a single location. But the plan would be quite involved if you were planning a multiple-focus curriculum consisting of four types of interventions, with fifteen to twenty discrete modules for five levels of 400 marketing professionals in a worldwide organization. The plan for this particular situation might include a phased design, development, and implementation plan for the start-up stage, with multiple revision dates, and a complex "training update" protocol for the targeted employees. In this example, it is obvious that the organization's strategic management objectives or business goals, especially in the marketing dimensions, are critically essential to the immediate planning project and for periodic updates of the plan and of any HRD interventions that result from the plan.

Regardless of the project dimensions, the more thought and details you include in the plan, the more useful it will be in both the short and long term. However, a word of caution is appropriate. Your plan should include all pertinent micro-details of the project. My personal preference is best expressed by the phrase "The more the better." Briefing documents to senior managers, the client, or client group, however, should reveal that you "did your homework," yet be aimed at illustrating the *most critical items* in the plan. You should deliberately emphasize the fact that you incorporated the use of the organization's strategic management plans and context into your plan for designing performance improvement activities. In other words, be proud to "strut your stuff" on the strategic side of the work!

Endorsement by the Planning Partners

Once a final plan has been constructed, you must ensure that the partners concur on the results. If they do not, then modifications must usually be made until the planning partners reach consensus. If decision recommendations are an outcome of the project results, then little will be accomplished later when a minority opinion or position is maintained by a team member who holds a position of authority or personal influence in the organization. This is even more critical when the person holding a minority position is a direct (or a principal) stakeholder in the project outcomes.

It is essential that the political as well as the professional attributes of every needs assessment and planning project be considered very carefully when you configure and direct the project. To do otherwise is potentially to destroy the credibility of the results and, in the long term, destroy support for the HRD function, as well. Professional recovery from these types of losses is extremely difficult and can have permanent effects.

When the work has been completed, the planning partners are thanked for their contributions to the results. Recall that, most likely, several of the team members will continue to be with you throughout later stages of the work. The balance of the team is discharged. All team members should be personally thanked for their participation and contributions to the project in the form of a formal letter with endorsement from the highest organization official in HRD.

The analysis, assessment, and planning results described above provide the boundaries and a firm foundation for generating the remaining components of the Strategic Systems Model on which this book is based: competency models, competency-based curriculum planning, competency-based performance improvement intervention(s), and formative and summative evaluations. In the long run, a thorough needs analysis, assessment, and planning effort improves the probability of having efficient and effective performance improvement opportunities—if, of course, those options are the most appropriate and cost-effective solutions to solving organization problems.

Numerous useful items on these topics are available in the literature. Selected items from among those choices have been included in the references for this chapter. Specifically, you might want to review Callahan (1985); Dodge (1987); Kaufman (1982, 1991); Mills (1987); Nowack (1991); Rossett (1987); Ulschak (1983); and Witkin (1984).

CONDUCTING A STRATEGIC ANALYSIS

Strategic Analysis and HRD

Completing a strategic analysis as a dimension of a needs analysis, assessment, and planning project sounds complicated. Many HRD professionals are not familiar or experienced in this discipline. Thinking about the traditional role of HRD in organizations provides a clue to the reason why they are unaware of this dimension of organization life.

In the past, more frequently than is preferable, HRD professionals have not had a recognized and responsible role in the strategic management planning and development process in organizations. Therefore, they generally do not have firsthand experience with strategic management thinking and planning. HRD professionals have come a long way in gaining an understanding of their role in the area of strategic management. This has led to their increased participation at the strategic decision-making levels of their organizations. As a matter of course, a goal of every senior HRD manager should be to have "strategic status" in his or her organization.

It is critical for long-term success to ensure that strategic analyses and those who decide or influence the strategic directions of organizations are integrally involved in every major organization HRD project. This is a way for an HRD department to gain visibility and, in conjunction with other measures, inclusion in the strategic management team of the organization.

Preliminary Steps for Conducting a Strategic Analysis

With some basic guidelines in hand and a willingness to search out and talk with a variety of persons in an organization, you will find that the strategic analysis process can be an enlightening and invigorating experience. If the HRD department or function does not yet have access to the strategic thinkers and planners in the organization, then ways must be found to gain that access.

In her recent article on strategic management and planning, Leila Gainer (1989) suggests various ways by which HRD professionals can become part of an organization's strategic management team. An important first step toward this goal is learning about the strategic thinking and management processes that the organization uses. The HRD professional must also collect considerable data on the internal and external dimensions of his or her organization as a step to participating in the strategic management process. This includes collecting information on broad issues concerning the organization, the organization's human resources, and the organization's strategic management objectives, initiatives, and directions.

In-depth information on the organization and strategic role of training and detailed case examples can also be found in a companion book to Gainer's article. The companion document was authored by Carnevale, Gainer, and Villet (1990). These references are very useful to anyone who wants or needs to learn more about ways to gain "strategic access" within an organization.

Umbrella Strategies

Gainer recommends the use of four management "umbrella strategies" as a way of understanding organizations. Part of a broad conceptual model of John A. Pearce, II (Pearce & Robinson, 1985), these umbrella strategies constitute a very useful guide for collecting data for an organization's strategic management and goals directions. "Grand strategies," which organizations use in various combinations to manage their organization, are also included in the model. The grand strategies are the raw materials used to define the umbrella or broad, conceptual strategies. The umbrella strategies and the grand strategies (in parentheses) subsumed under each include:

- Concentration—(concentration)

- Internal-Growth—(market development, product development, innovation, joint venture)

- External Growth—(horizontal or vertical integration, concentric or conglomerate diversification)

- Divestment—(retrenchment, turnaround, divestiture, liquidation)

(The above from Gainer, 1989, pp. S-9 and S-10; Pearce & Robinson, 1985.)

The strategies are seldom applied singularly within an organization, and they often will appear to have been applied in conflict with each other. At times this will be evident when different strategies are applied to individual work units, businesses, or operational divisions within an organization.

Although the objective of Gainer's article is to provide HRD professionals with information and suggestions for becoming part of the strategic process in their organizations, the contents of her article are also useful (when reframed) as guidelines for conducting a strategic analysis for a needs analysis, assessment, and planning project. The following information is an adaptation of selected portions of Gainer's article, modified for that purpose. This information is presented with the permission of the American Society for Training and Development, for which I am grateful.

Guidelines for Conducting a Strategic Analysis

These guidelines will help you conduct the strategic analyses needed to support decisions in defense of creating competency-based performance improvement opportunities and systems in an organization. With these analyses in hand, you will be able to establish the relationships between proposed competence-improvement opportunities and the achievement of the organization's strategic goals and objectives.

To do a strategic analysis, three profiles are needed and, therefore, recommended for development by the team of needs analysis planning partners:

- An Organization Environment Profile

- An Organization-Specific Human Resources Profile

- A Strategic Management Profile

Together, the three profiles provide the materials needed to understand the strategic management environment in which competency-based performance improvement systems will function.

An Organization Environment Profile

An organization environment profile includes an investigation of the internal and external environments in which an organization operates. The data required for constructing an organization environment profile are the answers to the fourteen following questions:

1. Is the organization's industry, constituency base, or political influence stable or evolving?

2. What are the growth trends with regard to the organization's industrial growth expectations?

3. Who are the competitors or collaborators for the organization?

4. What is the organization's competitive advantage over its competitors? What opportunities for collaboration exist and what is the probability for the success of the collaboration?

5. How will the organization capitalize on its competitors' strategic vulnerabilities or otherwise fill a gap left by a similar or allied organization?

6. What has contributed to past successes of the organization?

7. What employed strategies contributed most to its success?

8. What forces have initiated the search for a new strategy?

9. What technology (or technologies) will the organization use?

10. If new technology will be used, what new processes will be used, and when will they be fully operational in ways that will impact the achievement of organization goals?

11. What, if any, innovations are anticipated that could change the character of the competitive or collaborative environment? How would these innovations affect the organization's competitive or collaborative advantage?

12. What new management initiatives or procedures will be instituted by the organization and what is (are) their expected effect(s) on achieving organization goals?

13. How will the future regulatory, legislative, or political environment affect organization performance?

14. What functional (or technical) strategies will be employed by various work units or divisions (or the entire organization) to affect the overarching organization strategy? Why and how will these strategies be utilized?

Organization-Specific Human Resources Profile

Knowing the strengths, weaknesses, and other characteristics of the organization's human resources is critical to the development of a good quality strategic needs analysis. Answering the twelve questions below will provide the data needed to develop the organization's human resources profile.

1. A work force description includes answers to the following: What are the current strengths and weaknesses of the organization's work force? Is the work force technical? Skilled? How were workers prepared for their jobs? What type of training is required for them to maintain and enhance their job competence? Are employees flexible and adaptable to changing conditions?

2. For any particular corporate organization umbrella management strategy to be successful, what changes must occur in: Jobs? Organization culture? Work climate? Employees' competencies?

3. For any particular corporate organization umbrella strategy to be successful, will layoffs or other turnover be required? If so, how much and in what work units or with which occupations?

4. What is the strategic role of the union, and how will union contracts be affected?

5. How can training or education help the organization achieve its corporate strategic goals? To answer this, you must determine the potential training or education implications of an umbrella strategy on the affected functional area(s) of the organization undergoing analysis. (Detailed information on this topic is provided in the next section of this chapter.)

6. If training or education can help close gaps relative to achieving strategic goals, what kinds of specific programs are needed?

7. How will management's or the work force's present views of training or education affect the success ratio of future training or education initiatives?

8. What delivery mechanisms are most cost-effective and useful for each training or education initiative?

9. Is an employee development assistance plan (i.e., tuition reimbursement) available, and what role can it have in the enhancement or development of employees' competence?

10. Is there a training or education evaluation process in place, and does it track the return on investments made for training or education?

11. Does the organization routinely review existing training or education opportunities in light of future or pending strategic management decisions to determine the degree of fit between the two systems?

12. What is the degree of consistency among training, selection, hiring, appraisal, rewards, and career development with regard to the achievement of the corporate goals that are impacted by strategic management decisions?

Organization Strategic Management Profile

To develop a strategic management profile for the organization, you must first isolate the organization's strategic directions under one (or more) of the four "umbrella strategies" mentioned above. If you are working with a sub-unit of the organization, you will determine the organization's strategic direction as well as the strategies established for the sub-unit. It is essential that you determine the relationships which they share, identify where they differ, and explain the differences. As you collect data, you will not only confirm or deny your initial impressions of the umbrella strategy or strategies being used, but you will also begin to understand which of the "grand strategies" are being used. Recall that many organizations will generally use more than one of the "grand strategies" at a time.

As with the organization environment and organization human resources profiles, you or your team members will need to interview both persons within and external to the larger organization to collect data. These might include interviews with customers, recipients of services rendered by the organization, political figures, and so forth. To use the following research questions, you will first need to isolate the organization's strategic management plan and approach under one (or more) of the four umbrella strategies. Next, you will focus your investigations by identifying the grand strategies which are present. (For detailed information, consult Gainer's article or Pearce and Robinson, found in the references at the close of this chapter.)

Each umbrella strategy is defined below, and one or more research questions are suggested to help you complete your investigation. Except for the Concentration Umbrella Strategy, the remaining umbrella strategies include more than one grand strategy. Specific research questions are included when a particular grand strategy might significantly affect performance improvement planning decisions.

Concentration Umbrella Strategy : The organization concentrates on its recognized strengths—whether in its products or services—within its markets. The strategy is to invest its resources in its current initiatives.

1. What are the strategic emphasis options, which ones were chosen, and why were they chosen?

2. Work force competence must be maintained and enhanced; how are existing or proposed training or education systems impacted?

3. What organization culture or work force innovations impact existing or proposed training or education systems? These innovations could include, for example, emphases on work force diversity, quality, and team work.

Internal-Growth Umbrella Strategy : The organization encourages innovation, expands its markets, develops new or related products or services, or establishes joint ventures or coalitions with other organizations to strengthen its own position. The overall strategy is to build upon existing strengths. Emphases are on market development, product development, innovation, and joint venture.

The first eight issues below can be addressed when using any Internal-Growth Umbrella Strategy. The last three issues relate to specific grand strategies.

1. How rapidly and extensively does the organization want to grow and what market factors suggest that it can increase its competitive advantage?

2. How does the organization plan to grow (e.g., market development, product or services development, innovation, joint venture, collaboration, or a combination of these) and on what time schedule?

3. Will new facilities or operations be opened, and if so, how many and where, over what time frame, and how many new employees will be needed?

4. Will a new customer or client base be pursued? If so, what types of new employees will be needed? How many will be hired, what training will they need, and will the workplace competencies of existing employees be "retreaded"?

5. What new products or services will be introduced? How often will they be introduced? Will new equipment be needed? What are the training implications?

6. What is the timetable for putting new products or services on the market? What qualifications must the sales force have and what role will training have? Will new workers need to be added? What are the training implications?

7. Are new facilities planned? If so, what are the training implications? How will the sales staff for the new facilities be trained?

8. If foreign expansion is part of the scenario, what are the training or education implications?

9. If a "product (or service) development" strategy is used, then the following items should be considered for research:

- What are the technological implications of product or service development?

- What are the marketing and distribution implications?

- How will training be provided?

- What will be done to create a climate of incremental innovation (i.e., one that nurtures product or service improvements and spinoffs)?

- Will the new projects fill a niche or break new ground?

- How will the sales force be prepared to sell a groundbreaking product or service?

- What are the training implications?

10. If an "innovation strategy" is used, does the HRD department act as an observer, reactor, or catalyst to innovation? How will information flow in the organization systems, including the training or education systems, in pursuit of an innovation strategy?

11. If a "joint venture" strategy is used, are the cultures of the joining organizations similar? Which organization's philosophy will prevail in the joint venture scenario? What will be the new organization's orientation to training or education? How will training or education be provided in the new organization? If a foreign culture is involved, are there persons in both organizations who can and will facilitate a successful union of the national cultures? What are the training implications of the union of the cultures?

External-Growth Strategy: The organization expands its existing resources or strengthens its market position or constituency base through the acquisition or creation of new businesses or constituencies. The emphases are on horizontal or vertical integration. Diversification could include concentric or conglomerate diversification. The overall strategy is to focus existing resources on the development of new or different resources.

1. Overall, when an External-Growth Strategy is used, three generic factors will impact the training or education responses:

    • How will an organization's acquisition change the industry or service profile?

    • How will competitive or collaborative advantage be enhanced?

    • How rapidly and extensively does the organization plan to grow?

2. When an "integration" strategy is adopted, the following research questions should be answered:

    • Will the purchased organization's business be similar or dissimilar to the host organization?

    • How will total integration proceed with respect to facilities, employees, equipment, organization cultures, behavioral norms, and belief systems, and what new management initiatives will impact them?

    • What are the impacts on the host and acquired organizations of legislative, political, or regulatory demands, and how will these be managed?

    • What are the training or education implications of the merger?

    • How are training and education valued by both organizations and in the merger?

    • How will HRD persons from the organization entities coalesce to form a cohesive HRD team?

    • How will HRD in the merged organization support the achievement of the new organization's strategic goals?

3. When a "diversification" strategy is chosen, three questions should be considered in doing a strategic management analysis:

- How many separate buy-outs or purchases are planned?

- Are senior managers trained to make informed decisions about the future of the acquired organization and its utilitarian value to the parent organization?

- What are the training or education implications of building a management team that succeeds in the proposed arena?

Disinvestment Strategy. The organization, due to economic or financial losses, decreases or dissolves its operation in order to minimize losses to its stakeholders or constituents. This strategy could include retrenchment, turnaround, divestiture, or liquidation.

1. In general, why and how has the organization been competitive in the past and what changes have resulted to create the present status of the organization?

2. When a "retrenchment strategy" is chosen, you will:

   - Identify the steps that will be taken for retrenchment

   - State why these steps were chosen

   - Determine what functional strategies will be used by the operating units

   - Identify the role of the training or education function

   - State ways training or education costs can be contained or reduced

   - Identify how training or education can help reduce costs in the operating units

   - Overall, create ways training or education can be successfully used to increase the organization's success

3. A "turnaround" strategy requires answering the following questions:

- What is the profile of the organization's industry?

- Is the industry stable or evolving?

- Who are the competitors?

- How has the organization redefined its goals in light of the above?

- How will resources (human, technological, process-oriented, financial) be acquired or reallocated to support turnaround?

- How must the organization culture, behavioral norms, work-related values, and management practices and procedures be modified in order to achieve the turnaround goals?

- What are the impacts of recent regulatory, legislative or political events?

- How must employees' job competencies be developed and how will training or education be used to accomplish these goals?

Employees, in this context, could include existing employees, rehires from an earlier furlough period, or new hires.

4. When a "divestiture" strategy is adopted, the core organization attempts to survive and remain in operation while it divests itself of other functions or businesses. These are the key questions that should be answered:

   - What regrouping strategies will be adopted?

   - What are the implications of competence gaps in employees' performance with regard to sustained organization performance under the new strategy?

   - What are the best alternatives for closing the gaps, given the constraints on the total organization?

5. When a "liquidation" strategy is chosen, the organization soon will no longer exist. Displaced employees could require training for different or allied occupations, and outplacement counseling might be needed. Training might also include developing employees' competencies in life-career assessment, stress reduction, and change management. Psychoeducational counseling services might be offered.

Suggestions for Your Work

The following suggestions will help to ensure that your work with strategic analysis is a success.

- Remember that strategic management analyses are not difficult to perform if you use a systematic and organized approach to the process. The information on strategic analysis at the close of this chapter gives you a framework for developing your research plans.

- Once you have completed a thorough strategic management profile for the total organization, the information it provides will be useful for numerous other needs analysis, assessment, and planning projects. Many training or education needs within the organization likely could be imparted by the elements of the same or updated strategic profile you create for your initial project.

- If you do the total organization profile first, then you can also create subordinate strategic management profiles for numerous sub-units of the organization as they are needed. In very large organizations, this can be a *very* profitable investment for assessing the situation and then sorting out the pseudo-needs from valid needs for competence-development programs.

- It is a "given" that change and a need for flexibility are high priorities for organizations in the present and immediate future. Therefore, once you have created an initial strategic management profile, don't be disappointed to discover that it must be updated only a few months (or even weeks) after you completed it. To make this process easier to handle, I suggest that you encourage the inclusion of a forecasted strategic management direction in your profile.

• You might also want to include an open matrix that will allow you to keep a log of events or activities following publication of the profile. Maintaining this log will help you "track" strategic movements—not only those that are internal to the organization but external as well. For example, if you read that a product or service competitor will invade a market and this will affect your client organization's position in that market, this information—along with any supporting documentation—can be entered on the log. When it is time to update your profile, the information is chronologically organized and available at a moment's notice. Also, brief conversations with key persons who can provide information on an organization's strategic positions are a valuable source of help in this area. Your log can be used to record information obtained from those sources. Once you set up a master profile and log, it is very easy to maintain them.

• *Develop and maintain the discipline of doing ongoing strategic management analyses and the maintenance of those profiles as a critical component of your needs analysis, assessment, and planning work.* It will help you to become and remain vital to your client or client group since you will transmit a strong message that training or education warrants a strategic role in the achievement of *their goals.*

• When you collect information for strategic analyses, give each person who is interviewed a brief statement of how you will use the information they provide to close employee performance gaps. Incorporate frequent references to the need for competence as leverage for achieving organizational goals. Few persons will argue with the fact that employee and organization competence are important for organization success. You must directly communicate that your business (HRD, that is) is to significantly contribute to improved employee and organization competence, which will ultimately help the organization achieve its strategic goals and objectives.

SUMMARY

In this chapter, you were provided with a ten-step approach for completing a front-end needs analysis, assessment, and planning process, leading to a plan for creating competency-based training or education systems. There is a major difference between this approach and others. The difference is the emphasis that is placed upon using a collective training or education approach for improving employees' competence. A collective approach emphasizes training or educating individuals relative to their contributions to the achievement of an organization's strategic objectives, consistent with its strategic management initiatives.

The final plan that results from an application of this ten-step process must include:

- Information on the organization context

- A clear description of employees' competence needs

- A statement of how meeting those needs will "collectively" contribute to the achievement of organization goals

- The proposed competency-based training, education, or other priorities for addressing and meeting those needs

The emphasis in this chapter has been on doing all needs analyses, assessments, and planning at the strategic level of an organization. The final section of the chapter presented a framework and guidelines for doing strategic management analyses.

REFERENCES

Callahan, M. R. (Ed.). (1985, February). Be a better needs analyst. AS*TD Info-Line Series*. Alexandria, VA: American Society for Training and Development.

Carnevale, A. P., Gainer, L. J., & Villet, J. (1990). *Training in America: The organization and strategic role of training*. San Francisco, CA: Jossey-Bass.

Dodge, R. E. (1987, August). Getting started with a needs assessment: A nuts and bolts approach for putting one together. *Performance and Instruction*, pp. 16-20.

Gainer, L. J. (1989, September). "Making the competitive connection: Strategic management and training. Supplement to *Training and Development Journal*, *43* (9), pp. S-1 to S-30.

Humphrey, V. (1990, October). Training the total organization. *Training and Development Journal*, *44* (10), pp. 57-64.

Kaufman, R. (1982). *Identifying and solving problems: A systems approach* (3rd ed.). San Diego, CA: University Associates Publishers.

Kaufman, R. (1987, October). A needs assessment primer. *Training and Development Journal, 41* (10), pp. 78-83.

Kaufman, R. (1991). *Strategic planning plus: An organizational guide.* Glenview, IL: Scott-Foresman Professional Books.

Mills, G. E., Pace, R. W., & Peterson, B. D. (1987). *Analysis in human resources training and organization development.* Reading, MA: Addison-Wesley.

Nowack, K. M. (1991, April). A true training needs analysis. *Training and Development Journal, 45* (4), pp. 69-73.

O'Donnell, J. M. (1988, July). Focus groups: A habit-forming evaluation technique. *Training and Development Journal, 42* (7), pp. 71-73.

Pearce, J., II, & Robinson, R. B., Jr. (1985). *Strategic management: Strategic formulation and implementation* (2nd ed.). Homewood, IL: Irwin, Inc.

Rossett, A. (1987). *Training needs assessment.* Englewood, NJ: Educational Technology Publishing.

Samuelson, R. J. (1991, March 6). The culture of competence (and incompetence). *Washington Post,* p. A19.

Ulschak, F. L. (1983). *Human resource development: The theory and practice of need assessment.* Reston, VA: Reston Publishing Co.

Witkin, B. R. (1984). *Assessing needs in educational and social programs.* San Francisco, CA: Jossey-Bass.

Chapter 3

CONCEPTS AND METHODS FOR DEVELOPING COMPETENCY MODELS

In this chapter, five methods for developing competency models are introduced and briefly described. The five methods are then individually examined and the concepts associated with them and the steps for using them are explained. The discussion of the fifth method is prefaced by a look at the concept of flexible job design and modeling, and how it differs from more traditional job analysis and design methods. The chapter concludes with several suggestions for planning and completing a competency model development project, including the factors that influence the decision on which method to use, and with suggested project standards for the work.

IN RELATION TO THE STRATEGIC SYSTEMS MODEL

The strategic goals and objectives of an organization and the results of a front-end needs analysis, assessment, and planning project are the inputs to, and drive the competency model development stage of, creating a competency-based performance improvement system. This is Step 2 of the Strategic Systems Model. The relationship of the competency model subsystem to the other subsystems of the Strategic Systems Model is illustrated in Figure 3.1, on the following page.

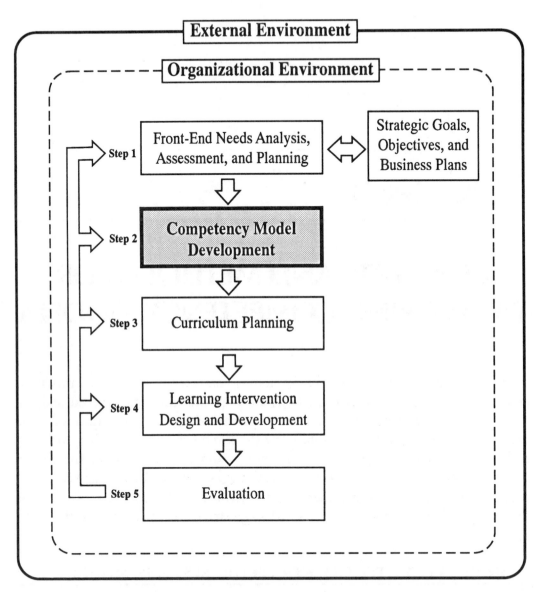

Figure 3.1: The Competency Model Development Subsystem of the Strategic Systems Model

INTRODUCTION TO COMPETENCY MODEL DEVELOPMENT METHODS

Organizations have successfully used five methods (or variations of them) for building job competency models, including the

- Job Competence Assessment Method

- Modified Job Competence Assessment Method

- Generic Model Overlay Method

- Customized Generic Model Method

- Flexible Job Competency Model Method

Job Competence Assessment Method. The Job Competence Assessment Method relies on the use of a rigorous, empirical research procedure called Job Competence Assessment, which helps determine what job competencies differentiate exemplary from average job performance. Exemplary and average performers are interviewed about the dimensions of their job performance. Once the competencies have been determined, they—in conjunction with other job elements—are used to construct the job competency model.

Modified Job Competence Assessment Method. The Modified Job Competence Assessment Method uses the Job Competence Assessment research procedure, with the modification of having the exemplary and average performers, who would normally be interviewed face to face, write or otherwise record their critical behavior stories for use by the researcher.

Generic Model Overlay Method. When an organization uses the Generic Model Overlay Method to acquire a competency model, it selects or obtains a prepared competency model and then overlays or superimposes it on a job within the organization.

Customized Generic Model Method. The Customized Generic Model Method relies on the researcher's tentative identification of a universe of candidate generic competencies that fully characterize the attributes of the exemplary and average performers of a job in the organization. The universal list of competencies is then researched and interpreted within the job and the larger organization context. As a result, the specific competencies that characterize the successful employee are verified or denied by the research. Other attributes for the desired competency model are also researched. The job competencies and these other attributes are then used to develop the competency model.

Flexible Job Competency Model Method. The Flexible Job Competency Model Method relies on having a wide variety of comprehensive information sources for inclusion in the research base. A feature of this method is the identification and use of future assumptions about the organization and the job. Depending upon the organization's preferences, internal and external sources of information can be used. The use of this method results in the availability of job roles, job outputs, quality standards for the outputs, and behavioral indicators for each job competency.

Competency models provide the adhesion or "glue" that is necessary among the elements of an organization's human resource management system. By this I mean that competency models help organizations take a unified and coordinated approach to designing the human resource management system, including job design, hiring, performance improvement, employee development, career planning or pathing, succession planning, performance appraisals, and the selection and compensation systems for a job. Therefore, any investment an organization makes in competency model development work has benefits beyond the usefulness of the results for HRD purposes.

THE JOB COMPETENCE ASSESSMENT METHOD (JCAM)

The notion of human competence came to the forefront of HRD through the concurrent work of psychologists Robert White and David McClelland. White (1959) isolated a human trait he named "competence." McClelland was the first to challenge the value of intelligence testing and the resultant use of an "intelligence quotient," or IQ score, as a predictor of successful living. McClelland (1973) observed that although performance is influenced by a person's intelligence, other personal characteristics, such as motivation and self-image, operate within the individual to differentiate successful from unsuccessful performance in a job role and in other life roles.

The work of McClelland and his associates resulted in the creation of a research process called the Job Competence Assessment Method (JCAM). In an article on the subject, George Klemp, Jr. (1982) wrote:

Job competence assessment is a powerful new solution to the problem of how to hire and train people for maximum effectiveness. By pinpointing the key knowledge, abilities, and other personal characteristics needed to do a job well, job competence assessment departs dramatically from classical job analysis. It starts with a simple premise: the best way to find out what it takes to do a job is to analyze the job's outstanding performers and then to study what they do that makes them so effective. Job competence assessment is therefore not so much assessment of the job as assessment of the person who does the job. (p. 55)

JCAM is a rigorously analytical, empirical method for determining the competencies that, in conjunction with other job elements, are used to construct the competency model for the job. Figure 3.2 on the following page presents some representative competencies and behavioral indicators from a competency model that was developed for safety professionals, using the JCAM. It is a useful frame of reference for the discussion which follows.

Competency Model Development Steps

Competency model development projects that use JCAM require the completion of these basic steps:

1. Research the job components (i.e., job tasks and activities, roles, organization environment and issues) and the requirements for *exemplary* job performance.

2. Research the attributes of the exemplary performers and construct the job competency model.

3. Validate the job competency model.

The use of the JCAM requires the availability of at least a trained survey researcher and support persons who can conduct the survey research tasks. A focus group is used for the completion of the tasks of only Step 1 below, with a large amount of assistance from the researcher and the support staff. The remaining steps of the JCAM are completed by the researcher and the support staff, with considerable assistance and support from the HRD specialist. If the research resources are not available in the HRD department, they must be obtained elsewhere.

Involvement Orientation

1. Promotes Participation

. . . consistently acts to build broad involvement, ownership, and commitment to plant safety programs.

- Recognizes that the essence of a safety program is involvement and ownership

- Seizes opportunities to promote employee participation and ownership in safety programs

- Works to get buy-in and involvement by appealing to a common goal and employees' individual contribution of suggestions, ideas, and effort

2. Team Building

. . . devotes major effort to accomplishing objectives through the use of teams.

- Identifies obstacles and opportunities for group functioning (e.g., size, composition)

- Understands [and] uses the motivating qualities of group accomplishments

- Uses specific techniques to guide group or team (e.g., pushes for development of a group charter to provide clear direction)

3. Development of Others

. . . acts with the realization that developing safety leaders is a key part of multiplying own effectiveness.

- Assigns others tasks that are designed to develop their abilities

- Gives others training and/or suggestions to help them do better

Influence

4. Strategic Influence

. . . consistently acts to build own credibility and influence key people on safety issues.

- Recognizes primary role as being with employees and seizes opportunities (i.e., is a floor presence)

- Recognizes interests and backgrounds of key decision-makers in the process of influencing and selling ideas

Figure 3.2: Selected Competencies and Behavioral Indicators from a Competency Model for Safety Professionals, Developed by Using a Job Competence Assessment Methodology

Source: Cobb. 1990. Reprinted with permission.

Each of the three steps requires the completion of specific research tasks. The manner in which the tasks are designed and completed in actual practice will oftentimes differ across organizations and even within divisions or strata of a single organization.

The three-step process described below is, in part, based on Klemp's (1982) report of the JCAM. Other information included in the presentation was obtained from a number of sources, including my own experience, personal conversations with practitioners, and published sources such as Richard Boyatzis (1982); David McClelland and Richard Boyatzis (1980); George O. Klemp, Jr. (1978, 1987); David McClelland (1976); and Ron Zemke (1982).

Step 1. **Research the job components (i.e., job tasks and activities, roles, organization environment and issues) and the requirements for exemplary job performance.**

The first task in the research process is to determine and document the job components. To accomplish this, a focus group is formed. The focus group should consist of persons who are job experts. Persons who have held the job and who are currently the manager(s) of those who hold the job, or other persons who have outstanding experience or expert knowledge of the job, should be included as members of the focus group.

The JCAM research process requires the direct involvement of key players in the organization. Depending upon the level or visibility of the job (or jobs) within the organization, this panel might or might not include organization officers, executives, senior managers, or influential corporate/organization leaders. Under any circumstances, the client or client group must have confidence in the members of this panel; they must be respected and credible representatives of the function.

The focus group defines the job performance requirements as a set of job outputs. These are the measures of effective job performance. Some examples include customer satisfaction indices, profits, numbers of adverse actions, case through-puts and closures, productivity indices, quality measures, and other such measures.

The focus group also describes the major job tasks and activities that contribute to the achievement of each of the job outputs. A job task or activity is critical for performance only when it can be shown to directly relate to the achievement of one or more job outputs.

Next, the focus group develops a comprehensive draft list of personal characteristics (e.g., the knowledge, skills, thought patterns) that they believe the exemplary job performers hold. Behavioral evidence of each personal characteristic (known as the "behavioral indicators") is also developed.

The focus group must be guided to document the full complement of technical and other personal characteristics that are common to, and used by, *both* the exemplary and the average performers. In a review of an early version of the JCAM, Zemke (1982) reported: "Its strength is that it isolated critical features of high performers. A weakness is that traits or behaviors which don't vary between high and low performers fail to appear in the final competencies" (p. 30). He also reported that "needs for technical job knowledge tend to be lost in this [i.e., an early version of the JCAM] process since 'entry level' knowledges and skills tend not to distinguish high and low performers, especially in higher level job classifications" (p. 30).

The list of characteristics is sent to those who hold the job and they are requested to rate each characteristic according to its importance for exemplary performance. The data is analyzed and an inventory of the characteristics is prepared. This inventory represents the respondents' "best estimate" of the characteristics that are held by the exemplary performers.

The final task for the focus group is to identify the exemplary (or outstanding) job performers. Members of the focus group are privately asked to identify exemplary and average job performers. Exemplary and average performers are also identified using other data on performance, such as productivity measures, sales levels, grievance levels, and so forth.

Persons who currently hold the job can be asked to nominate those peers whom they believe are exemplary and average performers. Peer nominations have high validity. This recommendation is supported by research results obtained by Lewin and Zwany (1976) and by Kane and Lawler (1978). Two lists are constructed: one of the exemplary performers and the other of average performers.

Step 2. Research the attributes of the exemplary performers and develop the job competency model.

Job observations are one approach that can be used to ascertain the immediate job context and the work environment in which employees perform their day-to-day duties. The observer's objective is to detect an overall sense of the work, climate, the styles of interaction, and the actual job tasks and activities. Job observations are used, however, only when they will significantly contribute to, or supply information needed for, the construction of the competency model. A major reason for this is that they are costly to conduct. However, there is another reason.

The observation data provides the researcher with a limited dimension of job performance—that which can be directly observed. The more elusive elements of job performance, those elements that are not easily observed, are captured by conducting Critical Behavior Interviews (CBI). The use of the CBIs is especially useful for identifying the soft competencies required for successful job performance. Thus, they make a major contribution to the data required to construct competency models for many professional and managerial jobs.

The CBI is a variation of the critical-incident interview process (Flanagan, 1954). Trained interviewers are used to conduct the sessions. The interview is tape-recorded with the permission of the employee, confidentiality guidelines are established with both the employee and the employer, and strict adherence to those guidelines is *always* maintained.

CBIs are conducted with 8-12 exemplary performers and an equal number of average performers. The early developers of the JCAM discovered that the quality of the persons interviewed and not the number of persons interviewed was the most significant factor in conducting the research (Klemp, 1982).

A CBI lasts between two and two-and one-half hours. Both the exemplary and average performing employees are interviewed. The interviewer does not know the performance level of each employee being interviewed. Each employee is asked to identify two job situations in which he or she felt particularly effective or whose outcome was pleasing. The employee is asked to describe each situation in very specific detail. The interviewer encourages the employee to give as many details of the incident as is possible to recall.

Next, the interviewer asks the employee to identify two situations where he or she was not pleased with the outcome, felt frustrated, or was otherwise dissatisfied with the results. Again, the employee is encouraged to give as many details about the experience as possible.

A comparison of the employee's stories effectively reconstructs the employee's job experience, and through analysis, the positive and negative job factors become evident. The major outcome of the CBI process is the researcher's insight into an employee's actions, inner thoughts, thought patterns, convictions, intentions, and feelings regarding the job—i.e., into the type of job attributes generally impossible to determine directly by using job performance observation methods.

Transcripts of the interviews are produced from the tape-recorded sessions. Trained specialists analyze the data or information found in the transcribed CBIs. The draft "best estimate" list of characteristics of exemplary performers that was researched and developed during the first step of the JCAM is used to tabulate and systematically encode the presence of potential competencies that are identified from the transcribed CBIs.

Elementary statistical comparison methods such as analysis of variance routines are used to identify the critical competencies that clearly distinguish the exemplary from the average performers. Recall that a personal characteristic becomes a competency only when there is proof that it contributes to successful job performance.

Two important sets of competencies are identified from the analyses:

COMPETENCY MODEL FOR ELECTRONIC PUBLISHING MANAGER

EXEMPLARY PERFORMER COMPETENCIES

These job competencies distinguish an employee's performance.

- Matches corporate capability with customer needs by applying advanced word-processing and electronic publishing techniques to create camera-ready copy

- Matches corporate capability with customer needs by applying advanced techniques for electronic requirements, illustration, graphic design, printing, and document binding

- Cultivates and maintains a high level of self-esteem

- Resolves severe conflicts with customers in ways that result in win-win outcomes

- Maintains proper vigilance regarding project performance in order to avoid fatal outcomes

. . .

COMPETENCIES SHARED BY THE EXEMPLARY AND AVERAGE PERFORMERS

These are the minimum, non-technical competencies required for satisfactory performance by all employees.

- Closes an electronic publishing contract with a customer that satisfies or exceeds the customer's requirements and lies within basic corporate capability

- Plans, schedules, and monitors the progress of electronic publishing projects in ways that result in the timely delivery of project outputs

- Delegates work to subordinates in ways that accomplish expected project outputs in a timely manner

- Selects software, hardware, other technologies, and human resources in ways that result in the production of outputs that satisfy customers' requirements

- Maintains productive, cooperative relationships with customers in the face of conflicting or counterproductive circumstances

- Maintains own physical and psychological stability over extended time intervals while balancing professional and personal needs

. . .

TECHNICAL COMPETENCIES

These are the minimum technical competencies required for satisfactory job performance by all employees.

- Completes traditional pre-press practices to create camera-ready copy

- Completes camera-ready copy by applying intermediate knowledge and skill with electronic publishing and word-processing packages

. . .

Figure 3.3: Segment of a Competency Model Illustrating Three Categories of Competencies

1. Competencies held by *only* the exemplary performers

2. Competencies held by *both* the exemplary *and* the average performers

The competencies held by *both* the exemplary *and* the average performers are the minimum job competencies. The competencies held by *only* the exemplary performers are the competencies that significantly *distinguish* exemplary from average job performance. These are the major sets of competencies that are used to build the competency model. Recall that, in addition, the total complement of technical job competencies that are used by the exemplary and the average performers must be included in the final competency model.

Figure 3.3 (on the opposite page) includes a segment of a competency model that was recently developed for the job "Electronic Publishing Manager." The contents illustrate the three types of competencies mentioned above: those held only by the exemplary performers, the minimum job competencies, and the technical competencies. Notice also the range of affective, cognitive, and psychomotor competencies required for effective job performance.

Your model should also include one or more behavioral indicators for each of the competencies. For example, in Figure 3.2, under "Team Building" competency, the item "Identifies obstacles and opportunities for group functioning" is a behavioral indicator for the competency. Since certain competencies are of special interest to the users of the model, the competencies for the exemplary performers, the technical competencies, and others of particular importance to the client can be designated in the model through standard text documentation methods.

Depending upon client requirements or needs, the job outputs and the job tasks and activities can also be included in the competency model report. Additionally, a matrix can be included that illustrates the relationships the job tasks and activities have to the role the competencies play in their accomplishment.

Step 3. **Validate the job competency model.**

The next step is to validate and then construct the final job competency model. When you validate a competency model, you are enhancing the credibility of its contents. The validation technique (or techniques) for competency models depends upon the time and resources that are available for completing the work and upon the critical necessity of validating the model in the first place.

The degree of validity needed for a competency model depends upon the use (or uses) that will be made of the model. Competency models that are used for employee selection, performance evaluation, or compensation purposes must have particularly high validity. In general, the question of how valid a competency model must be should be answered on a case-by-case basis. The answer lies in determining the costs associated with *not* having a valid model. For additional information on the issues raised here, you should review Harlan, Klemp, & Schaalman (1980); Pottinger, Wiesfeld, Tochon, Cohen, & Schaalman (1980); Block & Rebell (1980); and Huff, Klemp, Spencer, & Williamson (1980). Any competency model developed for an organization application must be consistent with providing fair and equal treatment of all employees affected by its application or use. Furthermore, the model that is used must have the endorsement of senior management or other key leaders within the organization. For these reasons, time must be committed to validating the competency model as part of the project.

There are at least three approaches for validating a competency model:

1. The replication of the original research

2. The application of alternative research procedures

3. The use of a panel of jurors consisting of external consultants with expert knowledge of the job

Using Research Replication Procedures. The first approach for validating a competency model, the replication of the original research, uses identical research procedures or techniques and at least two different sets of "research equivalent" subjects from the target population.

In order to replicate the original research, you identify a sufficient number of exemplary and average performers when Step 1 above is planned, and form two groups of "research equivalent" subjects, Group A and Group B. Let's assume that 24 exemplary and 24 average performers were identified during Step 1, above. During Step 1 the researcher randomly assigns 12 exemplary performers and 12 average performers to each of the Groups A and B. Next, the research team conducts CBIs with all members of both groups, eventually resulting in transcripts for a total of 48 exemplary and average performers.

Group A data, for example, could have been used to create the competency model during Step 2 above. During this, the validation stage, the analysts develop a competency model for Group B, using identical analysis and development methods. The contents of the competency models for Group A and Group B are then compared, the differences are contrasted and comprehended, and a final competency model is created. Additional job experts who were not involved in the initial research process can be called upon to assist in handling any remaining differences or concerns.

Using Alternate Research Procedures. The second approach for validating a competency model requires the application of alternative research procedures (other than the replication technique) that may be either similar to or different from those that were used to develop the primary competency model. There are various ways to do this. One alternative is for the focus group to survey a panel of job experts or others who are highly knowledgeable about the job, its requirements, and its setting. The members of the panel are asked to provide their opinions on the elements of the competency model that resulted from the initial research process. The survey design and approach will depend upon the subject-matter of the job, the time available to complete the survey work, and the technical support available within the organization (or obtainable through contractual services) to analyze and evaluate the results.

A second alternative is to test employees on the competencies. This alternative can be problematic for validating the soft competencies included in the competency model. Statistically valid and reliable measures of these competencies might require, for example, a cluster of test items that act as a surrogate for one or more dimensions of the competencies. Preparing these test items specific to a competency, or researching the availability of instruments that validly and reliably measure the presence of the competency, can be a time-consuming and costly experience. Sophisticated statistical analysis techniques are often also required to perform adequate analyses. This type of activity will require having (or having access to) the correct professional resources for completing the work.

Using a Panel of Expert Jurors. The third approach to validating a competency model is to use a panel of jurors who hold expert knowledge of the job and its setting. The members of the panel give their best professional judgments about the contents of the model. The jurors must be chosen very carefully and they must have proven credibility and recognition in their area(s) of expertise, both internal and external to the organization. Each situation dictates the best sources for recruiting the panel members and the criteria for their selection.

The validated competency model and a professionally prepared report of the project should be given to the client. This is usually done as part of a client or client group briefing that is conducted by presenting an executive summary of the results. A brief follow-up session or telephone conversation with the client several days following the briefing gives the client an opportunity to have time to review the report and to ask any questions or to suggest revisions that should be made.

It is essential to understand the benefits and costs associated with the use of the JCAM. Those factors are discussed below.

Benefits of Using the Job Competence Assessment Method

As a method for job analysis and, in the larger context, for competency model building, JCAM has numerous benefits over other methods. In particular:

1. The JCAM is highly useful for analyzing jobs whose performance dimensions and attributes are difficult to observe and define (i.e., jobs that require a large portion of soft competencies).

2. The JCAM can be applied to a wide variety of jobs. JCAM's ability to detect the more elusive elements of job performance make it an invaluable tool for virtually all competency model development projects since it produces a highly comprehensive set of competencies for a job.

3. The JCAM is criterion-referenced (i.e., relative to what the exemplary performers do) rather than norm-referenced (i.e., relative to what all employees who hold the job do). The competencies that significantly impact job performance are easily identified.

4. The JCAM investigates the internal realities of a job. The competencies that result from an application of the JCAM are referenced to actual, specific job performance behaviors rather than to the opinions or hypotheses that persons offer regarding job performance requirements.

5. The JCAM is very useful for identifying the affective attributes required for successful job performance.

6. The JCAM produces competency models that can be used immediately to create training or education opportunities that emphasize exemplary performance by employees. Inferences based on the job behaviors are unnecessary since the JCAM documents expert performance.

7. A performance improvement intervention or program that is based upon a valid competency model, such as that of the quality produced by an application of the JCAM, supports the marketing of the HRD intervention or program to the client and to others, including employees and others who are internal and external to the organization.

Cost Factors

Although the reported benefits of using the JCAM are tremendous, a certain level of investment must be made if this method is used. In order to make a decision on the extent of that investment, you should weigh the cost of using the JCAM against the benefits that will be realized. The benefits should outweigh the costs.

Seven major cost factors that influence a financial profile for the use of the JCAM can be immediately identified:

1. The JCAM is not a particularly cost-effective competency model development method for use in a job environment that is unstable or dynamic. When the job outputs and the job role requirements are in flux, the competencies required by employees to fulfill those roles and to produce the job outputs will, of necessity, frequently change. This could necessitate frequent replication of the research in order to maintain the validity of the competency model.

2. An application of the JCAM requires the use of a qualified researcher, as well as interviewers to conduct the CBIs. Unless qualified specialists are readily available, it will be necessary to identify, train, and compensate these interviewers.

3. The tape-recorded CBIs must be transcripted. This requires the availability of clerical support and the proper equipment to complete the task.

4. The review and analysis of the transcripted sessions requires the use of specialists who are trained to recognize and interpret the evidence of the competencies found in the transcripted CBIs. The training must be either internally designed and delivered or purchased externally. In order to engender ownership of the results, specialists from within the organization must also be recruited and trained, and they will need released time from their other job duties to complete the review and analyses of the transcripts.

5. If statistical comparisons are made to isolate the characteristics of the exemplary performers (Step 2 of the JCAM), then a statistical analysis resource will be needed. Although the statistical analysis requirements of the JCAM are minimal (e.g., the application of analysis of variance techniques), this resource must be either available within the organization or externally recruited.

6. If the employees to be interviewed are not geographically co-located, considerable time and expense must be invested for travel and communications with the interviewees and possibly with other persons. This can rapidly escalate the budget for a project.

7. The time frame required for completing a typical application of the JCAM is quite extensive when compared with the time frames of other competency model development methods. Even when the number of persons to be interviewed is not large, time is consumed by such tasks as coordinating interview schedules, briefing management in the host organization units, training interviewers and analysts, procuring needed resources, transcribing the interview tapes, and conducting meetings.

Although there are potentially significant costs associated with the use of this method, the high-quality results that are realized must be taken into account. When the use of rigorous, empirical methods is an appropriate response to a competency model development project, this method is the preferred choice.

Case Report of the Use of the JCAM

For reviewing a case report of an application of the JCAM in a very large organization context, the work of Flanders and Utterback (1985) is highly recommended. This case report describes how a three-tier competency model that describes the job competencies for Federal Government supervisors, managers, and executives was researched and prepared.

The model was implemented for training and educating Federal supervisors, managers, and executives. The elements of the three-tier competency model that evolved from the research were used to construct an employee competence inventory. By receiving feedback on their performance from their immediate manager, peers, and subordinates, Federal supervisors and managers were able to prepare individualized performance improvement plans that included various training or education experiences. The competency model was also a foundation for curriculum and instructional planning within Federal training program offices.

MODIFIED JOB COMPETENCE ASSESSMENT METHOD

The Modified Job Competence Assessment Method is the same as the JCAM, with only one exception. Instead of conducting one-on-one interviews with the exemplary and average performers for the subject job, the interview questions used for a CBI are listed on paper and employees are asked to write critical behavior stories. An alternative to this is to transmit the CBIs electronically. Their stories essentially reconstruct their job experiences, but, in many cases, with less detail than in a face-to-face interview.

An obvious disadvantage of this method is that when the data are collected without the advantage of live interaction between the employee and the interviewer, probing questions from the interviewer on aspects of the CBIs cannot be asked. An alternative is to ask the responding employees to include their telephone number with their responses so they can be contacted by the survey staff in case a follow-up information interview is needed or preferred.

A second disadvantage of this technique is that oftentimes the responding employees are reluctant to invest the time and effort required to compose and prepare quality narrative responses to a survey of this type. Therefore, the nonresponse rate could be higher than it would be using other, less demanding information reporting methods. If this approach is used, the cover letter that accompanies the questionnaire or instructions for writing the critical behavior stories should emphasize how important an employee's response is to the achievement of the organization's immediate and strategic objectives.

Another technique that encourages participation is making a telephone call to the employee and enlisting his or her support *prior to sending a formal data or information collection request*. This gives the employee an opportunity to ask questions. Respondents will frequently inform the analyst of pending schedules or projects that could delay or prohibit their participation. The benefits of the analyst knowing these facts in advance of sending a formal request are obvious. Many delays and the loss of critically important data can be avoided by making these calls in advance of a formal written request.

This technique is very useful when the employees to be polled are not centrally or geographically co-located. The costs of individually interviewing persons in several geographic locations can nearly prohibit some organizations from using the JCAM. This procedure is especially useful when an organization must interview employees who are working abroad.

Another approach for data collection is the use of a tape-recorded response to a written request to the employee. For the researcher to use this approach, the employee must have access to a tape-recording device. A blank audiocassette and a self-addressed, stamped envelope are included with the written request. A 90-minute audiocassette can be used, but a 120-minute length is preferable since a face-to-face CBI interview is usually planned to last at least two hours.

Although the data collection process has been altered, a preliminary telephone call should be made to acquaint the employee with the project and to determine whether it will be feasible for the employee to participate. During this conversation, the employee receives information on his or her role and guidelines for responding to the research questions. When the tape recording is received by the analyst, a written transcript is prepared in the same manner as it would have been prepared using the JCAM, and the analyst encodes the information using the same techniques. Once the contents of the transcripts are reviewed, the analyst has the opportunity to follow up by phoning the employee and asking clarifying questions.

Yet another information-gathering technique is to have the employee videotape a response to the interview questions. This approach has an added advantage over the use of a sound-only tape because changes in an employee's affect (e.g., their nonverbal behaviors) can be observed. A disadvantage is that all employees who must be interviewed might not have access to a videotaping studio, facility, or other resource.

Organizations are increasingly acquiring two-way video and audio-teleconferencing capabilities through the use of satellite technologies. This is an exciting possibility for conducting the CBIs that are required when the JCAM is selected for developing a competency model.

In summary, when a decision has been made to use the JCAM but it is difficult to gain access to the employees who must be interviewed, the alternatives above offer some options for obtaining the required data.

GENERIC MODEL OVERLAY METHOD

This alternative method does not require the completion of the numerous research steps of the JCAM for developing a competency model. The process relies on the use or the transplantation of an existing, research-based competency model in the organization. A certain sacrifice in the degree of fit of the model in the organization might be necessary.

A dependence on existing competency models is not as problematic as it may sound. Over the past several years, a considerable number of competency models for a variety of jobs and occupations have been developed. In particular, a number of models for the professions and trades have become available from practitioners, professional societies, trade associations, credentialing groups, researchers, and vendors. Although there is no central clearinghouse for competency models and competency model technology, competency models are also appearing with greater frequency in the literature and in books specific to a profession or trade. Exchanging competency models and research reports on their development is becoming common practice among many HRD professionals. This availability reflects a growing trend in capturing the benefits of using competency model technology as a foundation for human resource management systems, including organizations' performance improvement systems.

How, then, is a Generic Model Overlay Method completed? The approach described here assumes that little information is known about the job and the competencies employees must have in order to perform the job in a fully successful manner. The suggested approach can be modified to meet internal organization requirements.

The first step is to complete the needs analysis, assessment, and planning step of the Strategic Systems Model (see Figure 2.1). Analyses must be completed at the strategic organization level.

Next, a draft competency model is researched and developed for the job in the strategic organization context. A focus group of job experts is constituted, and facilitated brainstorming with the focus group is used to create the first draft competency model. Three sets of competencies are created, including those which distinguish exemplary from average job performance, those held by both the exemplary and the average performers, and the technical competencies required by both groups of job performers.

The draft competency model is verified by having a group of exemplary performers of the job review the draft model. The exemplary performers are identified by members of the focus group. The exemplary performers are asked to suggest additions, deletions, or other modifications to the model and also to explain the reason(s) for their suggestions. Once the review of the draft model is complete, the focus group reviews the exemplary performers' suggestions and, if necessary, revises the model to its satisfaction.

The final competency model and the strategic context information are used to conduct a search for a research-based competency model (or models) that align as closely as possible with the final competency model. If a research-based model for the job is located, then slight modifications to it might be necessary in order to tailor it to the application environment. This must be done carefully if the research integrity of the model is to be maintained. If an existing competence assessment accompanies the generic model and this instrument is to be used, then modifications to the model and instrument should *not* be made. If modifications are made, then the instrumentation must be validated prior to its use.

Quite often, the best source of a research-based model is a vendor with specialization in whatever job or occupation is the subject of the search. Management and supervision occupations are well represented by vendors who have specialized in making available researched competency models for their client organizations. Unless the model you select is in the public domain, you must obtain permission to use it (or a portion of it) from its owner. A second source of these types of models is professional and trade organizations.

This competency model development method is usually adopted for one or both of the following reasons:

1. If a well-aligned, research-based competency model can be located, then considerable time and resources need not be committed to conduct in-depth internal research to develop the model. This can represent a considerable cost savings to the organization. The external model should be reviewed to determine whether it was developed for a comparable job population and an occupation with a similar organizational context.

2. A generic model overlay method is a very attractive alternative when an organization wants to do competence assessments that will be used to create individualized employee development plans. If the model was carefully researched and developed, then designing a competence assessment instrument based on it should be a straightforward process—or one might be immediately available from a vendor. When a generic competency model with an accompanying assessment instrument of known reliability and validity can be located, then the model and the instrument should be adopted for use if the proper "fit" with the organization can be assured. Otherwise, tailoring or customizing models and assessment instruments must be done with care.

When competency models (and the instruments based upon them) are obtained from sources external to an organization, the practitioner should discuss with the client or client group the advantages and potential limitations of this method, and review the assumptions that must be made when it is used. Why so?

First, an externally developed job competency model, no matter how well it was researched, will seldom precisely characterize the attributes of high performers and the other competencies required for successful job performance as it exists within the context of the receiving organization. In particular, internal research will probably be needed in order to isolate the exemplary-performer competencies.

Second, societal and organization context assumptions must usually be made about the contents of these models. Given the rapid change occurring throughout the world, static or rigid job competency models will find minimal direct applications in these changing world and business environments. Using an overlay procedure of the type described here makes an assumption that homeostatic work conditions existed from the time the model was researched until it was adopted. Depending on the subject-matter of the model, and the conditions both then and now, this assumption might or might not be valid. It is subject to examination.

Third, using an external model overlay method assumes that the language contained in the external model will be consistent with the language of the host organization and its culture. When the model's language is not contextually specific to the organization, the phrases, terms, and expressions could potentially be interpreted in a variety of ways by the users. This could lead to confusion, inappropriate or inaccurate assessments or conclusions, or improperly targeted HRD interventions.

Fourth, with this method there is always a danger that some competencies critical to successful performance will not be detected or included in the generic competency model. Only research in the application context of the organization can reveal the more subtle omissions. Glaring omissions are usually easily identified. How you might correct a known deficiency, however, depends upon the resources available to you and upon other circumstances within the host organization.

Fifth, the technical job competencies required for successful job performance by the exemplary and the average performers must be included in the competency model. Behavioral indicators must also be developed for each of the technical competencies if they do not already exist.

One way (although imperfect) to overcome problems related to the degree of fit between the elements of a generic model and the job requirements in the host organization is to treat the competencies within the model as a universal menu of competencies, as opposed to a fixed or inflexible model. Before adopting this method, however, you must be certain that the generic model includes *at least* the full range of competencies required for fully successful job performance. Furthermore, it must include the technical and other competencies that are required for exemplary performance. If one or more elements of a model are missing, then research in the host organization will be necessary in order to ensure that a comprehensive model is adopted. Before you select and use a generic competency model in this manner, check the contents and characteristics of it very carefully. Share it with the client or client group and obtain their endorsement of it before you use it. Remember: The competency model must include the universe of competencies required for exemplary and average job performance.

Here's an example of how an endorsed, generic model can be successfully used. Assume an employee and her manager are using a comprehensive, generic competency model that was imported into the work organization, intending to develop her job training plan for the coming year. One way to ensure that the model is an accurate representation of the employee's specific job requirements is to have the employee and her manager jointly rate and concur on the value of each competency statement relative to its importance for her successful or exemplary job performance. This process has two advantages.

First, the competencies that have the greatest impacts on job performance can easily be identified and understood by the employee and her immediate manager. The competencies that differentiate exemplary from average job performance can be identified specific to the job.

Second, by viewing the generic model as a "menu" rather than as a static model, both persons in the transaction have an opportunity to identify the competencies they believe are of the greatest importance for improving the employee's performance relative to the immediate demands of the job. When there is disagreement on the job outputs and/or the competencies required to achieve them, this becomes known very early in the transaction. These disagreements indicate that the expectations held by the two parties are inconsistent, and that they could be the source of a larger problem later on if not corrected at the present time. Furthermore, when shifts in the definition of an employee's work outputs occur, the practice of treating the elements in the competency model as a menu (rather than as a static model) opens opportunities for more flexible and focused communication and understanding between the employee and the manager. Changes are easily accommodated. Competency models can also be used by teams as a way of communicating and acting on the achievement of common expectations.

Despite its possible limitations, a generic competency model overlay method can be a useful approach for avoiding the expense of developing a competency model using the internal resources of the organization. In particular, competency models produced by professional societies or trade associations for jobs in their profession or domain have usually resulted from a professional commitment on the part of the membership to invest the resources necessary for a high-quality result. Competency models developed by professional societies or trade organizations are usually comprehensive and found to be highly useful by the membership of the sponsoring organization (for example, see McLagan, 1989b). If the requisite assumptions and additional work can be minimized or in large part overcome, then this method can be a very workable solution to the problem of obtaining a job competency model with a minimum investment of an organization's resources.

CUSTOMIZED GENERIC MODEL METHOD

In order to use this method, a generic competency model or a set of generic competency statements is used as the primary raw materials to develop a customized competency model that is specific to a job, its outputs, and the application environment where the job exists. This method can be applied to a single job or to several jobs. Application of the steps that follow will result in a fixed or static competency model for a job within an organization.

The steps for using the Customized Generic Model Method include the following:

1. Enlist initial client or client group support and develop a project plan.

2. Assemble and review all available information pertinent to the job. Prepare a job information paper or portfolio.

3. Research an initial set of job competencies.

4. Organize a focus group.

5. Convene the focus group and develop a draft, "best estimate" competency model.

6. Research the draft, "best estimate" competency model in the organization and develop the final competency model.

7. Brief the client or client group on the project results. Prepare the final project products.

Each step is discussed below.

Step 1. **Enlist initial client or client group support and develop a project plan.**

You must *always* ensure the active involvement of the client or client group at virtually every stage of competency model development. Without that involvement and the concurrence of the client on the final project products, the use of the competency model within the organization has a low probability of acceptance and, therefore, of success. The HRD specialist is primarily responsible for overall project leadership. The client or client group may (or may not) choose to name a project co-leader to share the responsibility for completing the project steps with the HRD specialist. This should be decided during initial discussions the HRD specialist holds with the client or client group.

Preparing a competency model represents a considerable investment of organization time and other resources. As such, there is no adequate substitute for having a detailed project plan. Particularly, when using this method, you must ensure that the project steps, work requirements, and project outcomes are clear to all parties *before* detailed work begins. Initial responsibility for the preparation of a project plan rests with the HRD specialist or jointly with the HRD specialist and the project co-leader named by the client.

Step 2. Assemble and review all available information that is pertinent to the job. Prepare a job information paper or portfolio.

Gather as much information as possible about the job and project "issues." Assuming the job or jobs were a subject of front-end needs analysis, assessment, and planning, information generated at that time about the job requirements, the performance improvement issues, and other facts should be obtained and distributed to the project focus group. It is generally best to assemble this information in the form of a document or portfolio. Items like the job requirements, job outputs, tasks and activities performed, the organization or work environment context, and other pertinent information must be researched and completed. Some, all, or none of this information might be available, depending upon the situation. If the front-end work (described in chapter 2) was not completed, then it must be completed now. Once the information document or portfolio is ready, copies are distributed to the focus group members for their review and use throughout the project (see Step 5).

Step 3. Research an initial set of job competencies.

Search for and obtain either a competency model or a set of competencies that you sense are aligned with the job or jobs that are the subject of your work. A universe of average and exemplary performers' competencies and the technical competencies required for successful job performance should be anticipated as the search and procurement process is pursued. If a model or competency set(s) is located, determine the availability of the materials for your use. The copyright holder and/or the publisher must be contacted to determine whether the model or competency list can be used by you and your client, and the conditions of that use. The user must acknowledge the source of the information and permission to use it on any project publications that are prepared.

Step 4. **Organize a focus group.**

The composition of the focus group should be appropriate to the project requirements and product goals. Primary responsibility for the project rests with the HRD specialist and possibly a co-leader from the client or client group, if that option was chosen. Potential focus group members include the organization's senior managers, managers, subject-matter experts, and external persons such as its customers, clients, and so forth. The potential members are contacted and their membership is enlisted.

Step 5. **Convene the focus group and develop a draft, "best estimate" competency model.**

The focus group meets and begins work. The leader (or co-leaders) distributes the project plan, describes the work outputs already accomplished, explains each project product and its importance to the organization, reviews the concepts that will be used during the project, and presents a timetable for developing the products. The job information paper or portfolio is also distributed and discussed.

A draft, "best-estimate" competency model is the first product of the focus group. The first step of the classical JCAM is completed. The draft model includes the relationships of the job outputs to the competencies. The major job tasks or activities are aligned with the competency statements. The focus group members differentiate the competencies according to the technical, exemplary, and average performer categories that were described in the JCAM. Behavioral indicators are also composed.

Step 6. **Research the draft, "best estimate" competency model in the organization and develop the final competency model.**

The purpose of this step is to obtain verification of the contents of the draft competency model. It is essential for you to ensure that the list of competencies and other competency model elements are complete. The more comprehensive a competency model is, the more useful it will be for defining performance improvement interventions and other applications.

How this is done depends on the time and resources available to the focus group. It also depends on the type of results you require. You might possibly want, for example, to collect opinion data from a large number of persons within the organization. Or a decision might include the collection of CBI data only, or CBI data might be combined with opinion data. This could require you (or a contractor) to design a survey, including data collection procedures and forms, an analysis plan, and other elements required for completing a high-quality survey.

Given the volume of data collection and analysis work that must be completed, a research and analysis plan (which is separate from, or a subset of, the larger project plan) is essential to the success of the analysis activities. The plan must be very specific about how the technical work will be completed.

Decisions must be made regarding which individuals (or groups of individuals) will be studied, how their participation will be scheduled, and the organization political factors affecting their participation. A description of the survey population, its location and size, sampling plans, estimation formulas, data analysis methods, and so forth, must be included in the plan. This plan should also specify the types, uses, methods, and the rules or criteria that will be applied for building the competency model. Obviously the technical plans must be concrete prior to designing the data collection instruments (including interview protocols), the coding techniques for interpreting the interview data, and the statistical or other analysis procedures for analyzing and reducing discrete data to population estimates or values. Finally, decisions are required on how the analysis findings will be combined with other information to construct the competency model. Any specialized resources that are required to complete the work must be identified and procured.

Data collection can be accomplished in a variety of ways, such as through the use of structured individual interviews, specialized focus groups, checklists, questionnaires, and rating sheets. Organization resources and the professional capabilities available to the focus group will dictate the degree of sophistication possible in the application of a particular set of procedures.

Once the data have been collected, they are analyzed according to the project analysis plan, and the results are then interpreted. Interview data must usually be encoded against a set of categories, such as the researched list of capabilities from Step 1 of JCAM. Written data (e.g., as from questionnaires) must be reviewed for completeness, and low-level desk editing is usually required. When simple desk editing is not sufficient to improve the quality or the utility of the data, additional effort must be made either to return to the respondent for more information (if that person can be identified) or to seek an adequate replacement respondent. Replacements are usually used only when the total number of potential respondents is small. Large quantities of data are processed using a personal or mainframe computer. Every project can be significantly different in the way this step is handled.

Step 7. **Brief the client or client group on the project results. Prepare the final project products.**

On completion of the research and analysis phases above, a competency model is constructed. Supporting documents are prepared, explaining the elements of the model that describe the research processes used to create it. The client (or client group) and/or senior managers are briefed. Revisions to the project products are made once those reviews are complete.

In conclusion, this method produces an organizationally defensible competency model for a job if the specific suggestions included above and accepted research standards are utilized during implementation of the critical stages of the research process.

FLEXIBLE JOB PERFORMANCE DESIGN AND MODELING: A FUTURE-ORIENTED APPROACH

Job analysis and design concepts and techniques are integrally important to the completion of competency model development projects. The purpose of this section is to briefly introduce you to flexible job performance design and modeling.

The Information Age is here. And with it has come rapid change in the work place, including how jobs are designed, the job roles that employees have assumed, the job outputs expected of them, and the competencies they need for successful performance. It has been difficult for organizations to maintain up-to-date performance improvement programs that can remain current with these changes and with the new or different demands for job competence that they require.

Traditional approaches to job design in organizations are based on an assumption of long-term stability in the environmental assumptions, job roles, outputs, the quality standards for those outputs, and the competencies that employees need to produce those results. In the contemporary business and economic environment, job design, job outputs, and the competencies needed for successful performance are predicted to be dynamic, unstable, and fluid rather than stable and fixed.

The degree of stability in a job or job family, its work unit, and the organization as a whole will affect the job design and competency model development approach that is selected. Therefore, you need to be aware of the concepts of a flexible job design and competency model approach, which will provide you with a frame of reference for considering and evaluating the appropriateness of various job competency modeling methods. The balance of this section is committed to helping you attain that awareness.

Concerning the dilemma that instability raises, Patricia McLagan (1990) notes, "Individual job designs are becoming, and must continue to become, more individualized and flexible. This presents major problems for traditional job design methodologies which hold the individual constant while developing job descriptions that can accommodate many personalities. In today's environment, individuals often shape their jobs. As they work, they broaden and deepen or reduce the scope of their output responsibilities" (p. 375). She defines flexible job design as "a procedure that leads an organization through a series of steps to specify precisely what outcomes it wants to produce and the kinds of jobs and job holders that will be required to produce those outcomes. The emphasis is on using participative methods and a very specific and concrete language to facilitate the precise descriptions of what an organization wants to do" (p. 370).

According to McLagan, a flexible job design and competency modeling method results in products that do the following:

- Systematically forecast future requirements for an organization

- View the organization as an open social system that constantly changes in response to external influences

- Emphasize job outputs as the *major* building blocks of organization design

- Identify the performance requirements for a job and the employee capabilities needed to produce the job outputs

- View job design as a process of assigning or reassigning outputs to jobs

- Support a view of job evaluation that places individuals in broad salary bands based on the overall types of outputs they produce

- Treat a description of performance goals as the job description

- Provide a conceptual framework for integrating all human resource functions in an organization

- Provide workers and managers with the information needed to fully participate in defining jobs, managing performance, and guiding development

- Support easy updating as organization strategies and conditions change

Furthermore, a flexible job design and competency modeling approach can be applied to the jobs for an entire organization, to the jobs in a work unit within the organization, or to a single job (McLagan, 1990, pp. 369-370).

Application of a flexible job design method produces the following outputs (McLagan, 1990, p. 371):

- Job output menus that show the outputs for a job and (optional) criteria for evaluating their quality

- Competency menus that specify the competencies required to produce the outputs

- Generic job role models

- Individualized job models for each job-holder (if preferred)

The job elements are researched within the organization context by seeking and analyzing the expert opinions of officers, executives, managers, selected individual performers, subject-matter experts, or others as appropriate to the project objectives. Participative research techniques are used to facilitate the development of the critical job elements with these persons.

Job design and the development of competency models become a straightforward process once the job elements are available. One approach to job design is to select the relevant job outputs and the competencies from the respective menus required for successful performance. Another approach to job design is to select the role (or roles) from a menu which constitutes the job. Job roles are determined through a cluster analysis of the job outputs. By selecting a role or roles, the outputs are known, and the competencies can then be selected. Therefore, the job outputs, and the competencies required to achieve them are the elements needed to define the work.

Numerous advantages are realized by adopting a flexible job modeling approach:

1. Job competency models that result from the raw materials are considerably more durable over time than are competency models derived from other methods—an important feature of this method.

2. These competency models are easy to update as the work requirements change.

3. By using a flexible approach, competency models can be determined for jobs that do not yet exist.

4. Competency models constructed in this manner are readily available for doing in-depth micro-level needs analyses, since they support the useof a variety of individual and group analysis perspectives.

McLagan (1990) points out that establishing a total flexible organization and job design method:

> Requires considerable effort and involvement on the part of the people in the organization. In that sense, it is not cheap. It also requires considerable facilitation skills. Outputs of the facilitator's role include obtaining management commitment to the process and showing managers that this approach confronts directly the major issues of the business and is therefore an integral part of their management responsibility. If the commitment of top management can be achieved, flexible organization and job design is a total-system design process. (pp. 383-384)

A flexible job design and competency modeling method—which is a systems approach to job and organization design—holds high promise for the effective and efficient design and documentation of jobs in the present and future work environments, assuming a certain level of investment by its user.

Flexible Job Competency Model Method

The methods for developing competency models included earlier in this chapter are useful for jobs that are relatively stable and have relatively consistent outputs over sufficiently long enough periods of time to make the investment in the use of strict empirical methods a cost-effective decision. Furthermore, the research process (or segments of it) must be periodically replicated to maintain currency in the contents of these models. Also, traditional model-building methods are inappropriate for jobs that do not yet exist within the organization context. The method of flexible job competency modeling described below is a generic, step-by-step process for developing the job elements required to build generic, flexible, and individualized job competency models.

Figure 3.4 illustrates the elements of a generic competency model. It was constructed for the role of HRD Program Designer by using the job elements that were researched as part of the *HRD Models* project. A flexible job design and modeling method was used to complete this project. You will find it helpful to refer

Program Designer Role

The Program Designer Role includes preparing objectives, defining content, and selecting and sequencing activities for a specific intervention.

Job Outputs

1. **Program/Intervention Objectives**

   Quality Requirements:
   • They identify the indicators or measures that can show how each objective has been achieved.

   • They are stated in terms of what the learner will know, value and/or be able to do.
   . . .

2. **Program/Intervention Design**

   Quality Requirements:
   • The sequencing of content and method reflects an understanding of the audience and of adult learning principles.

   • The designs support the organization business plans and objectives.
   . . .

Competencies

   1. **Adult-Learning Understanding:** Knowing how adults acquire and use knowledge, skills, attitudes; understanding individual differences in learning.

   2. **Competency — Identification Skill:** Identifying the knowledge and skill requirements of jobs, tasks and roles

   3. **Information — Search Skill:** . . .

   4. **Intellectual Versatility:** . . .

   . . .

   10. **Writing Skill:** . . .

Ethical Issues

   1. Maintaining appropriate confidentiality

   2. Being sensitive to direct and indirect effects of an intervention and acting to address negative consequences
   . . .
   6. Making the intervention appropriate to the customers' and users' needs

Figure 3.4: Portion of a Competency Model Constructed by Using Selected Job Elements from an Application of the Flexible Job Competency and Model Method

Source: McLagan, 1989a and 1989b. Reprinted with permission.

to the elements of this example quite frequently as you proceed through the steps that follow. The elements included in Figure 3.4 represent only a fraction of the contents found in the menus for HRD jobs from the *HRD Models* project.

Although the following steps use the singular form "job," it should be understood that several jobs might be the focus of the project. To complete the flexible job competency modeling method, take the following steps:

1. Assemble and review all available information that is pertinent to the job. Prepare a job information paper or portfolio.

2. Identify an expert panel consisting of senior organization leaders, managers, or exemplary subject-matter experts.

3. Develop present and future assumptions about the job in the context of the organization.

4. Develop a job outputs menu, including (optional) quality criteria for each output.

5. Construct a job competencies menu and the behavioral indicators for each competency.

6. Determine a menu of job roles through a cluster analysis of the job outputs.

7. Construct one or more generic job competency models.

8. Brief the client or client group on the project results. Prepare the final project products.

A discussion of how each step is completed follows.

Step 1. Assemble and review all available information that is pertinent to the job. Prepare a job information paper or portfolio.

The purpose of this step is to avoid "reinventing the wheel" in later project steps. It is wasteful to invest the time of busy employees in creating anew that which already exists either within or external to the organization. The front-end needs analyses, assessment, and planning data relative to the job and the organization's strategic context are the first sources of information that the HRD specialist must obtain (see

Step 1 of Figure 3.1, the Strategic Systems Model). If the work of that step was not completed, then a strategic analysis must be completed in this stage of the work.

If the job already exists in the organization, any available information on it should be assembled for later inclusion in the paper or portfolio. This could include job tasks or activities, the job outputs, expectations, historical information on the job, how it has evolved, and any information on its future in the context of the organization. Information on the roles and competencies required by employees who currently hold the job is valuable. Demographic characteristics of the present and projected future job holders provide valuable information on how the job factors are implemented. In summary, the HRD specialist should review the available information, organize it, and include it in a brief paper or portfolio for use by the expert panel that will develop the project products.

Step 2. **Identify an expert panel consisting of senior organization leaders, managers, or exemplary subject-matter experts.**

The composition of the expert panel will largely depend on the nature of what must be studied. For example, for jobs with high strategic organization impact, the expert panel would probably include senior managers or corporate officers. For other projects, you might need to combine senior managers or officers with subject-matter experts or other managers in order to ensure that different perspectives on the issues are available. Yet other panels might consist of only managers or only subject-matter experts. In general, however, senior organization managers or leaders are the most appropriate source of information on the contextual and strategic present conditions and future assumptions for the organization. The other managers and the subject-matter experts are a source of information on technical, operational, or other information required to develop the job outputs, roles, the competency menus, behavioral indicators, or models. The project dimensions and context will suggest how you should proceed.

The composition of the expert panel and whether or not it is divided into sub-panels or specialized work groups are decisions driven by the nature of the project and the importance of the job for achieving strategic organization goals. How this plays out will also be affected by the psychology and the sociology within the organization, the availability of the personalities, the time available to complete the work, and so forth. The participation of the panel members must be arranged and a schedule of activities, including estimates of the time that must be committed to the project by each member, must be communicated.

Some organizations have included their customers, regulators, legal authorities, and others on the expert panel. This practice results in having a wider spectrum of opinions on not only how the organization is perceived externally, but also on how it is actually responding to those who receive or use its products, services, and information. Members drawn from the external organization environment can successfully contribute to the project results if the process is properly communicated and managed.

The facilitator for the expert panel must have highly developed facilitation competence. This person must be respected by the panel members, and especially respected by those panel members who are senior managers, managers, or leaders in the organization (i.e., the decision- or policy-makers in the organization).

For some projects, members of the expert panel(s) might not be able to conveniently meet and complete their work in a common location. In this case, the data must be collected remotely. This can be done by using the postal service or by electronic means. A useful survey method for completing this type of research is called the Delphi Technique (see Rath & Stoyanoff, 1983). The *HRD Models* project, which was sponsored by the American Society for Training and Development, researched HRD job roles, outputs, quality criteria, competencies, and the ethical issues associated with them. *HRD Models* is an excellent example of a project that relied upon survey research techniques that were designed to accommodate a geographically dispersed survey population (McLagan, 1989a, 1989b).

Step 3. **Develop present and future assumptions about the job in the context of the organization.**

The development of the present and future assumptions about a job must be grounded in a strategic organization context. The paper or portfolio that was prepared in Step 1 is the primary resource for this strategic context. This paper or portfolio, you will recall, included the front-end needs analysis, assessment, and planning results that were originally completed by using a strategic level of investigation and analysis. It should include broad information on the future strategic directions for the organization. The expert panel will develop context assumptions following a review of this paper or portfolio.

Context assumptions describe present job requirements and forecast future job requirements by describing *highly probable* future conditions that will affect the organization in which the job exists. These assumptions could include, for example, predictions about organization structure; technology; work force demographics or values; the legal or regulatory environment; the competitive environment; a need for different, new or additional products or services; or changes in sources of supplies or suppliers' services. Because they are a major information source for defining the competencies currently needed by workers and for predicting those competencies that will be needed later, it is essential that content assumptions are thoughtfully identified and agreed upon at a level in the organization appropriate to the job and its importance for the achievement of strategic organization goals.

Context assumptions are identified through structured, facilitated discussions and brainstorming. Consensus on the context assumptions among the panel members is essential. Since those assumptions are a foundation for the remaining project products, they must accurately describe both the present and future work conditions for the job or jobs under investigation or development. Once again, a highly competent facilitator must be used for this work.

Step 4. **Develop a job outputs menu, including (optional) quality criteria for each output.**

This menu includes job outputs that an organization provides to external entities or that individuals in an organization provide to each other, in order to achieve the organization's objectives. Outputs consist of products, services, or information. Associated with each output is a set of (optional) quality criteria that describe excellence for the output. The contents of the menu must describe the outputs that are key (given the assumptions identified in Step 3) to any other function or group internal or external to the organization. The job outputs menu and the quality criteria are developed by the expert panel by using brainstorming and arriving at consensus on the results.

McLagan suggests two ways to categorize job outputs: by core discipline and/or by their span of control. The latter is important if you want to place a value on the output for job evaluation purposes. "Core disciplines" represent outputs associated with a class or body of knowledge (e.g., electronics). For example, for the core discipline "management," some typical job outputs could include employee performance improvement plans, facility operating guidelines, sales goals, and case completion requirements.

Describing job outputs by their span of control requires identifying the value of the job outputs relative to the impacts of the decisions that must be made about them (McLagan, 1990, p. 372). There are six categories for identifying the span of control for job outputs:

1. Simple, discrete, prescribed tasks (lowest level)

2. Semiskilled operations that are performed

3. Statements about how existing processes will be used

4. Broad resource allocations

5. Action and program priorities

6. Broad organization goals or objectives (highest level)

Early identification of the core discipline and span of control for the job outputs has two advantages. First, these values provide clues on how the expert panels should be constituted. Second, these values suggest ways for designing flexible competency-based curricula that can be vertically integrated (i.e., across spans of control) as well as horizontally integrated (i.e., within or across core or subject-matter disciplines).

For each job output, optional quality criteria may also be generated. The quality criteria describe exemplary outputs. As the movement toward improved quality accelerates, organizations will more frequently include the development of quality criteria as a requirement of this work.

Step 5. **Construct a job competencies menu and the behavioral indicators for each competency.**

McLagan (1990, p. 374) suggests that five categories of competencies are useful for creating a competency menu that is linked to a job outputs menu. The competencies are those that are required to produce the job outputs. They include three skills categories: physical, interpersonal, and intrapersonal. In the knowledge domain, broad business and/or industry knowledge and specialist knowledge are included.

When the span of control for a job increases or becomes more abstract (and therefore less concrete), the competency statements tend to become broader. McLagan points out that under these circumstances:

> Task descriptions are less useful than descriptions of the broad knowledge and skills that a performer will draw on to make judgments and decisions about appropriate actions to take. An exhaustive competency menu would contain a finely grained list of the key skills and knowledge required for producing a job's outcomes. However, in our work it is more common for the menu to describe broad knowledge and skills, thus relegating finer levels of competency identification to the . . . "individual job model." (p. 374)

In light of the curriculum planning requirements that will be encountered later in chapter 4, a finely grained list of the key competencies is one of the most useful products for suggesting various curriculum design options, patterns, and plans. For example, a competency menu for a set of jobs might include "listening skills" as a critical competency for several of the jobs in the organization. A knowledge of this information is important for curriculum planning purposes across levels of the organization. First, this broad competency must be broken down into actual, specific performance dimensions for each job in the organization in order for performance improvement curricula and instructional activities to be designed. We must know the specific manifestations of "Using Listening Skills" for jobs or levels of jobs within the organization. This information is also needed for designing formal classroom experiences, for creating plans for on-the-job coaching, and for creating criteria and structures for job rotation assignments, special projects, and other performance improvement opportunities.

The panel of experts is used to create the competencies and competency menus. If additional subject-matter expertise is required at this stage of the design work, guest experts can be invited to work with the core panel of experts for whatever time period is appropriate for achieving the required outcomes.

Practitioners who use this method for competency modeling often provide the expert panel with a list or a collection of competencies that are relevant to the job or jobs under investigation. If a job already exists, competency statements might already be available. The competency list tends to "prime the pump" or start the brainstorming process with the panel members. Caution should be used, however, since providing too much information might inhibit the amount of creative energy that the panel invests in the work. You will need to monitor this on a project-by-project basis.

One way to develop a list of "candidate" competencies is to do an exhaustive literature search for the job or jobs under consideration. An organization, for example, chose to emphasize "leadership" as the most critical characteristic of managers at all levels of management within their organization. To ensure that this focus was accomplished, contemporary leadership literature was thoroughly researched and synthesized into a leadership design for the organization. An expert panel used this design, in conjunction with other information, to create flexible, generic competency models for each of three adjacent levels of management within their organization. The project was successful.

Either after the competency menu has been developed or during menu development, the behavioral indicators for each competency are developed. The behavioral indicators illustrate when a competency has been acquired or mastered by an employee. One or more levels of mastery can be created for each competency. These can include, for example, definitions for basic, intermediate and advanced levels of mastery. The expert panel develops the behavioral indicators and mastery levels through facilitated discussions. Once again, other job experts can be invited to work with the core panel on an ad hoc basis.

The products that result from this step include:

- A menu of job competencies and their alignments with the job outputs

- Behavioral indicators for each competency

- Mastery levels for the competencies (optional)

Step 6. **Determine a menu of job roles through a cluster analysis of the job outputs.**

To define job roles, the job outputs are cluster-analyzed into logical, practical subsets. Each job outputs cluster is named as a role. The roles collectively define the total job. For example, the roles of needs analyst, instructor/facilitator, and researcher could be included in a collective definition of the job "HRD Practitioner." Since a job role can consist of one or more job outputs, along with the competencies required to produce outputs, then the competencies required by an employee to fulfill each role can be identified.

The expert panel, possibly with the help of an analyst, develops the job roles.

Step 7. **Construct one or more job competency models.**

Using the raw materials developed in the earlier steps, constructing flexible generic or individual job competency models is a straightforward process. Model building can be accomplished in either of two ways:

1. By selecting the relevant job outputs. Because the job outputs are linked to the competencies, the competencies can be identified in this way.

2. By selecting the job roles from the list of roles. The outputs and the competencies then immediately follow.

Step 8. **Brief the client or client group on the project results. Revise the results where indicated. Prepare the final project products.**

The project results are presented to the client in executive summary form. The presentation should be jointly delivered by a highly respected member of the expert panel, with the support of the HRD practitioner. Reactions to the process or products should be encouraged, and any revisions indicated should be made following the briefing. Once the sponsor concurs on the products, they are published in final form.

A flexible job competency model method has great promise and numerous advantages for defining the moving job targets that have become characteristic of business practices in the " Information Age." The availability of sets of job roles, job outputs, and competencies makes curriculum design and planning a flexible, yet straightforward process. Modular curriculum elements can be designed in a variety of ways and in combinations that are the most useful, effective, and efficient ones for the organization. Curriculum designs and the learning activities based on them can more rapidly be made available as circumstances change.

Comments

In conclusion, the following comments on a flexible approach to job competency modeling and its applications are offered.

Because a flexible approach to the job competency modeling process provides a wider universe of raw materials (e.g., competencies, job outputs, roles, and so forth) than other methods, changes to job competency models for specific applications and jobs are easily accommodated.

Managers and their employees have the raw materials they need to build individualized competency models and job performance profiles based on those models. As shifts in the job roles, outputs, and competencies are manifested, it is relatively easy to modify performance contracts and the design of performance improvement profile mechanisms.

A flexible approach to competency modeling provides the HRD specialist with a wide range of raw materials for curriculum and instructional planning and development. The resource base is richer with a flexible development approach than it otherwise might be with other competency model methods. A result is that the performance improvement opportunities created by using these raw materials are focused on the critical factors that make a significant difference in performance in the organization. These performance improvement activities are easily modified when shifts in the raw materials occur.

PLANNING AND COMPLETING A MODEL-DEVELOPMENT PROJECT

In nearly all cases, the HRD department or function will be responsible for the leadership of the competency model development project. This work is usually handled by a senior-level HRD specialist with at least some survey research competencies and well-developed interpersonal competencies. Organizations often opt to use consultant services for the development of competency models, or for at least the completion of some of the more technical aspects of a competency model development project.

The major requirements for the successful completion of a competency model development project include:

- Ensuring that the client or client group is given an opportunity to name a co-leader with the HRD specialist for the competency model development project

- The development of a project plan in close collaboration with, and with the concurrence of, the client or client organization

- Ensuring the availability and allocation of the resources required to complete the project, including external contracts, when necessary

- Arranging the project logistics

- Providing or arranging for project staff training, if necessary

- Preparing for and delivering briefings to the client, client organization, or others on the progress of the project or its results; maintaining the active involvement and participation of the client at all stages of the project

- Developing project reports or managing others in their development

- Obtaining project reviews and endorsements from the client, the client organization, or senior managers in the organization, as appropriate to the project

- Coordinating the next steps that will be taken to implement the use of the project results

Role of the HRD Specialist

Generally, the HRD specialist will do the following:

- Always insist on the development and adherence to a formal, written project plan that has been jointly developed with the cooperation and concurrence of the client or client organization

- Present the final plan and receive endorsement of it from the client or client organization *before* resources are committed to it and work is started

- Ensure that the client is fully represented at all project stages. It is strongly suggested that the client provide a project co-leader to work with the HRD specialist as a full, co-equal leader

- Informally and formally brief the client on a regular basis and request the assistance, suggestions, and endorsements needed at key project stages

- Be very clear with the client or client organization on what the project results will include, and what they will not include

- Be prepared to explain the project objectives and technology to non-experts

- Be open to listening and adopting technical or other suggestions appropriate for conducting the project, yet weigh every alternative measure in the context of achieving high-quality project results.

Role of the Client or Client Organization

The client will do the following:

- Comprehend and commit to the time and expense requirements for completion of the work

- Ensure that, at a minimum, a representative is meaningfully involved in the project from its inception until its completion. Co-leadership with the HRD function is preferred.

- Provide assistance to the HRD specialist to obtain or allocate resources, especially when resources from the client are required in order to successfully complete the project

- Participate in the formulation of the project research plan and assist in conducting the research

- Provide access to elements of the organization when that access is critical to the success of the project

Which Competency Model Development Method Should I Use?

Most organizations are complex and individual organization nuances make it unrealistic to definitively recommend one particular method for completing a competency model development project. Listed below are several questions whose answers will help you determine the most useful competency model development method for your application.

In particular:

1. What is the size of the target population for which a competency model is needed?

2. What is the geographic distribution of the target population?

3. Can the HRD department or staff gain access to the target population? How much access to critical elements of the organization is possible?

4. Can key players, including managers of the target population, be made available for the project, and if so, with what frequency and duration?

5. Are the job requirements stable over time? Is the job design situation stable or unstable? How "future-oriented" should the model be, if at all? If a future-oriented model is needed, what resources are required and available for forecasting the job competencies?

6. How will the competency model be used for training or education system planning and development? How extensive will the system be?

7. What HRD (and other) resources (e.g., statistical) are available to complete the technical tasks of competency model development? If internal resources are not available, can contract or consultant help be obtained? Whose approval is required and what is the probability of receiving that approval? How much and what type of "selling" must be done to obtain these resources?

8. Which method for competency model development has the greatest probability of acceptance, support, and success, given the culture and current environment within the organization? Is the organization chaotic, stable, or some combination thereof?

9. How much time is available to the HRD staff and the client to develop the competency model?

10. Are the impacts of the organization's strategic management objectives upon the job clear to those currently in the job and to their managers? What is the source of the workers' information on the organization's strategic management initiatives and their role in and contributions to achieving them?

11. How important is the project and the availability of a competency model to the employees' manager(s) and to senior management within the larger organization—i.e., does anybody really care if this project gets completed or not?

12. Will the organization's leaders, managers, and other influential persons understand and tolerate the creative and analytical processes that are characteristic of most methods for developing a competency model? How much application of creativity and analysis to the project will be tolerated?

13. Are HRD professionals and the HRD department or function respected by the client or larger organization, and to what degree? What will be the perceived level of credibility for obtaining the results?

14. How much is already known about the job or occupation family for which a competency model is needed? Will this information be available and useful for developing the competency model? Does an "expert performance system" already exist? Is it documented, either with workers or their managers, or in the minds of other key persons in the organization?

15. What is the collective general intellectual capacity of the organization, and especially of its managers and senior leaders? Once the concepts, procedures, and the results of the research are presented, will managers and senior leaders comprehend, accept, and support the implementation of the project results?

16. Is it critical to empirically determine the competencies that distinguish the average from the exemplary performers?

Project Standards

Whatever competency model research method is used, the project leader(s) should attempt to achieve the following:

- The highest level of validity that is possible under the circumstances surrounding its development

- Maximum organization endorsement and support for the research process and the project results

- Maximum alignment with the organization's strategic management initiatives and objectives

- A comprehensive competency model (including those competencies that reflect the thoughts, thought patterns, mindsets, convictions, and other attributes or characteristics) that differentiates the exemplary and the average from the poor performers, and that includes the technical competencies required for successful performance

- The project results expected (i.e., the model and supporting materials), delivered to the client on the agreed schedule

SUMMARY

My intention in this chapter was to help you learn about the meaning and nature of job competence, ways to analyze and assess it, and how to document it in a form that is useful for subsequent stages of planning performance improvement curricula in an organization context. Several methods for developing job competency models were described. Competency models or menus (depending on the method used to develop them) can be an in-depth source of information on the organization context, job roles, future or predictable influences on a job, the outputs and quality requirements for them, the job competencies required to achieve those results, and the behavioral indicators that signify when an employee has acquired the competencies.

JCAM is a rigorous, empirically based process for researching and developing a competency model. When JCAM is applied, it produces job models of high validity that distinguish the competency attributes of exemplary and average job performers. However, when the circumstances affecting job performance change, the research process must usually be replicated in order to keep the model up-to-date.

Other methods for developing a competency model were presented, and the requirements for using them and the results that can be obtained from their use were discussed. The flexible method for developing competency models has exceptional promise for ensuring that the job designs and the competency models for those jobs will remain current and responsive to the exceedingly high demands imposed by current and predicted future business conditions.

Once a valid competency model or a menu of critical job elements is available for a job (or a group of jobs), they can be used as a subset of the materials that are the inputs for creating a curriculum plan, which is the major output of the next step in the Strategic Systems Model.

Additional information and perspectives on the topics included in this chapter can be found in the following references.

REFERENCES

Block, A. R., & Rebell, M. A. (1980). *The assessment of occupational competence. Competence assessment and the courts: An overview of the state of the law* (ERIC Report No. ED 192 169/CE 027 168). Springfield, VA: U.S. Dept. of Education.

Boyatzis, R. E. (1982). *The competent manager: A model for effective performance.* New York: J. Wiley.

Carr, C. (1992). *Smart training: The manager's guide to training for improved performance.* New York: McGraw-Hill.

Cobb, J. C. (1990, August). Behind 'enemy' lines: A metaphor for the job of the safety professional. *Sociological Practice Review, 1*(2), pp. 128-131.

Cobb, J., & Gibbs, J. (1990). A new, competency-based, on-the-job program for developing professional excellence in engineering. *The Journal of Management Development, 9*(3), pp. 60-72.

Eubanks, J. L., Marshall, J.B., & O'Driscoll, M.P. (1990, November). A competency model for OD practitioners. *Training and Development Journal, 44* (11), pp. 85-90.

Flanagan, J. C. (1954). The critical incident technique. *Psychological Bulletin, 51* (4), pp. 327-358.

Flanders, L. R., & Utterback, D. (1985, May-June). The management excellence inventory: A tool for management development. *Public Administration Review*, pp. 403-410.

Gilbert, T. (1978). *Human competence.* New York: McGraw-Hill.

Hall, J. (1988). *The competence connection: A blueprint for excellence.* The Woodlands, Texas: Woodstead Press.

Harlan, A., Klemp, G. O., Jr., & Schaalman, M.L. (1980). *The assessment of occupational competence. Competence assessment in personnel selection: Current practices and trends* (ERIC Report No. ED 192 165/CE 027 160). Springfield, VA: U.S. Dept. of Education.

Huff, S. M., Klemp, G. O., Jr., Spencer, L. M., Jr., & Williamson, S. A. (1980). *The assessment of occupational competence. Summary: A synthesis of issues* (ERIC Report No. ED 192 170/CE 027 165). Springfield, VA: U.S. Dept. of Education.

Kane, J., & Lawler, E. E. (1978). Methods of peer assessment. *Psychological Bulletin, 85*(3), pp. 555-586.

Klemp, G. O., Jr. (1978). *Job competence assessment.* Boston, MA: McBer and Co., Inc.

Klemp, G. O., Jr. (1982). Job competence assessment: Defining the attributes of the top performer. In *The pig in the python and other tales* (ASTD Research Series, Vol. 8, pp. 55-67). Alexandria, VA: American Society for Training and Development.

Klemp, G. O., Jr. (1987, October). *Job competence assessment: Defining 'success factors' of job performance.* Boston, MA: Charles River Consulting, Inc.

Lewin, A. Y., & Zwany, A. (1976). Peer nominations: A model, literature critique, and paradigm for research. *Personnel Psychology, 29*, pp. 423-447.

McClelland, D. C. (1973). Testing for competence rather than for 'intelligence.' *American Psychologist, 28*(1), pp. 1-14.

McClelland, D. C. (1976). *A guide to job competency assessment.* Boston: McBer and Co., Inc.

McClelland, D. C., & Boyatzis, R. E. (1980, January). Opportunities for counselors from the competency assessment movement. *Personnel and Guidance Journal*, pp. 368-372.

McLagan, P. A. (1989a, September). Models for HRD practice. *Training and Development Journal, 33*(9), pp. 49-59.

McLagan, P. A. (1989b). *Models for HRD practice.* Alexandria, VA: American Society for Training and Development.

McLagan, P. A. (1990). Flexible job models: A productivity strategy for the Information Age. In J.P. Campbell, R. Campbell & Associates, *Productivity in organizations: New perspectives from industrial and organizational psychology.* San Francisco: Jossey-Bass.

Pottinger, P. S., Wiesfeld, N. E., Tochen, D. K., Cohen, P.D., & Schaalman, M.L. (1980). *The assessment of occupational competence. Competence assessment for occupational certification* (ERIC Report No. ED 192 167/CE 027 162). Springfield, VA: U.S. Dept of Education.

Rath, G., & Stoyanoff, K. (1983). The Delhi Technique. In F. L. Ulschak, *Human resource development: The theory and practice of need assessment.* Reston, VA: Reston Publishing Co.

Rollins, T., & Fruge, M. (1992, January). Performance dimensions: Competencies with a twist. *Training, 29*(1), pp. 47-51.

Smith, H. W. (1985, July). Implementing a management development program. *Personnel Administrator*, pp. 75-86.

Sternberg, R., & Wagner, R. (1986). *Practical intelligence: Concepts of competence in the everyday world.* Cambridge: Cambridge University Press.

Sutton, E. E., & McQuigg-Martinetz, B. (1990, April). The development partnership: Managing skills for the future. *Training and Development Journal, 44*(4), pp. 63-71.

White, R. (1959). Motivation reconsidered: The concept of competence. *Psychological Review, 66*, pp. 279-333.

Chapter 4

CREATING A COMPETENCY-BASED CURRICULUM PLAN

Curriculum planning is an important HRD function because it works in a powerful way to improve the overall effectiveness and efficiency of HRD outputs. It also provides a framework for responding to the reactive and proactive demands of organization clients for training and education services from the HRD department, consistent with an organization's strategic priorities and available resources. This chapter includes a presentation and explanation of key techniques for creating competency-based curriculum plans consistent with a "total organization" philosophy.

IN RELATION TO THE STRATEGIC SYSTEMS MODEL

A review of the Strategic Systems Model found in Figure 4.1 (on the following page) illustrates the role of curriculum planning in a competency-based training or education system. Curriculum planning is Step 3 of the Strategic Systems Model. The inputs to the curriculum planning step are the products from the competency model development stage; the outputs of the curriculum planning step are the inputs to instructional design and development of competency-based learning opportunities.

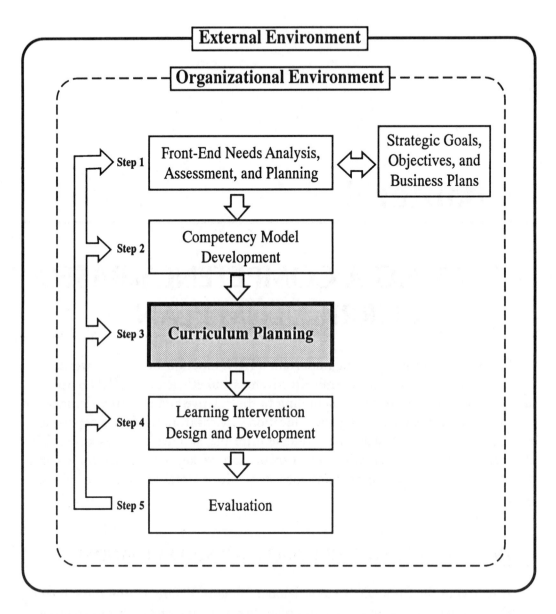

Figure 4.1: The Curriculum Planning Subsystem of the Strategic Systems Model

CURRICULUM ISSUES AND HRD

Considering the extent of information available on other HRD topics, there is comparatively little information on curriculum planning for organization performance improvement opportunities available in HRD literature. William Rothwell and H. C. Kazanas (1988) offer a reason for this deficiency:

> While much has been written about curriculum issues in elementary and secondary school settings, relatively little has focused specifically on settings outside traditional schools. One reason is that, until the last twenty years or so, people did not think much about planned learning after formal schooling. However, it is now apparent that everyone is a lifelong learner. It really does not make much sense to assume that learning ends with completion of formal schooling. (p. 4)

Learning after the formal completion of elementary or secondary education is no longer an option but an important necessity for most persons. Organization HRD departments are keenly aware of this fact, given organizations' need for employees who are expertly competent in areas of job performance that were virtually unknown only a few years ago. As such, organization-sponsored human resource development has become a growth industry, and that growth is predicted to continue well into the next several years. How HRD opportunities are conceived, planned, and organized have major cost implications for the organization. Curriculum planning is the primary discipline that must be learned and applied if organization HRD programs are to be as efficient and as cost-effective as possible. At present, curriculum analysis and planning are largely neglected functions in organization HRD. One reason for this could be that organization leaders hold opposing views of the training function.

Rothwell and Kazanas (1988) reported on the state-of-the-art on curriculum planning. They noted, among their several points, that curriculum planning can be a reactive or proactive activity in organization HRD.

Reactive curriculum planning responds to the performance improvement created for a present or immediate situation. It is training for the present job. Therefore, "in the context of the reactive view [of curriculum planning] *long-term planning for training* is a contradiction in terms. The reason: Training is always a short-term response to existing problems. It is appropriate for dealing with temporary gaps between *available* and *desirable* skills in specific jobs" (Rothwell & Kazanas, 1988, p. 3).

On the other hand, those who maintain a proactive view of curriculum planning see training as a means of facilitating employee socialization into new work cultures. Since the socialization process is a long-term process, so is training. An organized training plan or curriculum for each job is organized to build employee skills over time so that individuals are able to cope with each stage (anticipation, accommodation, stabilization) of their socialization process (Rothwell & Kazanas, 1988, pp. 2-4). However, it is important to remember that "the purpose of training is not only to build individual skills gradually but also to support career plans" (Rothwell & Kazanas, 1988, p. 4). Therefore, the role of a curriculum function in organization HRD is determined, in large part, by how its leaders view the training function.

In the context of this book, curriculum planning and management are considered critically essential functions of the HRD department. Since HRD is a service function that must be responsive to meeting both long- and short-term employee performance improvement needs, it must be prepared to immediately respond to both reactive and proactive requirements. A curriculum plan provides a conceptual framework that is useful for identifying and evaluating options for rationally responding to new requirements in an effective and efficient manner considering the resources that are available. Curriculum plans give order, cohesiveness, clarity, and structure to an organization's existing, planned, or anticipated performance improvement requirements. Curriculum plans also help organizations avoid making errors such as over-training (educating) or undertraining its employees.

THE CURRICULUM SUBSYSTEM

An organization's curriculum planning subsystem links the contents of its competency models with the instructional design and development subsystem. It is a critically needed subsystem, indispensable to having an effective and efficient competency-based performance improvement system. Unfortunately, organization HRD departments often lose sight of this important fact, many times due to a need to put out the latest fire. As a result, they have a catalog of disjointed and uncoordinated performance improvement opportunities that should have cohesion. Quite frequently, an outcome of this condition is that the interventions transmit inconsistent, incomplete, or worse yet, inappropriate messages to their clients.

Factors

Many factors impact the design, planning, and operation of a curriculum subsystem within the larger training or education system for an organization. Some of the more obvious ones include:

• The size or dimensions of the organization's HRD function and other functions allied with it

• Complexities in the way the organization has structured and organized jobs, functions and employees to achieve organization results

• The degree of stability or instability in the industry (or industries) with which the organization is most closely allied

• The internal stability of the factors in the organization that most heavily impact the HRD function

• Relationships among the organization and its clients, customers, or constituents

Obviously when an organization's training or education requirements are varied and extensive, the curriculum planning project will reflect those factors. A systematic, organized, and analytical approach to making sense of the content dimensions of a curriculum and how they should be organized and sequenced reduces a complex situation to a manageable project. An organization's curriculum plan can include a combination of training, education, and development interventions, if necessary.

Approach Taken in This Chapter

Each curriculum planning project differs from all others, and usually in many dimensions. Therefore it is impossible to explain all the possible ways to handle the combinations of situations which you might encounter in curriculum planning work. Instead, several techniques that have been successfully used in organization-based curriculum planning are presented and explained.

The concept of organization curriculum planning is illustrated in the professional literature through case reports. However, the step-by-step details and illustrations of how that planning was done are largely absent. A considerable portion of the information found in this chapter was created by attempting to capture some critical, generic curriculum planning processes. I hope that you will find them helpful. These techniques will improve with use as practitioners search for ways to handle curriculum planning and management challenges in their day-to-day work.

"Curriculum Architecture"

Training and education programs in organizations are frequently little more than random collections of performance improvement events. They lack unity, clarity, structure, and a common goal, such as helping the organization achieve its strategic goals. Many of these programs evolve as a reactive response to crisis conditions or activities in organizations rather than as a result of a proactive, planned, and systematic approach that interrelates an organization's performance improvement activities and sequences them in a logical, coherent fashion. McKenna, Svenson, Wallace, and Wallace (1984) observed that "training efforts are not directed at problems that have the largest impact on the organization's performance. Instead, resources are allocated and rushed to the scenes of various conflagrations according to the importance of the person who spotted the fire" (p. 77).

A formal curriculum planning process organizes performance improvement programs, interventions, and other opportunities into logical, systematic, coherent, and sequential "wholes" or meaningful units. The value of such a strongly structural proactive approach was emphasized by McKenna et al. (1984), who referred to a curriculum plan of this type as "curriculum architecture." Proposing a solution for the problem of reactive response, they write:

> Your training department can escape this reaction mode by designing a "curriculum architecture" that organizes the company's various training needs into a logical sequence of courses or modules. With this cohesive design in hand, you will have a blueprint to help you plan and assign priorities to developing and maintaining your training program. You'll also have a weapon to stave off raids on your resources by well-meaning but ill-advised fire rangers. (p. 77)

A similar perspective on curriculum planning, this time specific to management training curricula, was given a year earlier by Julia Galosy, whose approach to curriculum building for management training is quite similar to McKenna's. Galosy (1983) commented: "The challenge of curriculum design is to build a coherent, sequential plan which will provide structure to the full gamut of management training" (p. 48).

Together, McKenna's and Galosy's ideas reflect the "call to arms" of this chapter, which is to bring cohesion, coherence, and order to an organization's performance improvement opportunities, and to maintain them. For an organization to accomplish this, it must have total organization level curriculum planning that is driven by the need to achieve strategic goals as a first priority. With a planning system of this type in place, reactive and proactive requests for performance improvement initiatives can be evaluated and responded to in the most appropriate and cost-effective manner possible, *given the total organization's curriculum priorities and available resources*. This level of curriculum planning and management provides the HRD function with a very powerful resource that it can use to rationally and responsibly respond to requests for HRD services.

Options and Opportunities for HRD

The application of the curriculum planning methods described later in this chapter should result in efficient and effective organization-wide competency-based performance improvement systems. As work progresses in curriculum analysis and planning, HRD staff will realize options and opportunities to:

- Remove unnecessary performance improvement program redundancies through broad-based curriculum system streamlining

- Make additions, revisions, or deletions to existing performance improvement interventions

- Recognize ways for expanding the realm of competency-based performance improvement opportunities beyond traditional classroom training or education through the use of innovative approaches to learning

- Ensure that existing and planned performance improvement opportunities are competency-based, are focused on learners' needs, and, ultimately, are concentrated on helping the organization achieve its strategic goals

- Identify ways to make use of structured, formal competency-based performance improvement processes that are appropriate to the organization context and culture

- Recognize performance improvement opportunities external to the organization that could be useful for promoting competence acquisition and performance improvement without the cost of duplicating services already available

- Market performance improvement opportunities within the organization. Planned, coherent, cohesive, and systematic training or education curricula engender in organization clients and employees a sense of credibility and confidence in the HRD function.

CREATING A CURRICULUM PLAN: THE INITIAL STEPS

Virtually all curriculum analysis and planning projects share the three action steps presented in this section. The steps might not be completed exactly as described below since various factors existing in the organization at the time they are implemented will influence their use.

Initiating Curriculum Projects

The primary responsibility for initiating curriculum planning projects in organizations rests with the HRD function, with extensive support from its clients. In terms of the Strategic Systems Model (Figure 4.1), the in-depth curriculum planning process begins once job competency model(s) or menu(s) have been prepared. It is not unusual, however, for curriculum planning issues to be surfaced by the client, as well as by the HRD specialist, during the front-end needs analysis, assessment, and planning stage of creating a competency based training or education system.

At the front-end or the macro-planning stage (i.e., Step 1 of the Strategic Systems Model), it is usually difficult to fully envision how a curriculum plan will look at a later project stage, although the broad dimensions and needs are usually apparent. Until in-depth competency or micro-needs analyses are completed for the job(s) that are to be included in the system and data are available for designing the curriculum plan subsystem, detailed curriculum planning must wait. Curriculum options take form as additional data on the job performance requirements become available.

Three steps must be successfully completed for any curriculum planning project. The successful completion of these steps cannot be too strongly emphasized:

1. Select a focus group and its leader.

2. Determine the scope of the curriculum planning project.

3. Review the competency model(s) or menu(s) for the job(s) that is (are) the subject of the project.

A detailed discussion of each step follows.

Step 1. Select a focus group and its leader.

The first task that the HRD specialist completes is to seek help for completing the project from those most affected by the project results. A focus group approach should be used, unless the project is limited to designing a very small-scale curriculum plan. An example of a small-scale curriculum is one that includes a limited number of employees for a single job (e.g., sales representative) and a minimal number of interventions (e.g., a one-day workshop or a three-day course). The complexities of the organization situation will suggest the level of curriculum planning effort that is required.

In chapter 1, emphasis was placed on the use, attributes, selection, and management of focus groups for designing competency-based performance improvement systems; those principles equally apply equally here. "Representativeness" and "content competence" are the two most important selection factors for the members of a curriculum planning focus group. If possible, you should include in this group several of the persons who participated in earlier stages of the project. The most appropriate persons to be included are subject-matter experts who are also exemplary performers of the job or jobs that are the subject of the project. Managers of the exemplary performers or representatives from the client organization should also be included. Persons who are invited to work on a curriculum planning focus group should have well-developed team participation competencies, including interpersonal competencies. Once the scope of the project is more clearly defined in a later step, additional persons can be added to the focus group, if necessary.

The leader for a curriculum planning focus group must be selected with great care. On this subject, McKenna (1984) noted: "Without a leader who has a clear understanding of what data must be generated, the method probably will not succeed. And even with a knowledgeable leader, group process can run into trouble if there are serious disagreements within the group that can't be resolved" (p. 82). For this reason, the HRD specialist (or manager) and the client should jointly select the focus group leader. The leader must have well-developed interpersonal competencies and must be comfortable with working with diverse personalities and complex issues.

The focus group should be activated and work started only after the HRD specialist has organized the early curriculum planning tasks and obtained the support materials needed for a successful work effort. Obtaining support materials can require a considerable investment in time and labor, especially when the required items are not centrally located.

Once the focus group is activated, raw materials should be provided immediately to the members, including any job information papers or portfolios that were prepared earlier, copies of the competency model(s) for the subject job(s) of the planning project, and any other information related to the content or scope of the curriculum. Additionally needed materials are identified and procured as work progresses on these initial project steps.

Later project steps will depend upon the initial scope that is determined for the project and the results that are needed. These steps usually cannot be determined precisely until curriculum analysis and planning work proceeds. Very broad action steps are advisable at this time since it is sometimes difficult to accurately predict all of the minute tasks that a curriculum planning project can require. The information supplied in later sections of this chapter will help you identify the tasks that must be done when the three initial steps have been completed.

Step 2. **Determine the scope of the curriculum planning project.**

The second step is to determine the scope of the curriculum planning project. The strategic goals of the organization that were identified during Step 1 of the Strategic Systems Model drive the curriculum planning mechanism and suggest relative priorities for the work. It is entirely appropriate for an organization to have curriculum plans for several dimensions of its HRD-sponsored performance improvement programs. Linkages among related programs are made in ways that are logical for the organization context.

A curriculum planning project must have realistic boundaries. Curriculum plan boundaries defined by major organization functions are common. However, no single method always works best for establishing those boundaries. The information below will help the focus group specify the scope of the curriculum planning project.

Questions for Determining the Scope of the Project

The scope of a curriculum planning project must be defined very early on in the work. Experience teaches that curriculum planning projects seldom conclude with entirely predicted results. Several aspects of each situation must be considered in order to define the scope of any curriculum planning project. The more critical ones are described below as a series of questions.

1. Which jobs are the subject of the curriculum analysis and development project? How are they related to each other?

2. What delivery systems or mechanisms are currently available for the proposed curriculum? Are they the most appropriate delivery systems for the curriculum? How sophisticated a plan can the available delivery systems support?

3. What performance improvement opportunities already exist, and how are they related to the present curriculum planning project? If the contents of existing opportunities are similar or are related to the present effort, curriculum integration with those systems elements will probably be both advantageous and necessary.

4. How many employees are to be trained or educated, and over what time period? What is the optimal time period for the full complement of employees to be trained? Are there any constraints on achieving the optimal goal? How will they affect the curriculum plan?

5. Where are the employees who are targeted for training or education geographically located? What are the curriculum planning impacts of the differing geographies?

6. What equipment, facilities, staffing, and training technologies are available (or required) for implementing the curriculum plan? Can some training or education be delivered by using specialized equipment or technologies while employees are on the job at remote sites?

7. What levels of budget and staffing will be available for implementation of the curriculum plan? What are the levels of HRD competence within the available staff for implementation of the plan? Can the implementation of the curriculum plan be successfully completed by those available to complete the work?

8. What competence development or acquisition strategies will be adopted for curriculum implementation?

9. Will the performance improvement program(s) be custom developed (e.g., internal to the organization or through contractors) or will off-the-shelf materials be purchased? Will the off-the-shelf materials be customized?

10. What extent of coverage (i.e., mastery levels) of the competency model(s) or menu(s) should be included in the curriculum plan? Which competencies should be developed, if any, as an on-the-job training or education intervention?

11. Will pre-intervention competence assessment profiles and individualized training or education plans be used? As a result, will the use of individualized modules be a part of the curriculum design and plan? How much individualization is needed? How much curriculum individualization can the organization afford, and is the organization willing to support it? What instructional resources are available to support individualization? Can such a curriculum plan be administered?

12. What prerequisite competencies must employees have before completing the performance improvement opportunities to be included in the curriculum plan? How will employees acquire those competencies prior to entering the proposed curriculum? Should a separate curriculum plan be developed for any prerequisite competencies that are identified?

13. Are the optimal content sequences for the curriculum understood?

Two Rules of Thumb

McKenna et al. (1984, p. 78) suggest two rules-of-thumb to guide decisions on the scope of a curriculum planning project:

1. When training needs or requirements become diverse, a narrow scope should be used in order to produce the most accurate and comprehensive curriculum architecture. When this approach is used, what will result is either several smaller curriculum architectures (or plans), each with a limited scope, or a larger, broad-based curriculum architecture that can be modularized or individualized for each sub-group of the target audience.

For example, curriculum planning projects could include several business units of an organization, employees from a variety of geographic locations, each with different needs, or a variety of functions. The amount of distinction or discrimination of the competencies that must be included in the intervention(s) depends upon the circumstances impacting the employees' performance. In other words, the competencies become contextual to the situation(s) where they are applied. These are some examples of factors that will impact the curriculum design and planning process.

2. Client, or client-organization ownership of a curriculum plan is critical to its long-term health and success. The more influential and committed the ownership, the greater the probability of the success of the plan once implemented.

All clients represented within the scope of the curriculum planning project must be represented in all project development stages. This requirement for successful design, implementation, and the life cycle of a curriculum plan is consistent with the principles on which this book is based, and that stress the importance of extensive client involvement.

Step 3. **Review the competency model(s) or menu(s) for the job(s) that is (are) the subject of the project.**

The next step the focus group completes is a thorough, comprehensive review of the competency model(s) or menu(s) that is (are) available for the job(s) included in the project. The purpose of this task is to ensure that the focus group members have a common frame of reference for the analysis and planning activities that follow later. It is important to remember that some (and possibly all) members of the focus group might be newcomers to the work associated with the application of the Strategic Systems Model.

If competency models or menus do not exist for all the jobs within the project scope, then they must be developed. This requires, at a minimum, the completion of additional tasks in the second step of the Strategic Systems Model (for further information on ex-post-facto model building, see Moody, 1990).

Upon completion of the initial project steps, several curriculum analyses must be performed by the focus group or by individuals working under the guidance of the focus group. The analysis results suggest curriculum planning options. A curriculum plan is then created. The focus group leader and the HRD specialist are responsible for briefing the client and for any follow-up tasks that might be generated by the briefing.

In the following section, curriculum planning activities that are needed to develop a curriculum plan for a single job at one level of the organization are described. This represents the most basic level of organization curriculum planning.

CURRICULUM PLANNING FOR A SINGLE JOB

Curriculum analysis and planning require the planner to distinguish, compare, and contrast employee competencies and job outputs in order to arrive at logical, sequential, and coherent content "wholes" that can be translated into a series or sequence of performance improvement opportunities. The tasks completed are essential regardless of whether one is planning a curriculum for a single job or for a cluster of jobs at different organization strata.

Hypothetical Case Information

To assist readers who are unfamiliar with curriculum analysis and planning, the tasks discussed later in this section are illustrated by references to a job in the hypothetical organization described below. The facts are as follows:

1. This job is held by 300 employees in several geographic locations. Job performance somewhat differs across job sites, but is very consistent overall. Employees can produce the job outputs. However, front-end assessments revealed that the outputs are not being produced at the expected quality levels. This has resulted in considerable losses of revenue and reputation with the organization's customers.

   The identified performance deficiencies can be corrected by a training intervention. This is the most cost-effective solution. In general, little attention has been given to competency development and performance improvement for these employees. It was suggested during the front-end planning stage (Step 1 of the Strategic Systems Model) that the development of a flexible job competency model was the appropriate approach, given the current and anticipated environmental conditions impacting the production of the job outputs.

2. The client will pay 75 percent of the total costs of designing, developing, and implementing the performance improvement system. The HRD department will pay the balance of the costs.

3. Job outputs and competency menus were developed by applying the Flexible Job Competency Model Method (see chapter 3). The targeted employees for this training include persons with diverse work experience and education backgrounds; therefore, it was decided that flexibility in job design, individual performance improvement planning, and individualized learning strategies were needed. The competency menu for the job that resulted from the research process included the following competencies:

   - Computer software knowledge and skills, as they are applied to managing client cases

   - Problem-solving skills

   - Knowledge of organization career programs

   - Positive self-confidence regarding the job role

   - Active listening and responding skills

• Values positive human relationships

• Writing skills

Seven job outputs and excellence criteria for each of them were identified, and these are linked to the competencies. The environmental factors for the job and the behavioral indicators for the competencies were also identified.

4. The curriculum plan that will result from the analysis activities will include, for the most part, centrally delivered performance improvement activities. When advantageous, some of the learning activities will be offered at other job sites or job site clusters. "Update seminars" will always be held at local job sites. A wide variety of performance improvement delivery mechanisms are available for implementing the curriculum plan.

Competencies-to-Job Outputs Analysis

The focus group must analyze and comprehend the internal relationships among the job competencies and the job outputs. In order to do this, a competencies-to-job outputs matrix is constructed (McKenna et al., 1984, p. 82). Extending the concept provided by McKenna et al., the matrix presented in Figure 4.2 (on the following page) includes the full range of "competencies" rather than only the "knowledge and skills" requirements for the job. A matrix of this type might have been constructed at the competency model development stage (Step 2 of the Strategic Systems Model) of the larger project. If it was, then the focus group should now review those results. Group members should agree that the matrix accurately reflects the realities of the job. If group consensus does not exist, the leader must work with the focus group members until consensus is achieved.

Competency	Job Outputs						
	1	2	3	4	5	6	7
1. Apply computer software skills to client cases	A	A			B	B	
2. Apply problem-solving skills	A	A					
3. Maintain positive self-confidence relative to role			A	B	A	B	A
4. Utilize active listening and responding skills			A	A	A	A	A
5. Demonstrate knowledge of organization career program			A	A	A	A	A
6. Values positive human relationships			A	A	A	A	A
7. Apply writing skills relative to job roles	A	B	B				

A = Competency is critically essential for achieving the job output.
B = Competency enhances the possibility of achieving the job output, but is not critical for it.

Figure 4.2: Competencies-to-Job-Outputs Matrix for a Hypothetical Job

A competencies-to-job outputs matrix is constructed by cross-referencing each job competency in the competency model or menu to one or more job outputs. At the most elementary classification level, a check mark is used to signify that a competency-to-output association exists. The meaning of the check mark should be explained in the legend of the matrix, even though that meaning might be obvious or quite simple.

A second level of analysis can very easily be introduced. A two-level (or higher level) classification system can be added to the matrix. To do this, each competency-to-job outputs assessment is rated at one of two (or more) levels. Figure 4.2 illustrates a two-level, or binary, classification system for the hypothetical job, in which:

A = The competency is critically essential for achieving the job result.

B = The competency enhances the possibility of achieving the
job output, but it is not critical for achieving the output.

When no entry appears in a cell of the matrix, then no significant relationship exists at the intersection of the variables or dimensions of the matrix. This convention is used throughout the remainder of this book.

The degree of sophistication used in the matrix and the levels of analyses that are completed depends upon the time available for the work, the availability of data and other information, and the analysis resources available to the focus group. In many applications, you will probably find that the analysis suggestions above work adequately. More extensive or detailed procedures might be used if cost savings are a major objective of the project.

How are the matrix data interpreted and used to make curriculum planning decisions? Two particular options are frequently considered. Each option focuses attention on a different curriculum planning emphasis. The application context will often suggest other possibilities.

Using a Competency Emphasis

When the focus group uses a competency emphasis, it examines the relative value or importance of each of the critical competencies to the achievement of a single or a cluster (or collection) of job outputs. When this approach is chosen, the emphasis of the curriculum planning is placed on the acquisition of the competencies and then on their use for the achievement of the job outputs. The rationale often given for this emphasis is the planners' interest in emphasizing the high degree of transferability of the competencies to the achievement of several job outputs. Another reason could be that the competencies have dependent or interdependent relationships with each other or with other curriculum subsystems. Focusing on competencies, then, ensures that the required relationships will be acknowledged and retained.

Using a Job Outputs Emphasis

On the other hand, the focus group might choose to examine the importance of the competencies to the achievement of the job outputs. This is accomplished by evaluating the loadings (or sum) of the various ratings in each column of the matrix. The resulting curriculum plan will first focus on the job outputs and then on the critical competencies employees use to achieve those job outputs. This kind of curriculum plan illustrates performance improvement opportunities that emphasize the achievement of job outputs, rather than the critical competencies, as a first level of emphasis. The weight of each competency's contribution to the achievement of each of the respective job outputs is then factored into, or becomes an element of, the curriculum plan. The curriculum plan that results still merits the description "competency-based," although its initial emphasis is on the achievement of the job outputs rather than on individual competencies. Factors in the application context will suggest the appropriate emphasis.

Analyses of these types provide options for specifying a curriculum plan. For example, using the matrix in Figure 4.2, the focus group might choose to take a mixed-emphasis approach to curriculum planning. This might mean focusing on job outputs in some parts of the plan, and then on job competencies in other areas of the plan. Regardless of the curriculum design emphases that are chosen, the performance improvement options must stress competence acquisition and its application to the achievement of job outputs. The curriculum plan must be clear regarding the rationale for the construction emphasis that was selected.

Curriculum Planning for the Job

Once the analyses above have been completed and the focus group members agree on the options, a logical, cohesive, and sequential curriculum plan for the hypothetical job can be constructed. This can be a creative process. More frequently than not, several planning options are envisioned. Figure 4.3 (on the following page) illustrates one possible curriculum plan the focus group might produce. In this curriculum plan, the competencies were emphasized as a primary focus for curriculum planning.

This focus group decision was consistent with the characteristics and needs of the target population. Some key employee performance improvement needs were revealed through the front-end planning and a micro-needs assessment of employees (which was sponsored by the focus group and completed by surveying the target population, using the competency model and performance evaluation items based on it). Specifically, the focus group discovered that the employees needed individualized performance improvement opportunities that would "round out" the acquisition of the competencies they used to achieve the job outputs. The front-end (or macro) needs assessment from Step 1 of the Strategic Systems Model revealed that the employees could produce the job outputs, but that the quality levels of the outputs were unacceptable. Accordingly, they needed to acquire selected competencies at a higher performance level in order to meet the quality criteria established for the job outputs.

The other approach to curriculum planning, which emphasizes achievement of the job outputs through the acquisition of the clusters of competencies required to achieve them, would (most likely) have been a more attractive option to the focus group if it was confronted with training a target population of entry-level employees for the immediate pursuit of the job outputs.

A curriculum plan for a single job can range from very simple to one which is quite detailed. At a minimum, the plan should specifically include statements of, or

Competency	Primary Application Context	Suggested Approach	Sequence
1. Apply computer software skills to client cases	Job results 1 and 2	• Vendor-provided software training • Internal, organization-specific training • Organization simulation exercise	3
2. Apply analytical skills	Job results 1 and 2	• Internal seminar with computer-based exercises and case method examples	2
3. Apply writing skills relative to job role	Job result 2	• Internal courses • On-the-job practice • Internal follow-up seminars	4
4. Maintain high self-confidence relative to role	Job results 3, 5, 7	• Three part workshop • On-the-job applications	*
5. Utilize active listening and responding skills	Job results 3-7	• Simulation exercise	5
6. Demonstrate knowledge of organization career programs	Job results 3-7	• Lecturette and application exercises utilizing multiple media	1
7. Values positive human relationships	Job results 3-7	• Case-method exercises • Self-and-others assessment • Individual consultations with a professional clinician	*

* When this symbol appears, the facilitator can present the instructional activities at a time that is most appropriate to the situation.

Figure 4.3: A Curriculum Plan for the Hypothetical Job Portrayed in Figure 4.2

references to, the critical competencies, the job outputs, and the type or form of performance improvement intervention that is suggested or planned for competence acquisition. The relationships among these elements must be clearly spelled out in the body of the curriculum plan.

A curriculum plan for a single job could (optionally) include references to the job tasks and activities, the specific quality standards for the job outputs, or the behavioral indicators for the competencies. The supplementary elements that should be included will be suggested by the nature of the application for which the curriculum plan is being developed. The sample curriculum plan found in Figure 4.3 includes the minimum elements noted above.

Curriculum analysis and planning are considerably more involved when several jobs in the organization are included in the planning process. The greater the volume of jobs or the number of organization strata, the greater the planning challenge. The next section focuses on a process for planning organization-level curricula that include several jobs and the documentation requirements for them.

CURRICULUM PLANNING FOR MULTIPLE JOBS

The first task required for planning a curriculum for multiple jobs is the development of the focus group's understanding of the jobs from an organization systems perspective.

Understanding Jobs in An Organization Context—The Jobs Cluster Matrix

The focus group should construct a jobs cluster matrix for the jobs that are the subjects of curriculum planning. A jobs cluster matrix is a valuable tool for gaining an in-depth understanding of organization structures. It is also valuable as a communication medium. Constructing the matrix is a useful exercise, especially for focus group members who might not be fully familiar with the functions, levels of management, or the job titles within the organization. It is common for focus group members (especially in very large, decentralized organizations) to develop new or modified understandings of the jobs, roles, and outputs of work units within the larger organization.

As a communication medium, the jobs cluster matrix is valuable for briefing client(s) or senior managers within the organization during and after the completion of the larger project. Organizations often use this matrix to explain organization elements to external persons, such as visitors, legislative or regulatory groups, and professional societies.

Figure 4.4 illustrates the kind of matrix that could be produced for a cluster of jobs (Galosy, 1983, p. 49). This example includes a cluster of five jobs across four diverse functions of a large corporation. The matrix includes the levels of the jobs within the organization hierarchy in the left column. The column headings designate the functional units within the organization where the jobs are located. The cells of the matrix include the job titles that are internally used with each function and at each level of the organization hierarchy.

	Engineering	Finance	Marketing	Mgt. Info. Sys.
Officers	Sr. V.P.	Sr. V.P.	Sr. V.P.	Sr. V.P.
Executives	V.P.	V.P.	V.P.	V.P.
Managers	Sr. Mgr.	Comptroller	Reg. Mgr.	Dir.
Mgr.-of-Supv.	Mgr.	Mgr. & Dept. Mgr.	Dist. Mgr.	Mgr.
Supervisors	Supv. & Prog. Mgr.	Supv.	Supv.	Supv.

Figure 4.4: Example of a Jobs Cluster Matrix

The jobs cluster matrix is a helpful reference for the next task in the curriculum planning process, the analysis of the jobs-to-competencies relationships.

Analysis of Jobs-to-Competencies Relationships—Jobs-to-Competencies Matrix

At this stage of the work, the focus group creates a new analysis tool, one that shows the relationships among the competencies for all the jobs within the scope of the project and the job titles and their levels (or some other appropriately descriptive term for those jobs). A sample jobs-to-competencies matrix is illustrated in Figure 4.5, on the following page (Galosy, 1983, p. 50).

Competencies	Supv.	Mgr. of Supv.	Mgr. of Mgr.	Exec.	Officers
Coaching	√	√			
Employee Counseling	√	√	√	√	√
Strategic Planning			√	√	√
Activities Planning	√	√	√		
Communications Skills	√	√	√	√	√
Delegation	√	√	√		
Conducting Meetings			√	√	√
Leadership	√	√	√	√	√
Self-Confidence	√	√	√	√	√
Environmental Assessment			√	√	√
Time-and-Attendance	√				
Global Networking					√
Technical Competence	√	√	√		

Figure 4.5: Example of a Jobs-to-Competencies Matrix

The relationships among the jobs and competencies are easy to recognize, sort out, and examine by analyzing the elements of the jobs-to-competencies matrix. To construct this matrix, you list on one of its dimensions the totality of competencies for all jobs within the scope of the curriculum planning project. List the job titles and levels (or some other descriptive term for those jobs or specialties) on the other dimension of the matrix. Next, use the competency models or menus for each job to complete the individual cells of the matrix. Figure 4.5 illustrates the jobs-to-competencies matrix for the management jobs included in the hypothetical organization portrayed in Figure 4.4.

Some early, though important, observations result from an elementary analysis of the contents of the matrix found in Figure 4.5. For example, notice that four of the competencies (Employee Counseling, Communications Skills, Leadership, and Self-Confidence) are critical competencies for successful managerial performance at all organization strata.

A curriculum implication of this finding is that a resulting curriculum plan will need to include a unified and integrated approach to the development of managers' competencies in these areas across all of the organization strata. The planners will want to examine the possible advantages (and disadvantages) of integrating selected elements of the Leadership, Communications Skills, and Self-Confidence curriculum components in mutually complementary ways. Similarly, the acquisition of competence in Employee Counseling will be influenced by the managers' acquisition of the Communications Skills competency. Analyses of the matrix contents—as this example illustrates—sets the stage for completing later curriculum analysis and planning tasks.

An elementary classification of the competencies was used in this example: A check mark in the body of the table signifies those competencies in the left column that are required to achieve the job outputs expected at each level of management within the organization. However, a more complex classification system can be used if it would be advantageous to the project objective(s).

For illustrative purposes, let's assume that you want to represent in your matrix the relative importance of each competency for achieving the job outputs, as well as the present average level of employees' competence for all relevant cells in the matrix. Instead of inserting only a check mark in each cell to show that the competency is required by the employees for the achievement of the job output, you could assign and insert an entry like "A/2" in the cell. Using this technique, two ratings have been assigned to the competency: The first, (A), is a rating of how important the competency is for the successful achievement of the relevant job outputs; the second, (2), is the (arithmetic) average proficiency level of the employees in the target population for the competency. (To determine the average proficiency levels for the competencies, the focus group would need to conduct a survey research project or some other form of research.)

A competencies-to-job outputs matrix should be completed for each of the jobs included in Figure 4.5. These matrices provide the planners with additional planning insights, especially for curriculum integration purposes.

Curriculum Integration

Curriculum integration is a curriculum planning process that ensures the inclusion and development of the critical job competencies, each at their appropriate levels of subject-matter content depth and breadth across all elements or strata of an organization's performance improvement curriculum. "Appropriate" means that the subject-matter content is developed at the precise level required to enhance the probability of the employees' achievement of the job outputs within expected levels of quality.

Horizontal curriculum integration is an application of the curriculum integration process to the competencies and job outputs for a single job. Horizontal curriculum integration can also include an application of the process to a class of jobs that lie within the same stratum of an organization.

Vertical curriculum integration applies the curriculum integration process to jobs that span two or more strata of an organization hierarchy.

The generic curriculum integration process is well illustrated by the following example. Let's assume we want to ensure curriculum integration for a management training curriculum in the hypothetical organization represented in Figure 4.5, and specifically for the Self-Confidence competency. A number of information items are needed to complete the curriculum integration task. Notice in Figure 4.5 that "Self-Confidence" is a critical competency for achieving the job outputs at *all* levels of management in the organization.

Assume that the focus group conducted a micro-needs analysis and assessment of the managers at each organization level. The results of their work were summarized in a two-way rating system, and these ratings were then encoded for inclusion in the jobs-to-competencies matrix. Two ratings were included for each cell of the matrix: one signifying the importance of the competency to the achievement of the job outputs, and the other signifying the average level of competence currently held by each of the five groups of employees.

A subsequent analysis of the matrix data, in conjunction with the job competency models, revealed that (1) the Self-Confidence competency is of greater value for successful job performance by supervisors and managers-of-supervisors than it is for the organization's officers, (2) the definition of the Self-Confidence competency differs only minimally across the five levels of organization management, and (3) major differences exist in the circumstances or situations that require an application of the competency across the five levels of management.

In order to ensure vertical integration, the planners must reflect these facts in the plans they construct for performance improvement opportunities at each stratum of the organization. The precise content, with appropriate emphases, must be planned by stratum. For example, the curriculum content for supervisors and managers-of-supervisors must reflect a more in-depth emphasis on the meaning and application of the Self-Confidence competency than would be placed on the competency for senior managers. The applications of the competency found in the supervisor curriculum, for example, must represent specific job situations where the competency must be applied. On the other hand, Self-Confidence would have a different meaning for a senior officer; most likely, this meaning would be associated with the larger life-career issues that confront senior managers.

There is another dimension which must be considered. The managers' acquisition and application of the Self-Confidence competency *impacts, and is impacted by,* the development and application of virtually all of the other critical job competencies within each of the respective levels of the management hierarchy. The curriculum plan must account for these relationships. This is an example of a need for horizontal curriculum integration among the competencies for curricula at each of the five levels of management of the organization hierarchy.

These examples illustrate the level of effort that is required to ensure effective and efficient competency-based curriculum planning in a larger organization context. Without this planning effort, curriculum inefficiencies and a lack of program effectiveness will surely exist. And at an organization's bottom line, these are ultimately issues of cost-effectiveness.

The Organization-Level Curriculum Plan

The curriculum planning process is completed by organizing the information into an organization level curriculum plan for the subject jobs. Figure 4.6 (on the following page) includes a framework for organizing and presenting the gross details of a curriculum plan that would result from analyses of the type described earlier, and from the additional analysis work described below. The information found in Figure 4.6 will be used to illustrate the ideas that follow, and additional definitions and techniques will be provided. Note that competencies can be categorized in a variety of ways to facilitate the curriculum planning and management process; each situation will suggest the most appropriate categories to use.

Definitions and Comments

A *core competency* is a principal or critically essential competency for the successful performance of a given job at a given level in an organization hierarchy or structure.

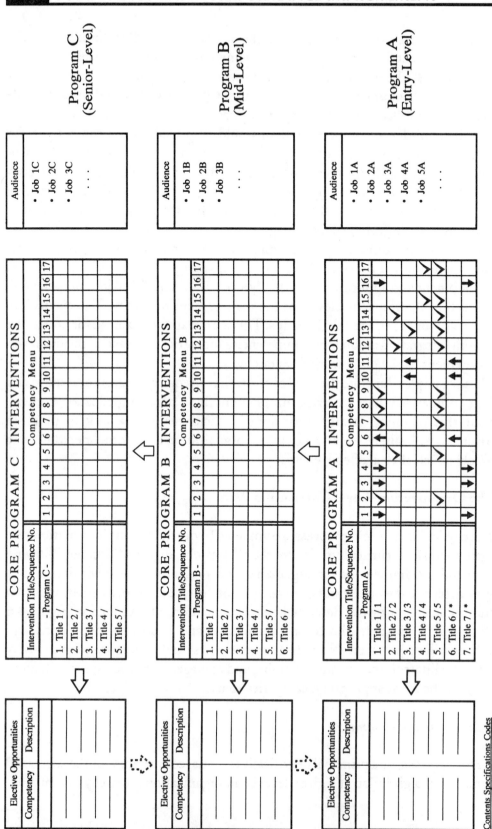

Figure 4.6: Curriculum Plan Template

A *core intervention* refers to a performance improvement opportunity whose subject-matter contents are based on one or more core competencies at a given level of an organization hierarchy or structure.

An *elective intervention* is an intervention which includes subject-matter content that supports or enhances the acquisition of one or more core competencies.

A *boundary competency* is a competency which shares a relationship with the competency requirements for a job that is either higher or lower in a hierarchy of jobs.

A *lower boundary competency* is a prerequisite competency for a job or a principal competency for the next lower order job in the job hierarchy.

An *upper boundary competency* is a principal competency for a higher order job in a hierarchy of jobs. Upper boundary competencies share strong relationships with one or more of the principal competencies for the job where the upper boundary designation was given. These competencies warrant special attention from the curriculum planner and from the designer or developer of the learning intervention(s).

Boundary designations for competencies are made for convenience by the curriculum planner, learning intervention designer or developer, and the evaluator. Learning opportunities must frequently be provided in order for employees to acquire lower boundary job competencies, although those competencies should have been acquired by the employee prior to assuming the job responsibilities. Finding this situation is not surprising, given the current need in organizations for maximum flexibility in job design and subsequently, for performance improvement activities. Accordingly, learning opportunities to help employees acquire lower boundary competencies must be anticipated during the curriculum planning step of the Strategic Systems Model.

On the other hand, including upper boundary job competencies among the learning opportunities for employees' present jobs provides them with competencies that will enhance their performance of the current job. It also provides employees with an education opportunity that will promote their understanding of the requirements of the next higher order job in the organization hierarchy (or, for that matter, even a job in another part of the organization). This type of curriculum planning helps an organization prepare employees for accepting an orderly succession of enhanced responsibilities in their current jobs and in the organization's more demanding jobs.

Interpreting An Organization Curriculum Plan Matrix

A review of the contents of the matrix in Figure 4.6 reveals how an organization curriculum plan can be conceptualized and communicated in the organization. This particular "curriculum plan template" illustrates how a curriculum can be organized into "Programs" for one or more jobs at each level of the organization hierarchy. Program A includes performance improvement opportunities for entry-level jobs, while Program C describes improvement opportunities for senior-level employees in jobs at Level C. Core and elective interventions are illustrated.

The job outputs were not included in this matrix in an effort to maintain readability. If not done earlier, individual matrices should be constructed for each job, illustrating the competencies-to-job outputs relationships embedded in the curriculum plan.

In Figure 4.6, ten of the seventeen competencies in Core Program A are essential for successful job performance for the job(s) at that level. Five of the seven performance improvement interventions provide competence acquisition opportunities for the ten core competencies. The sequence in which the interventions are to be delivered is noted in the table. Elective performance improvement opportunities were not defined in this stage of the curriculum planning process.

Although not included in Figure 4.6, the focus group outlined their recommendations for the Core Program A interventions. These are described below and provided as an example of some outcomes that can be realized from a curriculum planning project.

Intervention 1 is a highly experiential, formal training experience that develops four core job competencies essential to successful job performance immediately upon an employee's appointment to the job. Three lower boundary competencies are included to ensure that the participants have met the prerequisite levels of competence needed for the essential job competencies. One upper boundary competency is included in order to develop a participant's awareness of the types of performance requirements for employees in the next higher level job or category.

Intervention 2 emphasizes three related competencies that are needed six months following appointment to the job. The intervention is an intensive and very demanding simulation experience, delivered over a long weekend in a location away from the work place.

Intervention 3 is highly specialized in one of the competencies and includes introductory performance on two upper boundary competencies. The latter two competencies are sometimes performed by persons in Category A jobs, depending upon the conditions in the organization. The training requires a programmed, step-by-step approach to learning. Computer-based training methods are used. It should be completed nine months following appointment to the job.

Intervention 4 includes mindset competencies that require cognitive performance first, followed by clinical evaluation and experiential interpersonal interactions. This intervention is completed by employees once they have been on the job for at least a year.

Intervention 5 is an on-the-job application intervention. Its completion consumes the second full year on the job. A local employee development or training consultant monitors employees' achievements of the job competencies in a real-time setting.

Intervention 6 contains three upper boundary competencies. It is used as an "education" rather than as a "training" intervenion, but could be considered a training experience for employees who find a need to be competent in these areas due to changes or shifts in their job outputs or other requirements.

Intervention 7 consists of three lower boundary competencies, which are prerequuisite requirements for the jobs included in Program A. The activities are highly individualized so they can be completed on an as-needed basis by the job incumbents.

Graphic illustrations of the type included in Figure 4.6 can be used to illustrate only a limited number of attributes of curriculum subsystems. Adding attributes only causes unnecessary confusion. This tends to reduce the overall effectiveness of the curriculum planning effort. The focus group can modify the template if simplicity is needed. The legend in Figure 4.6 defines certain entries which are included in the cells of Core Program A. A table legend must always be included.

Performance Improvement Opportunities Matrix

Once a detailed curriculum plan is prepared, the plan can be illustrated in terms of how its elements are translated into specific performance improvement opportunities. A performance improvement opportunities matrix is prepared. A matrix of this type can be constructed for a single job or for several jobs within an organization hierarchy. Figure 4.7 (on the following page) illustrates one way to do this. The cells in the matrix, which are referenced to the information in Figure 4.6, reveal the types of performance improvement activities one might expect to see in a condensed version of a larger curriculum plan. Of course, the oɪganization would probably name the actual performance improvement events or opportunities that are specific to the cells of the matrix.

The matrix is useful for delivering briefings and for giving similar presentations on the ways that an organization's curriculum plan is translated into specific performance improvement opportunities. Additional information can be included in the matrix. However, too much information interferes with the purpose of having a condensed form of the plan in the first place. Once you have a first draft of your table, seek critical reviews from others, including those who have little or no knowledge of the information you are presenting. Also seek opinions from graphic artists or designers, advertising specialists, or similar persons. These persons usually have helpful suggestions on the best ways of communicating this type of information.

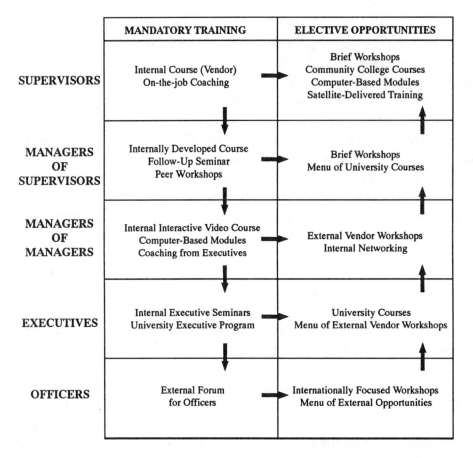

MANDATORY TRAINING	ELECTIVE OPPORTUNITIES
SUPERVISORS — Internal Course (Vendor) / On-the-job Coaching	Brief Workshops / Community College Courses / Computer-Based Modules / Satellite-Delivered Training
MANAGERS OF SUPERVISORS — Internally Developed Course / Follow-Up Seminar / Peer Workshops	Brief Workshops / Menu of University Courses
MANAGERS OF MANAGERS — Internal Interactive Video Course / Computer-Based Modules / Coaching from Executives	External Vendor Workshops / Internal Networking
EXECUTIVES — Internal Executive Seminars / University Executive Program	University Courses / Menu of External Vendor Workshops
OFFICERS — External Forum for Officers	Internationally Focused Workshops / Menu of External Opportunities

Figure 4.7: Hypothetical Organization Performance Improvement Opportunities Plan for Managers

Client Endorsement

Finally, client or senior management reviews and endorsements are critically important for the overall, long-term success of a curriculum plan. Estimates of the resource requirements for the project were anticipated and communicated to the client as part of the work for Step 1 of the Strategic Systems Model. The curriculum plan and the proposed performance improvement opportunities will revive the resources issue with the client. Since the client has had a very active role in all steps for project development, there should be few surprises about the costs for completing the remaining systems components. However, it is very important to apprise the client of the resources that are required to complete the project before work is initiated on the development of the learning interventions. The HRD specialist and the client's representative should carefully estimate and communicate the costs involved at this time. A firm commitment of resources from the client is essential before the design and development of the learning interventions begin (see Figure 4.1, Step 4).

SUMMARY

This chapter included techniques and explanations for competency-based curriculum planning in organizations. Curriculum planning organizes performance improvement opportunities and learning activities into logical, meaningful segments that help employees develop their competencies in ways that support the achievement of organization goals in the most cost-effective manner. Ultimately, the quality of an organization's curriculum plans have cost impacts on the organization.

Additional information on curriculum planning, concepts, issues, and activities can be found in Gottesman (1985); Moody (1990); Stolovitch & Keeps (1988); Svenson (1978); Pace, Peterson, & Porter (1986); Nadler (1982), Hannum & Hansen (1989); Rothwell & Kazanas (1988); Rothwell & Kazanas (1989); Palmer & Lesniak (1991); Rothwell & Kazanas (1992); and Rothwell & Sredl (1992).

REFERENCES

Galosy, J. R. (1983, January). Curriculum design for management training. *Training and Development Journal, 37* (1), pp. 48-51.

Gottesman, A. M. (1985, May). Cyclical curriculum review—A systems approach. *Journal of Systems Management*, pp. 30-31.

Hannum, W., & Hansen, C. (1989). *Instructional systems development in large organizations.* Englewood Cliffs, NJ: Educational Technology Publications.

McKenna, D. D., Svenson, R. A., Wallace, K., & Wallace, G. (1984, September). How to build a training structure that won't keep burning down. *Training*, pp. 77-83.

Moody, M. H. (1990, February). Ex-post-facto model building. *Training and Development Journal, 44*(2), pp. 55-59.

Nadler, L. (1982). *Designing training programs: The critical events model.* Reading, MA: Addison-Wesley.

Pace, R. W., Peterson, B. D., & Porter, W. M. (1986, March). Competency-based curricula. *Training and Development Journal, 40* (3), pp. 71-78.

Palmer, T. M., & Lesniak, R. J. (1991). Implementing a curriculum development project. In N. M. Dixon & J. Henkelman (Eds.), *Models for HRD practice: The academic guide.* Alexandria, VA: American Society for Training and Development.

Rothwell, W. J., & Kazanas, H. C. (1988). Curriculum planning for training: The state of the art. *Performance Improvement Quarterly 1*(3), pp. 2-16.

Rothwell, W. J., & Kazanas, H. C. (1989). *Strategic human resource development.* Englewood Cliffs, NJ: Prentice-Hall.

Rothwell, W. J., & Kazanas, H. C. (1992). *Mastering the instructional design process.* San Francisco, CA: Jossey-Bass.

Rothwell, W. J., & Sredl, H. J. (1992). *The ASTD reference guide to professional human resource development roles and competencies, Volume I* (2nd ed.). Amherst, MA: HRD Press.

Stolovitch, H. D., & Keeps, E. J. (1988). Curriculum development for business and industry. *Performance Improvement Quarterly, 1*(3), pp. 27-37.

Svenson, R. A. (1978, October). Planning a curriculum. *Training and Development Journal, 32* (10), pp. 4-7.

Chapter 5

DESIGNING AND DEVELOPING COMPETENCY-BASED LEARNING INTERVENTIONS

This chapter opens with a discussion of learning objectives in the context of competency-based HRD. The discussion emphasizes the importance of helping employees develop the affective job competencies. The balance of the chapter is committed to an explanation of a systematic instructional design and development process for creating competency-based learning interventions.

In the context of this chapter, the term "learning interventions or opportunities" has broad meaning. These activities could include, for example, formal classroom instruction, self-directed learning using a learning resource guide and ancillary materials, structured on-the-job experiences, such as the use of job aides, or a combination of these or other learning interventions or activities.

The term "delivery" is used mainly in two ways: (1) to designate that the learning activity is implemented or otherwise made available to the target population, and (2) that a formally taught or facilitated presentation of the material to be learned is provided to the members of the target population. Techniques for delivering (i.e., teaching or facilitating) learning interventions are not covered in this book since this information is available in the literature. Implementation strategies are not included for the same reason.

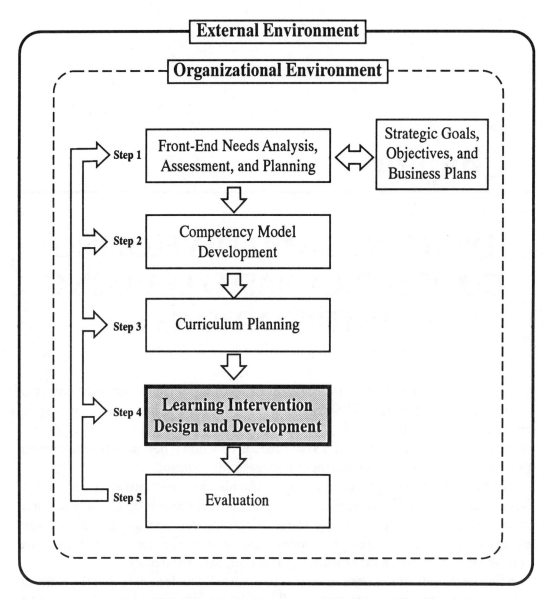

Figure 5.1: The Learning Intervention Design and Development Subsystem of the Strategic Systems Model

IN RELATION TO THE STRATEGIC SYSTEMS MODEL

This chapter provides information on the tools needed to translate the information from the front-end needs analysis, assessment, and planning phase (Step 1), the competency model development stage (Step 2), and the curriculum plan step (Step 3) to the design and development of learning interventions, which is Step 4 of the Strategic Systems Model. Figure 5.1 illustrates those relationships.

Before the instructional design step of the Strategic Systems Model is undertaken, how the curriculum plan and its contents (Step 3) are to be organized into broadly stated performance improvement interventions should be decided. The following presentation is based on the assumption that these decisions have been made.

LEARNING OBJECTIVES AND COMPETENCY-BASED HRD

In order to effectively and efficiently design competency-based performance improvement interventions, it is first necessary to identify the learning objectives (depending on the specificity of the curriculum plan) an employee must master and what degree of mastery an employee needs to acquire critical job competencies. The analysis and identification of learning objectives is an essential task of instructional design and development work. Planning for an assessment of achievement of learning objectives also relies on the designer and developer having a very clear statement of the expected outcomes of the competency acquisition process or intervention.

Tools are available to the instructional designer and developer for examining and evaluating the types of learning expected of employees during competency acquisition activities, and some of these are described in the remainder of this section. The role and importance of competencies and performance objectives in the affective domain of learning, in particular, are explained in relation to other types of learning. The actions required of HRD professionals to more adequately design and develop affective learning interventions for performance improvement are also discussed.

Domains of Learning Objectives

In 1948, a group of psychologists who were interested in achievement testing met at the American Psychological Association (APA) conference in Boston, Massachusetts, to tackle deficiencies in critical practice areas. What was needed, they decided, was a common terminology for describing and referencing human behavioral characteristics for school and college learning. It seemed to them "that some way of classifying and ordering the types of responses specified as *desired outcomes* of education might be useful" (Krathwohl, Bloom, & Masia, 1964, p. 4). After working on the problem, they concluded that two processes were important.

First, learning objectives must be defined in behavioral terms and must include a statement of the evidence—determined through tasks, tests, observations, etc.—relevant for judging the adequacy of the performance.

Second, a way of placing all learning objectives within a large overall scheme consisting of types, or "domains of learning," must be found.

Their work continued for a number of years and included numerous professional educators and psychologists as contributors. A result was the creation of a taxonomy of educational objectives. The taxonomy included three learning domains: cognitive, affective, and psychomotor. All learning outcomes, or objectives, can be placed in one of the three domains. Some objectives, however, share the properties of more than one domain.

The *cognitive domain* includes "objectives which emphasize remembering or reproducing something which has presumably been learned, as well as objectives which involve the solving of some intellectual task for which the individual has to determine the essential problem and then reorder given material or combine it with ideas, methods, or procedures previously learned" (Krathwohl et al., 1964, p. 6).

The *affective domain* includes objectives that "emphasize a feeling tone, an emotion, or a degree of acceptance or rejection" (Krathwohl et al., 1964, p. 7). These learning objectives have also become known in HRD as an individual's "attitudes."

The *psychomotor domain* includes objectives that "emphasize some muscular or motor skill, some manipulation of material and objects, or some act which requires neuromuscular coordination" (Krathwohl et al., 1964, p. 7).

A major advantage to HRD professionals of having this scheme for classifying learning objectives is that it helps curriculum planners, instructional designers, instructors, and evaluators more precisely know what is meant by the statement of a learning objective.

Importance of the Affective Domain

An application of the competency model development methods included in chapter 3 will result in the identification of a full range of competencies that span the three learning domains mentioned above. In professional jobs, many of those outcomes will be cognitive or affective learning outcomes. Technical jobs often include a substantial number of cognitive and psychomotor outcomes; however, they can also have a significant number of affective learning outcomes too.

In their landmark work on the classification of learning objectives in the affective domain, David Krathwohl, Benjamin Bloom, and Bertram Masia (1964) provided insights on how the achievement of one type of learning outcome (e.g., a cognitive outcome) affects the achievement of another (e.g., an affective outcome), and thus affects the interrelationship of all of the outcomes. This concept and its explanation have very real significance for how competency-based training or education systems are designed and developed.

During my research for this book, many HRD practitioners shared their thoughts with me, and they agreed that HRD programs need to give attention to the achievement of learning outcomes from each of the domains. They also indicated, however, that this is problematic because they know so little about analyzing, designing, and developing performance improvement interventions for learning objectives in the affective domain.

For this reason, they indicated (with rare exception) that they devoted little or no attention and instructional time to the achievement of affective outcomes by their employees. Hopefully the discussion below will alleviate this information deficiency and illustrate the importance of affective learning outcomes for developing employees' job competencies.

The Work of Krathwohl, Bloom, and Masia

Problems with affective objectives, similar to those described above, were discovered by Krathwohl, Bloom, and Masia, who in 1964 reported the following:

> We studied the history of several courses at the general education level of college. Typically, we found that in the original statement of objectives there was frequently as much an emphasis given to affective objectives as cognitive objectives . . . . However, . . . over a period of ten to twenty years, we found a rather rapid dropping of the affective objectives. (p. 16)

Although the cognitive, affective, and psychomotor categories are useful for classifying and analyzing learning outcomes, there is a holistic character to human performance that does not separate the outcomes of training or education. Krathwohl et al. (1964, p. 48) stated that nearly all cognitive learning objectives have a corresponding affective component if we look for it . They also concluded that "it appears that at all levels of the affective domain, affective objectives have a cognitive component, and one can find affective components for cognitive objectives" (p. 53).

Cognitive and affective learning outcomes are intimately related:

> In some instances the joint seeking of affective and cognitive [training or education] goals results in curricula which use one domain as the means to the other on a closely-knit alternating basis . . . . Perhaps it is analogous to a man scaling a wall using two step ladders side by side, each with rungs too wide apart to be conveniently reached in a single step. One ladder represents the cognitive behavior and objectives, the other the affective. The ladders are so constructed that the rungs of one ladder fall between the rungs of the other. The attainment of some complex goal is made possible by alternately climbing a rung on one ladder, which brings the next rung of the other ladder within reach. (Krathwohl et al., 1964, p. 60)

Krathwohl et al. (1964) offered several points that have implications for persons who are creating comprehensive competency-based performance improvement interventions. Specifically (pp. 54-57):

- The attainment of a learning objective in one domain can lead to the achievement of a learning objective in another domain.

- Emphases on one domain of learning (e.g., the cognitive domain) may tend to drive out the other domain (e.g., the affective domain).

- The emphasis on cognitive behavior in learning is an indication of the comfort many have when working in the cognitive domain.

- Good instruction is, in large part, the instructor's ability to attain the affective objectives by challenging the learners' beliefs (or mindsets) and getting them to discuss the issues associated with them.

- Over time, the emphasis upon cognitive learning outcomes at the expense of the affective outcomes can be lessened or stopped altogether by a conscious acknowledgment of its misplaced emphasis.

The final two points above are especially critical for contemporary HRD practitioners. First, instructional designers must include in their designs learning opportunities that will help the learner achieve affective learning outcomes by challenging learners' beliefs or mindsets and by getting them to discuss the issues that surround those beliefs. Second, HRD professionals must assume full responsibility for the inclusion of learning outcomes from the affective domain in their performance improvement activities. This implies, therefore, that the designer or developer must be able to recognize learning that must occur in each of the domains. Then, they must be competent at creating learning experiences that cross domain boundaries. There must be constant, conscious acknowledgement of a need for affective learning objectives in competency acquisition agendas. This opinion is shared by other HRD professionals—among them, Roger Poulet and Gerry Moult.

The Work of Poulet and Moult

Further insight on this topic was recently provided by practitioners Roger Poulet and Gerry Moult (1987). They examined the role of affective learning objectives and the achievement of job outputs in their work with the "Managing People First (MPF)" program, a wide-influence training system for British Airways. In the design of the MPF, Poulet and Moult (1987) reported that they "biased the balance between behavior-skill input and value input toward the latter. This gave [them] a unique opportunity to study the impact of values on the outputs—values both personal to the participants and inherent in the course" (p. 63). And the result? "We found that implementation [i.e., the transfer] of learned skills and behaviors was profoundly affected by whether the individual and corporate values were in or out of sync" (p. 63).

Their work led them to conclude that "the role of values in training had been neglected and that human resource departments were paying a high price for that neglect. Far too many training interventions are wasted, misused, or somehow fall short of expectations for reasons that remain a mystery to their designers and evaluators" (Poulet & Moult, 1987, pp. 62-63).

Regarding the inclusion of affective competencies in training programs, they observed: "Even training programs that appear to be exclusively technical, skill-based, or conceptual in content are mediated by the value systems, self-image, expectations, and ambitions of their participants. And it is these factors that determine the level of identification, acceptance, and implementation; that is, whether people really will do anything about their learning. This is the missing link in the transfer chain, and trainers disregard it to their own disadvantage" (Poulet & Moult, 1987, p. 63). Therefore, ignoring the affective competencies or learning outcomes in the design and delivery of training or education has probable effects on the degree to which the training content itself will be transferred to actual job performance.

Making the Paradigm Shift!

Many HRD professionals must make a significant paradigm shift in the importance they assign to affective learning outcomes in their designs if comprehensive competency-based performance improvement systems are to become a reality. At present, the tendency is to emphasize competencies that are largely cognitive or psychomotor in nature as elements of learning opportunities, at the expense of competencies that are more laden with affective attributes. Simply stated, practitioners frequently identify (or are conscious of) the full range of needs but choose to ignore the needs that seem impossible to translate into meaningful learning interventions, because they are unaware of how to do so.

Practitioners must balance their curricula and the learning programs and interventions that result from them by including a correct mixture of cognitive, affective, and psychomotor domain outcomes in the learning plans. For the approach in this book to effectively bring about strategic performance improvement in organizations, there must be a deliberate and consistent willingness to work in a holistic manner with the *total* employee, his or her job performance, and the organization. Affective learning outcomes can no longer be ignored if this is to happen.

If this paradigm shift is to occur in HRD professionals, they must challenge their personal comfort in emphasizing the cognitive over the affective dimensions of employee job competence when designing, developing, and implementing performance improvement curricula, programs, and interventions. On the other hand, however, they must also accept the limitations inherent in designing and delivering learning interventions on affective curriculum dimensions. Balance must be maintained. This shift in thinking and action is not easy to make if we have become accustomed to doing otherwise. Once a decision has been made to balance the three types of learning, how does the HRD practitioner proceed?

In order to make an affective competency "teachable," you must first break it down into its underlying dimensions or components. You must have a clear understanding of its dimensions, including its cognitive, affective, and psychomotor components and how they are interrelated. You must put the competency in an organization or environmental context and identify its ramifications and effect on the achievement of the job outputs. The next section of this chapter includes suggestions for analyzing affective job competencies.

It is also important to relate the competencies to the cultural dimensions of the target population. That is, how is each competency interpreted within the cultural and organization norms of the targeted employees? Sensitivity to cultural meaning is especially critical in a competence format since the affective dimensions of competency acquisition are intimately linked to individuals' cultural attributes.

Martin Scheerer (1954) observed that "behavior may be conceptualized as being embedded in a cognitive-emotional-motivational matrix in which no true separation is possible. No matter how we slice behavior, the ingredients of motivation-emotion-cognition are present in one form or another" (p. 123). Carefully interfacing the design and development of learning opportunities for cognitive and affective competencies can complement the learners' acquisition of both types of competencies.

There is no claim made here that employees will fully acquire and implement affective competencies on the job as a result of one or two formal learning interventions. In order to fully develop and implement some competencies, employees require the benefits of time, circumstances, and personal experience. Training or education interventions can supply critical knowledge and many of the concepts, techniques, and processes, as well as a certain amount of the experience. However, it usually can't provide *all* of the experience. Contextual learning is very critical. The designer or developer and the learning facilitator have the first responsibility for affective learning outcomes. The employee must supply the initiative and energy to acquire the personal attributes which most influence the achievement of job outputs. As HRD professionals, we must learn to live with the imperfection of our results. This outcome is far more preferable than that which results from making no attempt at all to develop employees' affective competencies.

In summary, the development of employees' affective competencies must not be ignored as elements of competency-based curricula and outcomes of learning interventions. Instead, the relationships of affective and cognitive competencies from the job competency model must be identified, and the development of competencies in one domain must be interfaced with competencies from the other domain in ways that support the development of competencies in the domains.

SYSTEMATIC INSTRUCTIONAL DESIGN AND DEVELOPMENT

Consistent with the theme of this book, a seven-step system for designing and developing competency-based learning interventions is presented in this section. The design and development process included here is an eclectic blend of practices used by many HRD practitioners and the theories and practices of individuals, notably Dick and Carey (1985), Gagne and Briggs (1979, 1988), and Gagne (1985).

Steps in the Process

Completion of the following steps will result in effective competency-based learning opportunities:

1. Complete an in-depth analysis of the characteristics of the learners, including their entry-level competencies and the work climate or environment.

2. Confirm and preliminarily organize the competencies to be included in the learning intervention or interventions.

3. Identify the subordinate competencies for each principal (or critical) competency. Sequence the competencies in the order in which they are to be acquired.

4. Elaborate the competencies as learner performance objectives. Design assessment items or activities to evaluate the learner's performance following instruction.

5. Design and develop the intervention learning plan and the instructional modules for the interventions.

6. Brief the client or client group.

7. Pilot test the performance improvement intervention. Make revisions as indicated by the formative evaluation results. Implement the program or intervention.

Need for a Plan

A key to the successful design, development, and implementation of learning opportunities in organizations is the development and adherence to a project plan for the design and development work. If you are an experienced instructional designer, you have probably recognized that the steps above are almost never completed in a precisely linear manner (see Overfield, 1989). The actions or results for the steps must be combined in various ways to achieve the design and development results. One constraint to linear progress, in particular, is that you need the availability and use of services from support persons to complete elements of the design and development steps. The designer usually must rely on the support of specialists in electronic media (e.g., computer equipment), graphic design specialists, and subject-matter specialists, to name a few. Therefore, depending upon the complexity and flow of the design and development work, constructing a project plan and adhering to it as closely as possible are "musts." Project management plans can be designed to include signature blocks for all who have a stake in the project. This technique is especially useful for managing large, complex projects.

Having a project plan that lacks consensus will usually result in confusion, disagreements, unfortunate professional-interpersonal conflicts, and finally, delays in achieving the design project results. There are seldom any "winners" and nearly always many "losers." When a design and development project fails at this stage or later, major concerns of credibility for the HRD department are usually raised by the client or client group. One way to improve the chances of a design and development project's success is to get a plan down on paper, and to get the concurrence of all contributors and the client!

Completing the Design and Development Steps

The next several pages are devoted to a discussion of the key points associated with the steps above. An exhaustive discussion of each step is not possible since each design and development project has different requirements. Several items can be found in the chapter references for additional information and assistance on the work required for completing each of the steps below.

Step 1. **Complete an in-depth analysis of the characteristics of the learners, including their entry-level competencies, and the work climate or environment.**

The in-depth analysis of the learners' characteristics helps the designer and developer to more specifically focus the emphases of the competencies on true employee needs. Elements of this profile will also suggest the most appropriate learning strategies for the intervention(s).

The determination of employees' entry-level competencies requires the design or selection, administration, and analysis of measurement devices for the competencies in question. Entry-level competencies could include both job and literacy competencies. In addition to entry-level competencies, employees should be measured on the degree to which they hold the actual job competencies.

The measurement and analysis processes will result in a micro-needs assessment of the target population's competencies. These data might have been collected in an earlier step of the Strategic Systems Model. If so, the results should be reviewed, and updated or supplemented if necessary.

These findings often will suggest that elements of the job competency model must be tailored in specific ways to meet the employees' specific performance needs. The designer and developer must also be attentive to the employees' performance capabilities with literacy competencies. This is a sensitive area of learning design and development work. It might not be possible for an organization to commit extensive resources to improving employees' literacy competencies. However, the design of learning interventions can be appropriately targeted to the learners' literacy levels once those are known from the analyses completed during this step.

The completion of this step, then, should result in a profile of the learners which will guide the development of later design and development work. The profile should have as much depth as possible depending on the resources available to collect and summarize the information. Using these findings, the designer and developer can specifically focus the training in ways that will ensure that it is meaningful to the employees and that it meets the objective of improved job performance.

What additional information should be collected? You might consider the following:

- The learners' prior and present work experiences

- The basic academic knowledge and skills levels of the target population (i.e., their literacy levels)

- Demographics of the target population

- Impacts resulting from the geographic distributions of the learners

- Learners' prior training and education levels in relation to the program or intervention contents

- The personalities of the learners

- The preferred learning styles of the targeted employees

- The attributes of the work climate (authoritarian, permissive, partici pative, etc.) where the competencies will be applied; obstacles that can potentially inhibit the use of the competencies and the achievement of the job outputs; as-yet untapped opportunities for employee achievement that exist within the environment

The analyses on the employees' competency needs and the profile of the target population are useful results for beginning work on the next step of the design and development process.

Step 2. **Confirm and preliminarily organize the competencies to be included in the learning intervention or interventions.**

Recall from chapter 4 that the job competencies from the competency model were analyzed on several dimensions and organized into a curriculum plan, and that a set of broad learning opportunities, called programs, were identified (see Figures 4.6 and 4.7).

The first task in this step is to confirm the appropriateness of the job competencies that were included in the curriculum plan, which is a critical foundation document for the design and development process. You must ensure that the elements you are working with are consistent with the characteristics of the target population. If significant time has elapsed since the curriculum plan was completed, you should definitely review it with the client and revise it as is necessary. Also remember to include any additional competencies that were identified in Step 1 above as an outcome of the analysis of the participants' attributes.

The second task is to establish a preliminary sequence or order for presenting the competencies in the learning intervention(s), if that was not (or could not be) confirmed at the curriculum planning stage. The competencies for most jobs usually share a wide variety of dependent, independent, or interdependent relationships with one other. These relationships are mainly influenced by their subject-matter content and by how employees use them (either singularly or in combination with other competencies) to achieve the job outputs. Sometimes the training schedule deadline and/or the job requirements will dictate which competencies must be included in each learning intervention and the schedule employees will follow to complete the interventions.

Preliminary sequencing might have been done as part of the curriculum plan; if so, the sequence included in the curriculum plan should be reviewed and confirmed, or used as a springboard for defining a revised sequence with the client. You must be very clear with your client on their expectations in this regard, and certainly in advance of tackling any of the later design steps. Developing instruction and other learning opportunities for the wrong competencies, for an inappropriate combination of competencies, or for incorrectly ordered competencies can be a costly misadventure, especially when technology-driven instructional materials or media are used for implementing the intervention.

The client and the HRD department must jointly create the overall intervention design plan for training the target population by deciding how the competencies will be organized. The answers to the following questions will provide you with some guidance for the development of the plan:

- How many separate (or distinct) interventions will be used? The project budget will heavily influence this decision.

- Which competencies will be included in each intervention?

- How much time will be allocated for employees to complete each intervention?

- What strategies (e.g., formal classroom instruction, on-the-job training, independent study) should be used for each of the interventions?

- How are the job outputs and the job tasks and activities related to competency acquisition?

Once these questions have been answered, the HRD specialist can represent the decisions in a Competency-based Learning Design Plan. The plan includes:

- A brief description of each learning intervention

- The duration of each intervention

- The competencies (or reference to a competency list) that will be acquired during each intervention

- The job outputs that will be emphasized

- The job tasks or activities employees perform during the intervention

- The job tasks or activities employees perform on the job following the intervention

Figure 5.2 illustrates a skeleton plan for selected elements of the following example.

Let's assume that a researched competency model and the curriculum plan specify fifteen competencies for the job, which collectively constitute a "program" included in the curriculum plan. Sequencing was not decided as part of the curriculum plan step; only the major program decisions were made. The HRD department and the client have jointly decided that the training program will consist of a series of integrated formal and on-the-job learning interventions to be completed by employees over the first thirty weeks on the job. It is decided that employees will acquire the

Phase	Learning Intervention Stage	Duration	Competencies*	Job Outputs*	Job Tasks or Activities*
1	Job Orientation	1 Wk.	1-15 (Overview)	A-H (Overview)	(a)-(f) (Overview)
2	Training Intervention I	1 Wk.	1-4, 6	A, C	(a)
3	On-the-job Coaching	8 Wk.	1-4, 6	A, C	(a)
4	Training Intervention II	1 Wk.	5,7, 10-12	B,D,E	(a) (b) (g) (f) (e)
5	On -the-job Coaching	8 Wk.	5,7, 10-12	B,D,E	(a) (b) (g) (f) (e)
6	Training Intervention III	1 Wk.	8,9, 13-15	F,G,H	(c) (d) (f)
7	On-the-job Coaching	8 Wk.	8,9, 13-15	F,G,H	(c) (d) (f)
8	Performance Assessment and Feedback	3 Days	1-15	A-H	(a)-(f)

*The competencies, job outputs, and tasks and activities are referenced to a hypothetical job competency model developed during Step 2 of the Strategic Systems Model. The Model contains Competencies 1-15, Outputs A-H, and Job Tasks and Activities (a)-(f).

Figure 5.2: Competency-Based Learning Design Plan

job competencies by completing three formal classroom-based instructional interventions of one week each, separated by intervals of eight weeks of on-the-job training.

Planning that will ensure adequate transfer of competency acquisition to daily job performance has been completed. The employees' on-the-job performance will be monitored by the immediate manager or a colleague who has been identified as an exemplary performer of the job. The monitoring will be a supportive relationship that includes coaching for improved performance. One to two months following the third classroom intervention, employees will return to the training environment to complete a brief seminar for job performance assessment and for receiving feedback for improved performance.

The client and the HRD department have agreed that the affective dimensions of employee performance are critical to successful job performance. To accomplish this, during the formal training intervention, the affective competencies and the performance objectives associated with them will be presented to the employees in an integrated manner with the other job competencies. However, they will receive special application emphases during their on-the-job performance, with coaching by the monitor.

Figure 5.2 includes an abbreviated Competency-based Learning Design Plan that illustrates some of the key conditions described in the example. Notice in Figure 5.2 that the job competencies, outputs, and the tasks or activities are referenced to the competency model. The plan outline can be modified to suit the conditions at hand. The plan provides an up-to-date blueprint to be used in later design and development work. It is a very useful communication document. The design plan *must* receive the endorsement of the client or client group before further design and development work continues.

> *Step 3.* **Identify the subordinate competencies for each principal (or critical) competency. Sequence the competencies in the order in which they are to be acquired.**

In this step, each principal competency is broken down into several levels of more finely graded subordinate or subcompetencies. Figure 5.3 illustrates how this process was applied to a principal competency. In this case, three subordinate levels of competencies are illustrated. You should remember that an employee will acquire and apply this competency in conjunction with other competencies. For this example, affective competencies are also required, as well as several prerequisite psychomotor competencies. This illustration will serve as a useful frame of reference as you read the remainder of this step.

Competency:	***Customer Contract Closing.*** An electronic publishing manager will close an electronic publishing contract with a customer that satisfies or exceeds the customer's requirements and lies within corporate capability.
Job Output:	A ***closed customer contract*** for an electronic publishing project

The Principal Competency and Select Subordinate Competencies

- Closes an electronic publishing contract with a customer that satisfies or exceeds the customer's requirements and lies within corporate capability

    - Develops and negotiates a contract proposal with the customer that meets the customer's needs and requirements

    - Compares the customer's needs and requirements with the corporate capability statement for electronic publishing, evaluates the findings to determine corporate service options, and determines the action(s) that must be taken to complete the job

    - Interviews a potential customer to determine critical project facts, including: budget guidelines for the project, delivery schedule, format or layout requirements, electronic requirements, graphic design needs, printing, and binding needs

    - Communicates the corporate capability statement for electronic publishing to a potential customer in ways that encourage the development and closing of a contract

    - Synthesizes the capabilities and limitations regarding the available hardware, software, other technologies, and human resources into a corporate capability statement for electronic publishing

        - Comprehends the capabilities and limitations of hardware, software, other technologies, and human resources that are available external to the firm (i.e., through subcontractors) in the electronic publishing or allied fields

        - Compares the similarities and contrasts the differences for the capabilities and the limitations of the hardware, software, other technologies, and the human resources available internal to the firm

            - States the capabilities and limitations of the hardware, software, other technologies, and the human resources available internal to the firm

            - Lists the hardware, software, and other technologies internal to the firm.

            - Lists the design, illustration, development, and technical capabilities of human resources available internal to the firm.

Figure 5.3: Illustration of a Principal Competency and Three Levels of Subordinate Competencies

In order to identify subordinate or subcompetencies, first you must know more about the type(s) of learning that must occur in order for the employee to acquire the competency. To do this, each competency is classified by a type of human capability it represents. There are two sets of tools available to you for completing this task: the taxonomy of educational outcomes and the work of Robert Gagne and Leslie Briggs.

The taxonomy of educational outcomes, which was an outcome of the 1948 APA work group, provided a framework for classifying the outcomes of learning using the cognitive, affective, and psychomotor domains. For the details of the processes involved in the classification system, consult Bloom (1956); Krathwohl, Bloom, & Masia (1964); and Simpson (1966).

A useful set of categories for determining the types of learning was developed by Robert Gagne and Leslie Briggs (1979). They identified five types of human capabilities, on which their theory of instructional design is based (pp. 49-58):

1. *Intellectual skills.* This includes learning how to do something of an intellectual nature. When an intellectual skill is being demonstrated, the learner shows how an intellectual operation is carried out.

2. *Cognitive strategies.* These skills govern an individual's learning, remembering, and thinking behaviors. The individual solves a variety of practical problems by efficient means. Creative problem solving is an example of a cognitive strategy.

3. *Verbal information.* This is essentially verbal knowledge. Verbal information is learned in both formal and incidental ways. The learner states or otherwise communicates information.

4. *Motor skills.* This involves carrying out motor activities in a variety of contexts.

5. *Attitudes.* An attitude is a persistent state that modifies an individual's choice of action with regard to objects, persons, or events.

In general, you can locate intellectual skills, cognitive strategies, and verbal information in the cognitive domain; attitudes in the affective domain; and motor skills in the psychomotor domain of training (or education) goals.

By using the human capabilities categories above to classify the principal competencies needed for successful job performance, it becomes easier to determine how adequately each type of learned capability has been covered by the competency development work. Furthermore, each category of competencies (or types of learned capabilities) has its own conditions of learning. Therefore, once the competency statements are identified within a category, the conditions of learning will be the same for all the competency statements within the category. This makes instructional design a considerably more efficient process. It also facilitates the completion of Step 5 of the instructional design stage: The designer identifies and plans the conditions of learning needed for the instructional process (Gagne & Briggs, 1979).

Once the type of learning represented by each competency is known, an analysis method from those provided below can be used to identify the subcompetencies. Several useful analysis methods for determining subordinate competencies and their relationships with one other have appeared in the HRD literature (e.g., Hannum & Hansen, 1989, pp. 126-129).

The Information Domain. To analyze competencies in the information domain, an elaboration analysis is recommended. When this approach is used, you search for the key idea of the essence of the information. Once the key idea(s) is (are) identified, each idea is elaborated. Further elaborations produce more finely graded elaborations, and so forth. A hierarchy of the main information items, and each of its sub-items, is prepared. This hierarchy will show the relationships and key elements of information that must be included in the instructional program.

The Cognitive Domain. Cognitive competencies require the development of a set of competencies subordinate to the principal competency. A hierarchy is constructed which shows the relationship of the competencies to the principal competency and/ or to one another.

Intellectual skills and their analysis and acquisition demand special attention. Gagne and Briggs (1988) observed: "One cannot have a course [of instruction] without intellectual skills." Thus, intellectual skills play a critical role in designing instructional programs or interventions. They cited two reasons for this: "First, [intellectual skills] are the kinds of capabilities that determine what the student can do, and thus are intimately bound up with the description of a course in terms of its learning outcomes. A second reason is that intellectual skills have a cumulative nature—they build upon each other in a predictable manner. Accordingly, they provide the most useful model for the sequencing of course structure" (pp. 50-51).

Therefore, designers and developers must pay special attention to the intellectual skills included in the intervention, since they strongly influence how the learning objectives should be sequenced.

The Affective Domain. For competencies in the affective domain, the recommended technique is goal analysis. Affective learning goals are among the most difficult to describe and specify. Recall that an attitude is a persisting state that modifies a person's choice of action in relation to objects, persons, or events. Mager (1972) pointed out that "a statement about attitude is a statement of prediction based on what somebody says or what somebody does" (p. 16). The application of goal analysis results in the identification of the behaviors that can be expected once the competency is acquired by the employee. These are analogous to the "behavioral indicators" found in the competency model. Mager (p. 72) describes and explains a straightforward five-step process for goal analysis in the affective domain. Although the behavioral indicators from the competency model will usually elaborate affective competencies, you might need to do further analyses on them for design and development purposes. Therefore Mager's (p. 72) steps for completing a goal analysis are presented:

1. Write down the goal.

2. Jot down, in words and phrases, the performance that if achieved, would cause you to agree that the goal is achieved.

3. Sort out the jottings. Delete duplications and unwanted items. Repeat Steps One and Two for any remaining abstractions (fuzzies) considered important.

4. Write a complete statement for each performance, describing the nature, quality, or amount you will consider acceptable.

5. Test the statements with the question: If someone achieved or demonstrated each of these performances, would I be willing to say he has achieved the goal? When you can answer "yes," the analysis is finished.

The Motor Domain. A technique known as procedural analysis is useful for competencies that lie within the motor domain of learned capabilities. To analyze a motor competency using procedural analysis, you determine the required set of individual movements and the routing or process used for sequencing the movements that will achieve the objective (Dick & Carey, 1985, pp. 53-55; Hannum & Hansen, 1989, pp. 127-128).

An application of the techniques above will result in the subordinate levels of detail for the competencies. Depending upon how narrowly (or broadly) you defined your principal competencies, a single competency might require the application of several of the analysis techniques, and each application might be required at several levels of lower order detail. When it comes time to complete analyses of this type, you will want to enlist help from job experts, including the job managers. In some cases, job experts external to your organization might be needed to give additional support or detail to your work.

Once the principal and subordinate competencies have been identified, their relationship(s) with each other are confirmed. Some designers prefer to show these relationships by using a diagram, chart, and/or a step-by-step outline. The objective here is to determine and to fully understand the relationships of the competencies with each other since these linkages must be made when the learning interventions are designed and developed.

Step 4. Elaborate the competencies as learner performance objectives. Design assessment items or activities to evaluate the learner's performance following instruction.

Notice from your activities in Step 3 that each elaboration produced more specifically defined competencies. In this step, each learning requirement is written in the form of a learner performance statement known as a *performance objective*. A performance objective describes exactly what a learner (and not the instructor or facilitator) must be able to do, under a given set of performance conditions, and with what outputs, to successfully meet the objective.

Figure 5.4 (on the following page) includes an illustration of a job competency and a set of performance objectives (in hierarchial order). The achievement of the performance objectives will lead to the acquisition and application of the competency. This illustration will serve as a useful frame of reference for the remainder of this step.

Defining learning events requires this level of specificity. Competency statements (both principal and subordinate) do not include specific, well-defined performance requirements. The competency statements are not specific enough for you to judge when a learner has acquired a competency. Since you need precise statements of the learner performance expectations to design and develop instruction, you must ensure that each competency statement is reduced to specific performance terms within the context of the job. These performance objectives also provide support for designing assessment items to subsequently determine whether learning has occurred and whether the competencies have been acquired by the learner.

THE COMPETENCY-TO-PERFORMANCE OBJECTIVE INTERFACE

Competency: Applies the use of twelve special word-processing functions by using the function keys.

Performance Objectives:

1:      Identifies eleven of the twelve first-level function keys for the XYZ software package, given an unmarked keyboard diagram.

2:      Describes the first-level functions, by function key number, and selects the correct outcome 100% of the time when shown a set of choices that illustrate a first-level function key application.

3:      Applies the use of the twelve first-level function keys with 100% accuracy while word-processing a passage of text.

Figure 5.4: An Illustration of the Competency-to-Performance Objective Interface

Making the transition from generic or process competencies to performance objectives can be problematic. You have several sources of information:

- The front-end needs analysis, assessment, and planning results. These results provide valuable information on the most critical job performance requirements in a strategic organization context. Depending upon the level of detail that was used to complete the front-end plan, you might have comprehensive enough information to complete your analyses.

- The job outputs, which were included in the competency model

- The job tasks and activities or actions that were associated with the competencies during the competency model- or menu-building process. If it was difficult to make those associations during the research stage, then another method will be needed to reach the required level of detail.

- Data obtained during the critical incident interviews with exemplary performers during the competency model-or menu-building process. If critical behavior interviews were not conducted earlier, then this source of information will not be available to you.

- A "job context analysis" (Douds, 1992). This approach produces precise information on the competency, and it provides detailed information on how each competency is utilized by the exemplary performers to achieve consistently high-quality job outputs. In this process, two to four exemplary performers from the target population are identified. The exemplary performers provide answers to three questions relevant to the use of the competency in the workplace:

    1. What are the job situations in which the competency is used?

    2. What are the particularly difficult aspects of applying the competency?

    3. How do you know that you are performing this competency in a truly exemplary manner?

When analyzed, the exemplary performers' answers to these questions will suggest a wide range of performance requirements and dimensions, and the performance objectives can be identified and defined as a natural outgrowth of the interview data analyses. Depending upon the application environment and your preferences, you might want to complete your context analyses at an earlier project stage; for example, at the curriculum planning stage.

Recall that a competency is a personal characteristic an employee has and uses for successful job performance. In the context of planned performance improvement interventions, learner or instructional performance objectives describe the actions, conditions, and outputs a learner will take (either singularly or in combination with other performance objectives) in order to acquire a competency.

Sometimes the acquisition of one competency will require the successful achievement of only one performance objective: The competency and the action component of the performance objective are one and the same. In this case, the performance objective informs the competency by describing the condition(s) of the performance and the criterion (or criteria) that must be met for successful competency acquisition. This situation is common when competencies and performance objectives are defined for very concrete jobs; for example, competencies that are common to less-skilled technical jobs. For more abstract or multi-dimensional competencies, such as those encountered in management or professional jobs, a competency might require the successful completion of several performance objectives where the relationships among them must be defined in hierarchial form. These are commonly referred to in practice as a learning hierarchy.

Analysis of the performance dimensions of the competencies and the definition and ordering of the performance objectives is one of the most, if not the most, challenging tasks of the designer and developer. When you are preparing a set of instructional performance objectives for a moderately abstract competency, be careful not to lose sight of the fact that competency acquisition is the terminal outcome of the employee's learning experience. *The learner must have closure on competency acquisition.* Therefore, it is important to establish the critical linkages of the performance objectives to the competency. One way to stay focused on the competency is to establish a learning hierarchy or path for the performance objectives that ultimately leads to competency acquisition.

Many practitioners have difficulty writing clear, definitive performance objectives. Oftentimes it is because they have not invested sufficient effort in the performance analyses needed in order to specify the job performance requirements. Defining performance objectives requires a moderate to high level of analysis competence, and well-defined verbal abilities.

The task of writing performance objectives is easier to complete when the designer thinks of each of the requirements for a good performance objective as a three-step process:

1. State the employee action(s) or performance that is desired.

2. Define the performance conditions.

3. State the criterion (or criteria) for judging an employee's performance as "successful."

The HRD literature abounds with helpful resources for designing and using performance objectives. Some references you might find useful to review include Mager (1975b); Dick & Carey (1985); or Gagne, Briggs, & Wager (1988).

High quality performance objectives have several advantages for instructional design and development:

> • They are essential for communicating to learners exactly what they are to learn, the performance conditions, and the criterion or criteria for successful performance.

- Well-conceived and written performance objectives support the design and use of evaluation instruments and processes.

- They significantly contribute information to useful instructional documents and other materials for the program or intervention for which they were designed. These products include such items as instructional materials for the learners, instructors' or facilitators' guides, marketing documents for the program, policy guidelines and documents, and program and student evaluation materials.

As you prepare performance objectives, it is helpful to have a frame of reference for determining the level of actual performance that will be expected of the learner for each objective included in the learning program. Earlier in this chapter, a taxonomy of educational objectives was discussed as a tool for classifying and describing educational objectives in three domains of learning: cognitive, affective, and psychomotor. Performance objectives each can be classified not only by their learning domain but also by a hierarchy of subdivisions within each of the three domains.

For example, in the affective domain there are five categories of performance: receiving or attending (the lowest level), responding, valuing, organization, and at the most complex level, characterization by a value or value complex. When a learner completes a characterization by a value or value complex, the learner's performance is at the highest level of performance in the affective domain. The dictates of the job requirements are the best indicators of which domain level should be used for each performance objective.

These classifications have four major contributions to the production of performance objectives:

1. They identify the sophistication levels of the learner performance objectives across the three domains of learning. This provides a basis for assessing whether or not the instructional contents are appropriate for the broader expectations and objectives of competency acquisition.

2. They help the designer and developer enhance the specificity of the performance objectives.

3. Because the specificity of the performance objectives is improved, the assessment of a learner's progress is made easier.

4. They help the curriculum specialist compare the similarities and contrast the differences in curriculum content within, as well as across, several programs or interventions.

Once again, the performance objectives should be classified by using one of the two methods recommended earlier for the competencies. I strongly recommend that you classify the performance objectives for your instructional design and development projects in this manner. This is another check that a proper balance is being maintained among the various types of learned capabilities which, when achieved, will lead to competency acquisition.

Once you are satisfied with the quality of the performance objectives, you should link them with the competencies they support. You should also show the order in which they will be accomplished by the employees during the intervention. This is the stage of design and development work when major errors or omissions must be identified and finally put to rest. Major errors, omissions, or flaws in the meanings or interpretations of the competencies or performance requirements needed for competency acquisition can have costly consequences if these problems are carried into the final stages of the intervention development work.

This is a good time to conduct a major review session with your client or client group. It is always useful to give them a detailed outline of the competency statements and the performance objectives well in advance of a work session with them. Ask them to review all of the elements and to make revisions (or recommendations for revisions) at that time. You should include the job activities or tasks that correspond to each competency and the job outputs that are achieved by or impacted by the application of the competency. The outline of information included in Figure 5.2 could be used to create the review document; the information elements in the figure can be tailored to specific needs.

The second task in this step is to design assessment items (or activities) to evaluate the learner's performance. Assessment as it is used in this context is of two types:

- Assessment of the learner's performance of the individual performance objective(s)

- Assessment of the larger intended instructional outcome—i.e., the learner's acquisition of the competency

At the performance objective level, learners can demonstrate their achievement in several ways. They can, for example, satisfactorily complete test items, demonstrate their competence through active, observable performance (e.g., give a speech), or demonstrate the achievement of some final job output or outputs in the broader sense. Mager's *Measuring Instructional Intent* (1975a) is a comprehensive resource for designing and developing an assessment of learning achievement. In addition to this resource, a number of references for the assessment of individual performance and program evaluation are provided in the references for this chapter and for chapter 7.

At the competency acquisition level, assessment seeks to determine whether the learner has acquired the competency and its subordinate and allied competencies. Recall that the competency model (which all instruction and learning is based on) includes a statement of the principal competencies, the behavioral indicators that indicate when a competency has been acquired, the job outputs, and the job tasks and activities associated with the competency. The assessment of competency acquisition requires the learner to exhibit the behavioral indicators and to produce the job output(s) associated with the competency, or combined with other competencies. This means, therefore, that the assessment of competency acquisition could consist of a simplistic to a highly complex process or set of processes. The job requirements, the nature of the competencies, the environmental context, and the kinds of job outputs impact how simple or how complex the learning assessment process will be.

Later in this chapter and in chapter 6, you will learn about several instructional methods that require a participant to demonstrate the application of one or more principal competencies in the context of the job setting. Simulations and the case method are good examples of these techniques. Other instructional approaches also accomplish these outcomes. These same activities also can be used to assess a learner's use of a competency or a cluster of competencies, as well as to assess many of the underlying instructional performance objectives. Therefore, as you proceed to the next step, you will want to think of creative ways to assess competency acquisition at interim stages of competency acquisition and at the completion of the acquisition process.

Step 5. Design and develop the intervention learning plan and the instructional modules for the interventions.

This step includes the design and development work that must be done to create an intervention learning plan and the instructional modules for the interventions.

The first task in producing a learning plan is to cluster the competencies and the performance objectives allied with them into modules in ways that constitute "conceptual wholes." The interventions and the modules each constitute small instructional subsystems. The competencies are grouped by assembling logical combinations of them into each module. An instructional module can include one or several competencies.

The second task is to organize the instructional modules into an overall learning intervention plan, which includes (at a minimum):

1. The names or titles of the modules

2. The sequence in which the learner should complete the modules; options for other sequences

3. Competencies and performance objectives included in each module

4. The learning strategy (or strategies) for each module, based on the learners' characteristics and the intervention content flow

5. Instructional media (e.g., workbooks, videos, job aids, and so forth) required

6. The time required by the learner to complete each module

7. A description of the assessment process for the competencies and the performance objectives included in each module

8. Other information about the module, and its relationships to the total intervention

The third task is the actual development of the specific details of the learning activities. This is the time when the designer and developer bring the job elements, information from the learning plan, and information from earlier steps in the design and development process together to create the learning activities for each module.

Chapter 6 includes information on numerous instructional strategies and media that are useful for developing competency-based learning activities.

The learning strategies and the content to be learned will suggest needs for certain media or materials. These include items such as computer software, tests, and assessment hard-copy materials, videotaped presentations, books, pamphlets, instruments, audiotape materials, transparencies, CD/ROM (compact disc read-only memory), and others. You are faced with identifying the sources and availabilities of media and materials, their costs, the time required to procure or to produce them, and your budget for making or buying what you need. Conversely, the media and materials available to you will significantly impact your learning design and development options.

The following section focuses on a significant instructional theory, Robert Gagne's Events of Instruction, and provides information on Gagne-Briggs' Conditions of Learning. This is followed by an instructional design paradigm called the Competency Acquisition Process (CAP), which was an outgrowth of the work of David McClelland and his associates. This information will prove to be quite valuable for the design and development work that must be completed.

For comprehensive information on instructional design theories and models and applications of them, consult Reigeluth (1983).

The Events of Instruction and the Conditions of Learning

Robert Gagne's theory of instruction is an invaluable aid to the design and development of learning activities. According to Gagne's theory, in order to develop and deliver instruction of any kind, the content to be delivered (which is dictated by the competencies and the performance objectives) must be broken down into one or more instructional events. Gagne, Briggs, and Wagner (1988) refer to the Events of Instruction as the "bricks and mortar of the individual lesson" (p. 177).

Gagne's theory relates "the external events of instruction to the outcomes of learning by showing how these events lead to appropriate support or enhancement of internal learning processes . . . . The province of an instructional theory is to propose a rationally based relationship between instructional events, their effects on learning processes, and the learning outcomes that are produced as a result of these processes" (Gagne, 1985, p. 244). Gagne (1985) orders these events into nine distinct categories. In the following description of these events, the singular of "competency" and "performance objective" should be interpreted to mean the plural form if that is appropriate to the application. The term "communication medium" as it is used here is a generic phrase that refers to instructional media, such as computer-based instruction, interactive videodisc instruction, and so forth.

Gagne's Events of Instruction (Gagne, 1985) are as follows:

1. *Gaining the learner's attention.* The instructor, facilitator, or some form of media gains the learner's attention, usually by using an abrupt stimulus change. The competency or performance objective is stated and explained in clear terms appropriate for the learner.

2. *Informing the learner of the learning objectives.* The facilitator or other communication medium uses simple words to tell the learners what they will be able to *do* as a result of acquiring the competency. This overview of the content to be learned raises a learner's expectations for the instruction and for their achievement of the learning material.

3. *Stimulating the recall of prior learning.* The learner is asked to recall previously learned knowledge or skills that are related to the lesson contents.

4. *Presenting the stimulus for new learning.* The facilitator, instructor, or other communication medium displays and illustrates or demonstrates the distinctive features of the content to be learned.

5. *Providing learning guidance.* The facilitator, instructor, or other communication medium makes the stimulus as meaningful as possible for the learner. Learning guidance is provided in two ways. The use of concrete examples is the first way. The second way is by the use of concrete terms and concepts—each idea elaborated on by reference to what is already in the learner's memory.

6. *Eliciting the desired performance.* The facilitator, instructor, or other communication medium asks the learner to perform in a specifically desired manner. Up to this point, the new capability reflected in the performance objective has been encoded for long-term memory storage by the learner. Now the learner is asked to demonstrate the new learning.

7. *Providing the learner with feedback following the performance.* The facilitator, instructor, or other communication medium informs the learner about the correctness or the degree of correctness of the performance.

8. *Assessing the learner's performance.* Although the learner has demonstrated that the learning which was intended has occurred, it is necessary to check that it has been stored in a reliable or stable manner. This stability or reliability is verified by having the learner demonstrate the performance several additional times. Practice exercises help increase the probability of stability of the learned material, and give the learner an opportunity for additional applications of the newly learned material.

9. *Enhancing the retention and transfer of the newly learned material.* Practicing the newly learned material contributes to the retention of verbal information, intellectual skills, and motor skills. However, Gagne cautions: "Although specific evidence is not readily available, it might be expected that practice has similar effects on the retention of cognitive strategies and attitudes. . . . Transfer of knowledge, skills, and strategies to new problems and new situations is a matter on which evidence continues to be sought" (p. 255).

Gagne's final event, the transfer of training (or education) outcomes (i.e., job competencies) to an employees job, is a persistent issue in HRD and deserves some attention here. It is not uncommon to hear that the competencies employees have acquired and practiced during a performance improvement intervention either are not, or cannot be, applied by the employees on their return to the job. (Note that this problem was reflected in Vignettes 1 and 2 of the Introduction.)

A number of reasons have been offered to explain this phenomenon; among them is that an employee's organization climate or work circumstances do not, for a wide possibility of reasons, support the application of the newly acquired competencies. From a learning intervention and design perspective, there are two immediate actions a designer and developer can take to improve the probability of the transfer of competencies acquired during an intervention to the workplace.

First, the instructional context and setting should match, as closely as possible, the realities of the employee's job context and requirements. Second, the HRD function must recognize and establish a partnership relationship with the client or client group that supports the use of the competencies in the workplace. Useful sources of additional information on the training transfer issue and transfer strategies can be found in Dixon (1990) and Broad & Newstrom (1992).

Gagne's theory of instruction states that learning will occur if each instructional event takes a form indicated by research to be most effective (i.e., that optimally supports the learner's internal processes required for learning) (Gagne et al., 1988, p. 256). Gagne and Briggs (1979) further break down each Event of Instruction into a description of the instructional techniques specific to each type of learned capability (e.g., motor skills, intellectual skills, and so forth). These are called the Conditions of Learning. Figure 5.5 (on the following page) includes the nine Events of Instruction and the Conditions of Learning they imply for the five types of learned capabilities (intellectual skill, cognitive strategy, information, attitude, and motor skill). For additional information on these ideas, consult Petry, Mouton, & Reigeluth (1987).

The Competency Acquisition Process

The Competency Acquisition Process (CAP) is an instructional design paradigm that evolved from the work of David McClelland and his associates. It has been successfully used to create competency-based management performance improvement interventions (Boyatzis, 1982, pp. 253-257).

When proceeding through the steps of the CAP learning events, the learner must do the following:

Instructional Event	Type of Capability				
	Intellectual Skill	Cognitive Strategy	Information	Attitude	Motor Skills
1. Gaining Attention	Introduce stimulus change; variations in sensory mode				
2. Informing learner of objective	Provide description and example of the performance to be expected	Clarify the general nature of the solution expected	Indicate the kind of verbal question to be answered	Provide example of the kind of action choice aimed for	Provide a demonstration of the performance to be expected
3. Stimulating recall of prerequisites	Stimulate recall of subordinate concepts and rules	Stimulate recall of task strategies and associated intellectual skills	Stimulate recall of context of organized information	Stimulate recall of relevant information, skills, and human model identification	Stimulate recall of executive sub-routine and part-skills
4. Presenting the stimulus material	Present examples of concept or rule	Present novel problems	Present information in propositional form	Present human model, demonstrating choice of personal action	Provide external stimuli for performance, including tools or implements
5. Providing learning guidance	Provide verbal cues to proper combining sequence	Provide prompts and hints to novel solution	Provide verbal links to a larger meaningful context	Provide for observation of model's choice of action, and of reinforcement received by model	Provide practice with feedback of performance achievement
6. Eliciting the performance	Ask learner to apply rule or concept to new examples	Ask for problem solution	Ask for information in paraphrase, or in learner's own words	Ask learner to indicate choice of action in real or simulated situations	Ask for execution of the performance
7. Providing feedback	Confirm correctness of rule or concept application	Confirm originality of problem solution	Confirm correctness of statement of information	Provide direct or vicarious reinforcement of action choice	Provide feedback on degree of accuracy and timing of performance
8. Assessing performance	Learner demonstrates application of concept or rule	Learner originates a novel solution	Learner restates information in paraphrased form	Learner makes desired choice of personal action in real or simulated situation	Learner executes performance of total skill
9. Enhancing retention and transfer	Provide spaced reviews including a variety of examples	Provide occasions for a variety of novel problem solutions	Provide verbal links to additional complexes of information	Provide additional varied situations for selected choice of action	Learner continues skill practice

Figure 5.5: Learning Events and the Conditions of Learning They Imply for Five Types of Learned Capabilities

Source: Gagne and Briggs, 1979, p. 166. Reprinted with permission.

1. Recognize the competency

2. Comprehend the competency and how it relates to job effectiveness

3. Receive feedback on performance of the competency

4. Experiment with demonstrating the competency or demonstrating it at a higher level of effectiveness

5. Practice using the competency

6. Apply the competency in a job situation and in the context of other competencies

Notice how the CAP steps reflect Gagne's instructional events. The heart of the learning is found in the first four steps of the CAP, with practice occurring in the fifth step. The final step emphasizes an important attribute of any competency-based intervention or program: the use of the competency in the job situation and in the context of other competencies. This step illustrates the holistic nature of competent performance and its application in any of life's contexts.

The first two steps of the CAP include instructional activities designed to ensure that the learner understands the competency in the context of job performance. Specifically, a learner must do the following:

- Recognize and comprehend the competency and instructional objective(s)

- See how the competency manifests itself in the context of the job

- Realize that the competency might manifest itself in several dimensions of the job

Depending upon the type of competency to be developed, the instructional activities would include describing the objective(s), providing content overviews, and providing examples. The examples used should include explicit demonstrations of the performance of the competency *within the specific context of the job*. If the job competency was carefully researched during an earlier stage, the behavioral indicators for the competency will be available as a foundation for choosing the performance examples. In addition, the representative job tasks, job activities, and job outputs information relative to the competency will be available. Three primary components should be made explicit in the performance example:

1. The competency

2. Its behavioral indicators

3. The job outputs that will be impacted or achieved as a result of the learners' use of the competency

Employees must recognize how exemplary performers think and act.

In these two stages of competence acquisition, I suggest you use assessment activities to ensure that in fact, the learners have recognized and comprehended the competency when it was performed. It is also important to ensure that the learners not only comprehend the competency, but that they comprehend it in the context of job performance and the organization. If that understanding is absent, then a greater variety of examples and group discussion might be helpful.

Once the competency has been recognized and comprehended, the learner is encouraged to *perform the competency*. The purpose of this step is to observe and determine the learner's experience and actual level of performance of the competency, and to provide the learner with consultative feedback on how to improve performance. If the learner is found fully competent at this stage of the CAP, the trainer should provide the learner with enrichment opportunities to perform the competency at a higher level of the competency. Careful front-end analyses of the target population are required in order to efficiently and effectively individualize learning activities for this step of the CAP.

At this stage of competence development, the learner may or may not have been sufficiently exposed to the performance requirement(s) for the competency, or may not yet have acquired sufficient prerequisite competencies or practice to successfully perform the competency. There might also be times when you will *not* want to have the employee attempt the required performance. The reasons for this could include, but not necessarily be limited to, the following conditions: The performance of some psychomotor behaviors (if not learned and performed with precision) might endanger the safety of the learner or others if the learner has not yet had sufficient experience; the performance might endanger the psychological safety of the learner or others; the learner has had no prior experience associated with exhibiting the performance; or the performance cannot (or should not) occur in the existing learning environment. You must use good professional judgment when making your decisions at this stage of instructional design.

Underlying all competence assessment methods and activities is the issue of the credibility of the assessment results of the employee's performance. The assessment processes and results you select must be meaningful to, and found credible by, the employee. If they are not, you will have considerable difficulty motivating the employee for later learning activities. For this reason and others, you should pay considerable attention to the competence assessment process and the vitality of the results. Conducting a pilot test of your process and enlisting the support of knowledgeable persons regarding the assessment instruments or processes you plan to use cannot be stressed too heavily. This is especially true when attempting to assess the performance of soft competencies.

One of the simpler forms of assessment is self-assessment. This can be accomplished in numerous ways. The use of self-administered tests, survey, questionnaires, exercises, and so forth are common.

Another popular form of assessment is the self-and-others assessment process. This approach is currently very popular in management training and education, and with other "soft competencies" jobs. One application of this technique is the self-and-immediate manager assessment combination. Its most common use involves a pre-interview meeting between the employee and his or her immediate manager. During this meeting, they mutually review the competency, examine its behavioral indicators or other measures, and discuss both the available information on the employee's performance and the pending training or education experience. An ideal outcome of this process is that the employee has a competency-related objective to accomplish and that its achievement is facilitated by the learning intervention.

In summary, learners in a competency-based learning situation must be given appropriate assessment exercises for each of the principal or critical job competencies and must receive feedback on the results of their performance. The assessment results help the learners focus their attention on areas where improvements are needed. Immediate performance feedback gives the learner motivation for completing the remaining events of the intervention. At this stage of competency acquisition, the learner is prepared to use the assessment feedback and earlier learning experiences to advantage. This is accomplished by completing additional learning activities.

The learning activities should be "individualized" to the maximum degree possible. "Individualized learning" means the employee is provided with an intervention that corresponds to his or her present performance level for the competency, and that can be completed by the employee in a flexible manner, consistent with organization resources. The degree to which the performance improvement environment can support individualized learning for competence acquisition is a multi-dimensional issue. Responding to this issue requires knowing about a number of factors:

- The value the organization places on individual as opposed to group learning experiences

- The necessary time required, and the facilities and equipment needed, including their availability

- The importance placed on the networking and information-sharing that results from group rather than from individually pursued learning experiences

- Other administrative information that impacts the delivery systems for the interventions and how employees are scheduled for them

You will need to consider your options regarding how much, if any, individualization of the learning experiences can be achieved.

To complete the competency acquisition process, the learner experiments with and demonstrates the use of the competency. The learner receives in-depth learning experiences on the competency and the subordinate and allied competencies, relative to their present level of performance of the competency. Gagne's Events of Instruction are helpful for designing the learning activities. Emphases are needed in order to provide elaborations on the content to provide prompts and guidance, to provide application opportunities, and to provide performance feedback.

Next, the learner practices using the competency in the context of the work and total organization setting. Corrective or supportive feedback is a key element of this phase.

In the final step, the learner applies the competency in a job situation and in the context of other competencies. Supportive or corrective feedback on the performance is also essential at this stage.

In summary, the CAP is an instructional paradigm that has been successfully used for training employees in management, a content area that is rich in soft competencies. It is an option to consider for designing and developing competency-based interventions. References to the CAP can be found in the work of Richard Boyatzis (1982).

Step 6. **Brief the client or client group.**

When the learning plan and the modules for each of the interventions have been developed, the client (or client group) is briefed prior to a pilot test of the intervention(s).

A condensed learning plan and an abstracted form of the modules for the interventions can be used for this briefing. You should ask the client to suggest any enhancements, modifications, or other suggestions regarding the plan. Recommendations for change must be carefully reviewed since certain changes can require considerable time to make and can affect many parts of the design and development work. Always determine exactly how critical or important the recommended changes are when they involve job performance issues. Also, if your client is willing to supply any critical resources (e.g., persons, money, equipment, software, materials, and so forth), now is the time to confirm the availability of the resource.

You should also provide the client with information on when to expect a pilot test of the intervention(s). Many clients will not understand the role and details of a pilot test. This needs to be explained to all stakeholders before it is used. And you should explain the role that the client and others play in the execution of the pilot test. Any resources you need the client to provide must be made clear at this time.

Step 7. **Pilot test the performance improvement intervention. Make revisions as indicated by formative evaluation results. Implement the program or intervention.**

A planned pilot test of the learning intervention(s) is conducted with learners from the target population. A formative evaluation plan and data collection or other assessment instruments that might be needed for data collection must be designed and acquired. Conducting formative evaluations of performance improvement programs is a subject of chapter 7.

Following a formal pilot test of the program or intervention, the results are reported to the client, recommendations for revision are made, and the program or intervention is revised where appropriate. A delivery schedule for the program or intervention is developed and implementation proceeds.

CONCLUDING COMMENTS

Bear in mind the following thoughts and suggestions when you design, develop, and implement competency-based performance improvement interventions using the contents of this chapter:

- Those who design and administer competency-based programs must be systems-focused and be able to create a variety of approaches in pursuit of program goals.

- As with any instructional program or medium, clerical or administrative support is an on-going requirement. The tasks performed by clerical staff include a wide variety of requirements, such as maintaining instructional materials, procuring supplies and services, setting up instructional areas, managing computer data bases, and a host of other requirements.

- If you intend to use learner-centered competency-based training or education interventions, remember that for a process like this to realize its full potential, HRD leaders and staff must have mindsets appropriate for using it. Instructional delivery must focus on the learner's full, active involvement in the learning activities, rather than focus on the instructor or facilitator performance.

Decision making regarding the design, development, and implementation of complex competency-based systems must be made in a timely fashion and as close to project plan as possible. Design and development decisions tend to drive later decisions downstream. A failure to make timely decisions can affect the program or intervention options.

Since competency-based instructional systems tend to be multi-dimensional and multi-media in nature, it is important to have the space and the access needed for conducting the instructional program. Certain learning technologies require permanent space connections and other facilities.

Finally, before you embark on a commitment to create training or education interventions, you should obtain media and graphic design support, writers, copy-editing services, printing services, and so forth. You should complete all projects using a single word-processing software package, and you should attempt to have compatibility among your software resources. You should also ensure that you have access to compatible equipment for producing the products you need.

Asking for extensive resources during project development rather than at the early planning and consensus stage can cause unfortunate problems for all involved. Therefore, many of the elements above should appear in your overall project plan. Anticipate all of your major needs and plan ahead!

In summary, a wide range of theories and practices are available to the instructional designer and developer in addition to those presented here. For additional information, consult Reigeluth (1983).

REFERENCES

Beck, L. (1983). Assessment centers. In F. L. Ulschak, Human Resource Development, *The theory and practice of need assessment*. Reston, VA: Reston Publishing Co.

Bloom, B. S. (Ed.). (1956). *Taxonomy of educational objectives, the classification of educational goals— Handbook I: Cognitive domain*. New York: McKay.

Boyatzis, R. E. (1982). *The competent manager: A model for effective performance*. New York: John Wiley and Sons.

Broad, M. L., & Newstrom, J. W. (1992). *Transfer of training: Action-packed strategies to ensure high payoff from training investments.* Reading, MA: Addison-Wesley.

Dick, W., & Carey, L. (1985). *The systematic design of instruction* (2nd ed.). Glenview, IL: Scott, Foresman and Co.

Dixon, N. M. (1990). Action learning, action science and learning new skills. *Industrial and Commercial Training, 22* (4), pp. 10-16.

Douds, A. Selected information on the context analysis procedure resulted from a personal discussion with Alex Douds on May 18, 1992.

Feuer, D., & Lee, C. (1988, May). The kaizen connection: How companies pick tomorrow's workers. *Training,* pp. 23-33.

Gagne, R. M. (1977). *The conditions of learning* (3rd ed.). New York: Holt, Rinehart and Winston.

Gagne, R. M. (1985). *The conditions of learning and theory of instruction* (4th ed.). New York: Holt, Rinehart and Winston.

Gagne, R. M., & Briggs, L. J. (1979). *Principles of instructional design* (2nd ed.). New York: Holt, Rinehart and Winston.

Gagne, R. M., Briggs, L. J., & Wager, W.W. (1988). *Principles of instructional design* (3rd ed). New York: Holt, Rinehart and Winston.

Hannum, W., & Hansen, C. (1989). *Instructional systems development in large organizations.* Englewood Cliffs, NJ: Educational Technology Publications.

Krathwohl, D. R., Bloom, B.S., & Masia, B. B. (1964). *Taxonomy of educational objectives: The classification of educational goals. Handbook II: Affective domain.* New York: McKay.

Mager, R. F. (1972). *Goal analysis.* Belmont, CA: Pitman Management and Training.

Mager, R. F. (1975a). *Measuring instructional intent.* Belmont, CA: Pitman Management and Training.

Mager, R. F. (1975b). *Preparing instructional objectives* (2nd ed.). Belmont, CA: Pitman Management and Training.

Overfield, K. (1989, November). Program development for the real world. *Training and Development Journal, 43* (11), pp. 65-71.

Pedler, M. (1983). *Action learning in practice.* Aldershot: Gower Publishing.

Petry, B., Mouton, H., & Reigeluth, C. M. (1987). A lesson based on the Gagne-Briggs theory of instruction. In C. M. Reigeluth (Ed.), *Instructional theories in action: Lessons illustrating selected theories and models.* Hillsdale, NJ: Lawrence Erlbaum Assoc., Publishers.

Poulet, R., & Moult, G. (1987, July). Putting values into education. *Training and Development Journal, 41* (7), pp. 62-66.

Reigeluth, C. M. (1983). *Instructional design theories and models: An overview of their current status.* Hillsdale, NJ: Lawrence Erlbaum Assoc., Publishers.

Scheerer, M. (1954). Cognitive theory. In *Handbook of Social Psychology, 1* (chap. 3). Cambridge, MA: Addison-Wesley.

Simpson, E. J. (1966). *The classification of educational objectives: Psychomotor domain.* (Research Project No. OE-5-85-104). Urbana, IL: University of Illinois.

Williamson, S. A., & Schaalman, M. L. (1980). *The assessment of occupational competence, Report No. 2. Assessment centers: Theory, practice, and implications for education* (ERIC Report No. ED 192 166/CE 027 161). Springfield, VA: U.S. Dept. of Education.

Chapter 6

LEARNING STRATEGIES AND MEDIA FOR COMPETENCY-BASED INTERVENTIONS

This chapter presents select learning or instructional strategies and media particularly useful for designing and developing competency-based learning interventions. A large number of strategies are discussed, including simulations, business games, and the case method, as well as a host of other less involved learning strategies. All of the strategies included here are "learner-centered" because they require active learner involvement and participation. The learner is responsible for the achievement of the learning goals. Mediated learning strategies and emerging training technologies are reviewed and discussed in the final section of the chapter. References for obtaining additional information are provided.

IN RELATION TO THE STRATEGIC SYSTEMS MODEL

Step 4 of the Strategic Systems Model requires the design and development of instructional or learning interventions that will facilitate employees' acquisition of the competencies and that will support the achievement of job outputs. The competencies were identified in Step 3 of the Strategic Systems Model. The material included in this chapter is a supporting resource for creating the learning interventions or opportunities that are required outputs from Step 4 of the Strategic Systems Model.

LEARNING STRATEGIES FOR COMPETENCY-BASED APPLICATIONS

Once the job competencies and the learning objectives are defined, the design and development of the learning or instructional subsystem is underway. The issue of the learning strategies is immediately confronted. Because instruction is a process that informs and shapes a learning experience (whether that experience is formal or informal, instructor-directed or self-directed), *how* it informs and shapes learning is of vital importance to its success. Learning strategies tackle this problem directly. They include all the various teaching-aid learning activities and supporting mechanisms that are used by the persons involved in the experience (Nadler, 1983, p. 162). The central question is, What learning strategies should I choose?

Learning strategies that are used for competency-based learning experiences should have the following characteristics:

- They should place major learning emphases on the competency, on how it relates to achieving the job outputs, and on the role of both the competency and the job outputs in achieving strategic organization goals.

- They should actively involve the learner and make the learner responsible for achievement at all stages of the learning intervention; i.e., they should be learner-centered. The strategy must emphasize what the learner will do and accomplish, *not* what the instructor or facilitator will do and accomplish.

- The instructional strategy or strategies should replicate the achievement of the job outputs in a simulation of actual work conditions, including the interruptions, stresses, political impacts, and other deterrents to the achievement of the job outputs.

- The instructional strategy should include highly visible opportunities for employees to gain insight into the problem of transference of competency acquision to its application on the job. Employees should learn about the full range of obstacles (from the most to the least common) that they may encounter when transferring the application of the competencies to the workplace for the achievement of job outputs, and they should learn ways to overcome those obstacles.

Although the required characteristics above naturally limit the list of potentially useful learning strategies available to you, the strategy selection process is still quite challenging. As Leonard Nadler (1982) has noted, "The selection of appropriate instructional strategies becomes more challenging with each passing year. The availability of sources is rapidly increasing as the market for HRD continues to expand. New producers continually enter the field. This is good, for it provides more possibilities, but it does complicate the selection process" (p. 162).

The selection and application of instructional strategies for competency-based performance improvement interventions should be guided by several fundamental considerations. Observations of, and experiences with, a variety of competency-based performance improvement settings have produced the following suggestions.

It is important to guard against an overemphasis on the application of any one technology or instructional strategy (e.g., brainstorming, flip chart discussions, games). There is no single learning strategy that is "most" appropriate for all applications, nor is there a "preferred" learning strategy.

The learning strategies you use must be consistent with, and conducive to, the environmental conditions in the application arena. The curriculum content, the attributes of the learners, the norms of the organization, the resources available, and the capabilities of the people who facilitate or direct the learning process critically influence the approaches that can be used. The designer and developer must be realistic about what can and cannot be accomplished with the available resources.

Learning strategies that use technologies for their delivery will most likely be "dated" from the moment the technologies become available. This is not an unfamiliar problem: Instructional technology has been advancing quite rapidly for over a decade. Writing on this issue in 1982, Nadler commented that:

> In the early 1950s . . . the 16mm projector was considered the ultimate technology. Today . . . there are other technologies that are more threatening, or challenging, depending upon the competency and experience of the Designer. The field has expanded to the point where the Designer may not be the appropriate person to make a decision about a specific instructional strategy, but instead calls upon a specialist who has a wide range of experience with a variety of instructional strategies. (p. 162)

Nadler's observations are more timely than ever, and his advice is still valuable and sound.

If you are an instructional designer and developer, you will probably conceptualize the overall design of a competency-based program and participate with others in the selection of the strategies; however, the precise details of how the instructional technologies are used to implement the plan might need to be worked out with the extensive, or the exclusive, help of several other specialists. If you find that you do need the help of specialists, guard against placing too much dependence on them; you must monitor their work at critical points of the project and must ensure they are producing what your organization wants and can use (Nadler, 1982).

Competency-based learning designs, in particular, must acknowledge and account for the characteristics of adult learners and the learning strategies that work best with adults. Adult learners expect, and deserve, to leave the experience with competencies that can directly and immediately be applied on the job. In the case of education opportunities, they must be able to recognize and use the competencies in a later assignment. Adults view HRD situations with a sense of immediacy and specificity. Job-specific performance improvement must acknowledge the learners' experience and the competencies they bring (or maybe do not bring) to the learning intervention. Adult learners thrive on having choices regarding what and how they learn.

Instructors and facilitators must be aware that adult learners appreciate being treated like adults when they are in a learning environment. All too often, adult learners report that their "instructional superiors" treat them as if they were children or adolescents. A good learning strategy can be rendered useless if the instructor or facilitator has failed to make the perceptual shift from the parenting role (which has traditionally been the role of the elementary or secondary school teacher) to the role of an adult teacher or facilitator. (For additional information on adult learning principles, see Knowles 1980, 1984; and Knox, 1986.)

You should accommodate the maximum amount of content individualization that you are capable of, given the constraints within the environment. As you design, attempt to find ways to use employees' experience and the competencies they bring to the job. Employees should be able to bypass instructional modules where they are competent in favor of other opportunities where either they can achieve at an advanced level or they can pursue the achievement of different competencies.

The degree to which the training or education program can be individualized is highly dependent upon the nature of the contents, the available resources, and the flexibility of the organization. When it is sensible to individualize learning, and the resources are (or can be) made available, it is highly recommended.

Numerous resources are readily available on learning designs and learning strategies that are specific for adults. Particular references include Nadler (1982); Eitington (1984); Gagne & Briggs (1979, 1988); Gagne (1977, 1985); Knowles (1980, 1984); Hannum & Hansen (1989); Craig (1976, 1987); and Frantzreb (1991). Further information on these sources can be found in the chapter references, and the authors noted above will refer you to yet other sources that you might find equally valuable. Literally dozens of useful resources are available.

Simulations

Simulations rank high among the most useful learning techniques for emphasizing a "training-in-context" concept, where the learning environment approximates the employee's workplace environment in as many contextual ways as possible. During a simulation, employees perform in situations resembling those they face daily in the workplace. This is a useful method for creating learning designs for both training (i.e., for the current job) and education (i.e., for a future or other job). In the educational sense, an employee can gain an understanding of exactly what a new job entails since actual job experiences are replicated. The strategy is adaptable to a very wide variety of competencies and jobs.

Hendrickson (1990) observes: "Training in context [through simulations] means taking the time to build reality into your training design. It also means understanding how job pressures and the organization climate affect the way work gets done. Most of all, it means that you have taken steps to help your trainees use new knowledge back on the job, where it will make a difference" (p. 70). He lists and describes eight steps for building an effective job simulation, adding post-intervention evaluation as a final requirement (pp. 65-70). In the presentation below, Hendrickson's approach was slightly modified to make it more compatible with the purposes and contents of this book, although care was taken to maintain the overall integrity of his work.

Steps for Building An Effective Job Simulation

The following steps must be completed in order to build an effective job simulation:

Step 1. Identify the learning objectives, relative to one or more job competencies, and in specific performance terms.

Step 2. Assemble a design team of "insiders."

Step 3. Describe the job activities, tasks, and the work routine for the target population over a logical time frame (e.g., daily, weekly, or annually).

Step 4. Identify the "gotchas."

Step 5. Integrate the competency(ies), job activities, tasks, routines, job outputs, behavioral indicators, learning objectives, and gotchas into an overall learning design.

Step 6. Add content breaks.

Step 7. Develop an assessment strategy.

Step 8. Conduct a pilot test of the simulation, revise as necessary, and implement the simulation with the target population.

Each step in the process is discussed in detail below.

Step 1. **Identify the learning objectives, relative to one or more job competencies, and in specific performance terms.**

All learning interventions begin with the job competencies and the achievement of the critical job outputs that competent performance ultimately makes possible. The competency model (or menu) developed for a job contains the basic information on job performance needed to develop a simulation. Depending upon how the model was developed and its resulting elements, you should have available:

- Competencies

- Job outputs (correlated with the competencies)

- Behavioral indicators for each competency

- Job roles

- Job activities and major tasks (correlated with the competencies)

- Front-end needs analysis and assessment data, and an overall plan for meeting the identified needs

As you have probably noticed, by doing the front-end work at the needs analysis and competency model or menu development stages (Steps 1 and 2 of the Strategic Systems Model), you have a good start for tackling the simulation design work. In this step, you will refine much of the competency model information collected earlier into the learning objectives. The competencies, the behavioral indicators, and the job activities are refined to identify specific knowledge and skills components (e.g., subcompetencies) and a logical sequence for learning them. Do not forget to include any prerequisite competencies that the learner is expected to have acquired prior to the intervention.

Step 2. **Assemble a design team of "insiders."**

Although the contributing members of your design team must be from within the organization, you can use external professionals to facilitate this and later design activities. If possible, the job experts should include high-performing or exemplary employees who contributed to the competency model research work, as well as one or more persons with expert job knowledge who were part of the front-end needs analysis and planning project for this job. Most of the time, you will want to have a multi-discipline team for this work.

After the design team is assembled, the bulk of the work is completed by the team and not by the HRD specialist. The HRD specialist's role is to facilitate the design team's work rather than to act as the "design expert." The HRD specialist frequently serves as an internal consultant to the design team in order to ensure that the results are of high quality.

Step 3. **Describe the job activities, tasks, and the work routine for the target population over a logical time frame (e.g., daily, weekly, or annually).**

The outputs of this step include a detailed description of the job activities for the chosen time frame. The time frame you select depends upon exactly what you want to accomplish as a result of the simulation exercise. Data must be collected on topics such as the interpersonal relationships that are required on the job, the human networks that are used, the intrapersonal competencies that are used for achieving job results or outputs, schedules that are followed, performance measures, and so forth. The meanings and purposes underlying the routine(s) are important facts for planning the simulation. The competency model and the routines for the job will suggest the bulk of the data you must collect in order to design a challenging and useful simulation.

Once the information has been collected, you should have the team state the goals of the simulation and relate the learning objectives to those goals. If your team cannot develop a logical match between the two entities, it probably means they have not thoroughly collected data and/or analyzed the data or the situation correctly.

Step 4. **Identify the "gotchas."**

Hendrickson characterizes "gotchas" as the things that get in the way of the achievement of the job outputs. Examples of gotchas include unclear lines of authority that interfere with decision making, quality goals that interfere with meeting production goals, unnecessary or arbitrary paperwork, and unnecessary and/

or unproductive meetings, which impede the achievement of work objectives that heavily impact critical job results or outputs. One reason traditional training and education programs are criticized for being too sanitary is that the gotchas are rarely, if ever, included in the training or education interventions.

Identifying the interruptions and roadblocks for any job is not a difficult assignment for the job expert. Once the major gotchas are listed, the work group should rank them according to their importance to simulating the job in the organization context.

Step 5. **Integrate the competency(-ies), job activities, tasks, routines, job outputs, behavioral indicators, learning objectives, and gotchas into an overall learning design.**

The job situations, the learning objectives, the job competency(-ies), the time-driven job routine, and the job outputs must be combined to develop an overall learning design. Achievement of the job outputs and the goals of the simulation will drive the overall design.

Once the step-by-step design is laid out, the gotchas and in-basket (and possibly other interruptions to job performance) are added as obstacles to achieving the critical job outputs. Linkages are then made among the numerous job situations from beginning to end.

Next, other job experts and HRD professionals review the design and provide feedback and suggestions for improvement of the products.

Step 6. **Add content breaks.**

Content breaks are added at critical points of the design to stress the learning objectives and how the participants are achieving them as a result of their participation in the simulation. Content breaks can be used to summarize or elaborate on key teaching points, to discuss alternative behaviors or processes that could affect the achievement of job outputs, and perhaps of most importance, to focus on the competency(-ies) and its (their) meaning and application within the context of the job.

Content breaks are very useful interludes for holding discussions on the internal thought patterns, or mindsets, that the participants use to perform their job. The contents of these discussions are similar to those an interviewer experiences with exemplary performers when conducting a behavioral event interview. Since the observation and assessment of mindset changes are difficult waters to navigate in any format—including a competency-based format—content breaks are one way to get at those difficult-to-observe behaviors.

Content breaks provide opportunities to discuss and to receive feedback on performance in a segment of the simulation. The content break can also be used for practice exercises or remedial learning activities for sharpening or even developing the participants' ability to more effectively comprehend and/or demonstrate a competency that needs strengthening.

A variety of learning techniques and processes are available for use during a content break. (Other learner-centered learning strategies are included later in this chapter.) Overall, keep your content breaks brief but challenging. You want to maintain continuity of the contents in the simulation activities and to ensure that the learner achieves all the learning objectives. Therefore, you must adhere to a firm schedule. This means your overall plan must be very carefully thought out.

Step 7. **Develop an assessment strategy.**

The assessment of a learner's performance is job context specific, given the visible nature of the performance environment. The achievement of the learning objectives, achievement of the job outputs, and evidence of the acquisition of the competency (using the behavioral indicators and possibly other factors) constitute the major assessment components of the learning process. A wide variety of assessment activities can be considered, including problem-solving exercises, the use of test items, individual and group exercises, simulated job performance situations, and so forth. Assessments of learning achievement for this method, as well as other assessment methods, are discussed in chapter 7.

Step 8. **Conduct a pilot test of the simulation, revise as necessary, and implement the simulation with the target population.**

For this step, you should choose participants from the target population who are not a "political risk" for any of the other participants. The group should be small, e.g., six to eight persons. Ask the group members to maintain a diary on their specific reactions to the entire instructional process. Have them record suggestions for improvement, such as places in the process where the objectives are not clear or where job realities are not accurately represented. It is especially important for them to note the prerequisite competencies that are required of the participating employees at each subject-matter content shift in the simulation. Have them suggest how a prerequisite competency could be developed by a participant either internal or external to the simulation.

Conducting a pilot test of a project, program, or intervention has its own process requirements. If you are unfamiliar with conducting a pilot test, you might want to review the article "Fail-Safe Pilot Programs" (Derven, 1989, pp. 63-64). Also, chapter 7 includes a pilot test process that you can adapt to a simulation.

To conclude the process, the design team should reconvene, review the findings of the pilot test, and revise and prepare the simulation for implementation and delivery with the target population.

The Benefits of Learning Simulations

A number of HRD professionals have reported on the benefits and challenges of learning simulations (Frantzreb, 1991; Haslam, 1990). Simulations offer numerous benefits for competency-based training or education enterprises:

1. They provide a dynamic atmosphere for learning and allow for job practice without penalties for individual actions. A wide variety of competencies subordinate to the critical or principal job competencies can be incorporated into a simulation exercise.

2. They are active, learner-centered, and learner-controlled experiences. A wide variety of competencies are amenable to development and acquisition using simulation learning strategies.

3. Simulations can be designed to encourage the learners to develop higher order intellectual competencies. These types of competencies are transferrable to a wide variety of job requirements.

4. Simulations can be used to effectively collapse many hours to many days of job experience into just several hours of employee training time. "Training time is reduced when the outcome is competency," says Haslam (1990).

5. Although simulations are more expensive to design and develop on the front-end than traditional learning activities are, training costs can be reduced over time. When simulations are individualized to specific learner needs, learners can spend time working on acquiring competencies in areas where they need to improve. In effect, this reduces (overall) the training hours required for competence acquisition.

6. Learners find thoughtfully designed and developed simulations very challenging and enjoyable.

7. Simulations can be created to accomplish team building and related learning and other organization development objectives.

8. Simulations provide opportunities for learners to participate in competence development activities that include opportunities to network with their peers from other functional disciplines or with employees from other parts of their organization.

The Challenges of Learning Simulations

On the other hand, simulations are a challenge to design, develop, and administer. Specifically:

1. They are usually complex and therefore require somewhat more front-end analysis, design, and development time than other types of learning interventions. Although, for computer-based simulations, Haslam (1990) observes that "more sophisticated authoring tools and software are reducing that development time considerably by helping developers prototype more quickly" (pp. 10-16).

2. Simulations can require the use of several types of media and materials, and decisions must be made on how much detail is needed. Do you have the variety of media, materials, or technology needed? Can you acquire what you need and do not have? These decisions are critical to project success and must be made *before* work begins.

3. The objectives of a learning simulation must be very clear from the inception of the design work. This means that a detailed, comprehensive front-end investigation of the learning and experiential requirements must be made.

4. The role of the facilitator is a critical one for the success of a simulation. Therefore, this person must be carefully chosen. The facilitator must encourage the learners to proceed, must provide guidance without deliberately influencing the decision-making process, and generally must maintain the group's focus on achieving the job outputs and other objectives for the simulation.

Further information on learning simulations can be found in Trollip (1990) and in Hannum & Hansen (1989).

BUSINESS GAMES

Business games (or "games" for short) are another experiential learning strategy that can significantly contribute to competence acquisition. Many persons classify games as a form of simulation exercise. Games, unlike certain forms of simulation, usually have a clear competitive element as part of their purpose and structure. A game can emphasize self-competition, competition with an external standard, competition among the players, or some combination of these.

Say Newstrom and Scannell (1990), " The law of association is a classic form of learning, and games are one way to use it" (pp. 227-228). But games should not constitute the bulk of a training or education intervention. They are best used to emphasize concepts that are introduced or developed as part of a larger instructional plan. Games are used to advantage when their purposes are clearly integrated with a very specific aspect (or aspects) of competence development and when they are used in moderation.

Newstrom and Scannell (1990) shared several tips for the successful use of games (pp. 227-228). The following is a synopsis of them:

1. **Be prepared.** Unless trainers have a good handle on the why, where, what, and how of using a game, they are going to fall flat on their faces.

2. **Be brief.** Games are excellent vehicles for reinforcing learning concepts or techniques, but they can't be the main thing. Don't let gaming become the tail that wags the dog.

3. **Have a purpose.** Have some objective in mind. Know what that game is supposed to do, prove, or reinforce.

4. **Involve people.** The participants' retention is best when in some way they are involved in the action.

5. **Have fun.** Training is serious business, and people should take it seriously. But you should have fun doing what you are doing.

6. **Don't be gimmicky.** Gimmicks can be far more destructive than instructive.

7. **Don't steal training games without giving credit to the sources.** This is imperative.

8. **Don't have strict categories.** Be flexible and creative. Don't get in a rut by doing the same thing all the time. Try new adaptations and revisions. Avoid becoming too methodical.

To the suggestions above I would add the following personal experience and thoughts. I once delivered a packaged training seminar (i.e., a seminar designed by others) that included games whose objectives were to uncover and explore intrapersonal and interpersonal issues (such as trust, integrity, and other sensitive issues) as part of a competency acquisition intervention. Because the learning activities can trigger dramatic, anticipated psychological responses from the participants, using games of this type requires special sensitivities and competencies from those who design, develop, and teach or facilitate the intervention. Those who preceded me as trainers for the event experienced serious problems with the instructional event in which this kind of game was used. They were neither prepared for the responses that resulted, nor were they capable of facilitating a positive set of outcomes for the participants. Yet, the learners' responses *were predictable.*

Two unfortunate outcomes resulted: Earlier seminar participants left the training event without a sense of personal psychological closure or other resolution of the personal issues which surfaced, and the reputation and perceived value of the seminars were diminished among the client group. You need not avoid the use of these activities; just be certain that you use them appropriately in your designs *and* that those who deliver the competence acquisition activities are qualified to deliver them, and to deliver them properly. *Protect* the psychological well-being of your learners while at the same time you help them become competent. Trainers who use sensitive game interventions require special facilitator competencies that ensure the learning is accomplished as intended while the participants' well-being is maintained.

For further information on games and simulations, including a list of sources for hundreds of games and simulations, you might want to consult Gentry (1990). Gentry also includes an extensive bibliography on these topics. The role of management games and simulations in education and research is reviewed in depth by Keys and Wolfe (1990).

The Case Method

The case method has been around for some time now. Like games, case method learning is classified by some people as a form of simulation of real-life persons, circumstances, situations, or events.

The *case method* is a process that includes having a group of learners read and critically examine an actual work situation or event, including the issues, circumstances, persons, actions, background information, documents, or other media surrounding the case. In a group setting, the learners discuss the issues and circumstances surrounding the case, and propose and defend solutions to the problems or issues of the case. There is usually no single, best solution to the problem(s) or issue(s) surfaced in the case.

The *case study* method, which is a form of the *case method*, is different from the case method in one important way. When the case study method is used as a learning strategy, the learners are presented with the facts and outcomes of a case without having the benefits of discussing the potential outcomes for the case using a variety of decision scenarios. In short, the learner is given the information as a finished product. Because of this limitation, the case method option is more preferable for instructional use. If you do opt for the *case study* method, make sure you carefully distinguish this approach from the *case method* in your instructional designs.

The case method has numerous uses, including the development of a learner's

- Problem-solving and decision-making competencies

- Interpersonal and intrapersonal competencies

- Higher order thought processes

- Communication competence

Proponents of the case method also claim that the learners improve their ability to accept responsibility for their discussions. From an organization point of view, the case method is useful for exploring major issues and policy matters that an organization faces. It is also valuable for creating organization-wide implementation strategies for policies, plans, or procedures.

The Benefits and Drawbacks of the Case Method

The benefits and drawbacks of the case method were comprehensively described in a recent "Info-line" series, a publication of the American Society for Training and Development. The major benefits and drawbacks were outlined, and with slight modifications, they are summarized below (Spruell, 1987, pp. 3-4).

On the "benefits" side, the case method provides learning through experience by simulating real-life situations in a limited time and with limited resources. The setting provides a safe environment for learning. The participants

- Learn through experience because they are active rather than passive during the experience

- Are forced to think as conceptual material is applied to real-world situations

- Partake of exercises that deal with real business facts and events rather than organizational generalities

- Learn that organization issues and problems do not have a single solution, but rather, several possible solutions

- Develop greater insights into their own and others' intrapersonal and interpersonal competencies, including their communications competencies

- Learn the values of diversity and how its presence and operation can become manifest in high-quality results

The case method is advantageous to the perspective taken in this book: The broad, overall goals of an organization surface and learners rapidly develop a "total organization" understanding of the big picture. This is an ideal way for learners to gain experience with strategic management issues. The correct use of the case method also increases a participant's understanding of the relationships among people, things, events, and the environment of the organization. Participants comprehend the acceptance of responsibility, independent thinking, objectivity, and the use of good judgment. Learners acquire the ability to identify potential problems and to recommend realistic actions.

The case method also has drawbacks. Since the learner is in a no-risk environment, there is no real, long-term responsibility for the decisions that are made during the process. Once decisions and accountability are made, the results or outcomes of those decisions cannot be observed in a real-world setting, plans or actions cannot be revised, nor can the results be known. An overemphasis upon the use of the case method limits the types of competencies that can be developed, and this overuse can cause the participants to lose enthusiasm for the process. Learners who are inexperienced with analytical methods or who have limited analytical competence can rapidly become frustrated with the case method process.

Use of the Case Method

In order to use the case method as an effective, learner-centered strategy, several critical pieces must be in place:

1. The situation on which the case is based must be complex. It should have both strategic significance for the organization and high relevance to an employee's job.

2. The learners must have the *potential* to handle—through the application of various types of analysis, synthesis, and evaluation activities—a large body of information. Participants must be willing to express themselves on a wide variety of topics and to appropriately challenge others' views while maintaining the capacity to accept opposing views.

3. The instructor or facilitator role is an especially critical factor for achieving successful outcomes with the case method. The facilitator

   - Must *not* assume the role of a teacher or guru

   - Must be able to facilitate what can, at times, be difficult discussions and interactions among the learners

   - Must give feedback without "putting words in a participant's mouth"

   - Must be sensitive to the needs of all participants who experience frustration with the case method as a learning strategy

   - Must oftentimes put away his or her own "expert knowledge" and assume the "helper" role

If any of these critical resource attributes are missing and cannot be obtained, you should use caution in proceeding with the case method strategy.

If you decide that the case method is an appropriate, workable learning strategy for a competence acquisition program, you should plan to develop the case (or cases) specific to your organization. That is, the case you develop should reflect the employees' workplace environment. Spruell (1987) offers a six-step method for case development, along with a reproducible job aid for the case planning development (pp. 6; 14-16). The six steps are presented here to give you a sense of what is involved in the case development process. If you decide to proceed, the reproducible job aid mentioned above could be useful.

Step 1. Clearly state the case objectives in terms of what the learners will achieve. What competencies will be pursued and acquired by the learners? To what degree will those competencies be acquired? What performance objectives must be achieved in order to acquire each competency?

Step 2. State the central case issue. This is different from, yet consistent with, the learners' objectives, and is usually an organization issue.

Step 3. Choose the case situation. The situation should raise the organization issue and present opportunities for developing the critical competencies needed by the learners. The situation should be neither too technical nor too political. You must be able to gather facts and objective opinions on the case. If excessive details are involved, or political alignments are strong, you will have difficulties with the process.

Step 4. Plan the research needed to develop the case. This means that you must decide whom to interview, what parts of the organization to cover, what processes need to be observed, what background information is needed, and what documentation is required.

Step 5. Conduct the case research through data collection relevant to the interviews and observations you will conduct, and through a review of documentation.

Step 6. Write the case. By this time, you should have extensive data on the problem (or issues) and its environment. You should select those data that are directly related to the case situation and the decisions the learners must make on the case. You are then ready to describe the events, circumstances, and people in the case situation. Avoid "avant garde" writing styles: Always be direct. Protect the identities of persons whose circumstances constitute each situation, and use care with the vocabulary, avoiding "cute" phrases, personal names, and the like.

Finally, evaluate your work by trying it out in a small pilot test. Try to achieve a balanced pilot test group. Depending upon the case situation, it is probably best to have both content experts and novices as part of the group. You will want to think carefully about this prior to setting the plans for the review process. You will almost always need to revise the case materials or methods prior to full implementation.

The case method has received a considerable amount of attention in the literature. Further information on the case method can be found in the following chapter references: Eitington (1984); Craig (1976); Argyris (1980); Berger (1983); Pigors & Pigors (1987); Armistead (1984); Kelly (1983); Gray & Constable (1983); and Hudspeth & Knirk (1991). Gray and Constable, Berger, and Argyris focus on the use of the case method in management development.

In summary, when cases are carefully developed (using the case method approach) and validated, they can be a powerful instructional tool for competence acquisition. However, you must balance their use with the application of other learner-centered learning strategies.

ADDITIONAL LEARNER-CENTERED LEARNING STRATEGIES

As noted earlier in this chapter, the number of learning strategies available to the designer and developer of learner-centered, competency-based training or education is sizable, and growing. Add to this the media now available (and rapidly growing), and the choices become even more complex. Four loosely organized classes of learner-centered techniques that, either singly or in combination with the techniques above, might be used to design and deliver competency-based programs are included below. The definitions included in the first three strategy classes are those given by Nadler (1982, pp. 170-180). Another source of active, learner-centered training techniques can be found in Silberman (1990). Additional suggestions can be found in Eitington (1984) and in Pike (1990). An advantage of these strategies is that they are relatively simple compared with the strategies described earlier in this chapter.

Class One Strategies

The first class of learning strategies relies on the demonstration of a behavior or a set of behaviors by the learners and/or the assessment of behaviors relative to a learning (or other) performance expectation for the learner. The techniques include skits, observations, peer-mediated learning, role-plays, and interactive or behavior modeling.

- *Skit.* A short, rehearsed, dramatic presentation, involving two or more persons, who usually act from a prepared script, and dramatizing an incident that illustrates a problem or situation.

- *Observation.* The learner observes and reports on an action or incident.

- *Peer-mediated learning.* The learners are grouped with their peers and facilitate each others' learning under the guidance of a group leader, who provides them with specially prepared materials.

- *Role-play.* A role-play is an interaction among two or more individuals on a given topic or situation. It is often used to provide practice for learners on previously presented material. This strategy has many variations, including multiple role-play and role-reversal.

- *Interactive or behavior modeling.* A means of learning new behaviors by observing model or ideal behavior, trying new behavior, and receiving feedback; the cycle is repeated until the new behavior is learned.

Class Two Strategies

All the activities in the second class of strategies share one notable characteristic: They provide the learner with opportunities to "experiment with" or "test out" specified performance requirements. The performance occurs in a controlled environment (much like a laboratory) and/or in a situation where a specific outcome (i.e., a product) or a set of outcomes is the terminal goal. Many of these strategies are similar in certain ways to simulations but lack one or more of the attributes of a full-fledged simulation as it was defined earlier. The strategies in this set include laboratory, clinic, discussion, fish bowl, sensitivity training, team building, discussion, work group, workshop, and seminar.

- *Laboratory.* An environment equipped for experimentation and testing by the learner. Can be used to accomplish a variety of instructional objectives, including cognitive, affective, and psychomotor objectives.

- *Clinic.* A session, or part of a session, where the learners react to some common experience they have earlier shared. Can also be used when part of the group has an experience they would like others to react to. The instructor serves as a resource person and carefully observes the activities in order to avoid losing the objective of the session.

- *Discussion.* A relatively unstructured exchange of ideas among members of a group on a topic of mutual interest.

- *Fish bowl.* A discussion group that is divided into an inner circle which discusses and an outer group which observes. A member of the outer group may "tap in" or exchange places with a member of the inner group.

- *Sensitivity training.* Not only "training" but also "education," this strategy involves a group which is deprived of leader, agenda, and norms. As the group struggles to fill those gaps, members exhibit behaviors which are then used as the basis for learning.

- *Team building.* Rather than a single strategy, team building is a concept that uses various instructional strategies to promote effective group interaction.

- *Work group.* Members work as a group to achieve stated objectives and produce a tangible product.

- *Workshop.* The purpose of this group learning experience is to highly involve the participants in the production of a product.

- *Seminar.* This is a form of learning where each learner in the group is expected to be at a sufficient level of content-competence on the seminar topic to actively participate. The instructor or facilitator serves as a resource person, with the seminar member taking responsibility for the interaction during the seminar.

Class Three Strategies

The third class includes strategies that are particularly useful (either singly or in combination with other strategies) for the development of psychomotor objectives. The strategies in this class include observation, demonstration, model, mock-up, and field trip.

- *Observation.* The learner observes and reports on an action or incident.

- *Demonstration.* A demonstration is a presentation that shows how to perform an act or procedure. Can be done by direct presentation or through the use of a prepared videocassette. A demonstration should be brief, allow for interaction with the learner, and then proceed to the next point.

- *Model.* Usually represents a physical object which is presented in a different form than usual in order to facilitate learning. A model can also be used to present ideas or to show the flow of a series of actions.

- *Mock-up.* A mock-up is a full-sized replica built accurately to scale.

- *Field trip.* A carefully arranged group visit to an object or place for on-site observation and learning.

Self-Directed Learning

Competency-based training or education programs or interventions can also include the use of self-directed learning strategies. Among the learning strategies for self-directed learning, the principal ones are as follows:

- Reading

- Computer-based learning

- Some forms of mediated learning, such as interactive video-disc packages

- Some forms of distance learning

- Programmed instruction

- Correspondence or home-study learning

- Special projects or assignments

- Tutorials

- Contract-based learning

- Annotated reading lists, bibliographies, or study guides

A drawback of some of these strategies is that they lack the advantages that result from involvement with one's peers or with others in the learning process. For some types of training or education, this is not an important consideration. This issue is driven by the nature of the competencies the learner must achieve. When learning is enhanced as a result of interactions with others (and this is especially the case when soft competencies are involved), careful consideration should be given to how to best use self-directed strategies. Sometimes it is possible to combine self-directed strategies with planned interactive sessions with other persons who are also completing the same self-directed program. Another option is for the learner to have periodic discussion and feedback sessions on the content matter with a subject-matter expert, coach, mentor, or HRD specialist. The program contents, objectives, and learning situations determine what type of professional is used in these sessions.

Job-Site Strategies

Yet other forms of learner-centered activities include the use of job-site strategies: coaching, apprenticeship, internship, externship, on-the-job training, job rotation, and variants of these. Depending on how these strategies are perceived and/or defined within the organization, some of them might be defined as training, while others might be viewed as employee education or development.

Although formal, structured job-site training and education programs are highly useful techniques, they tend to be problematic and to pose a challenge to organize, administer, and maintain. One of their more difficult aspects is maintaining accountability for each learner's performance. This accountability is usually the responsibility of line managers and others who do not report to the HRD function. Much work remains to be done on successfully meeting the challenges associated with competency-based job-site learning strategies, and the transfer of planned, formal training or education outcomes to the job site (as discussed in chapter 1).

Mediated Learning Strategies

Mediated learning designs and instructional strategies rely either wholly or in part on the use of various media or technology. Media is a word with broad applications which include items such as computer hardware and software, videotaped presentations, books, pamphlets, instruments, audiotape materials, videotaped lessons, transparencies, CD/ROM (compact disc read-only memory), and other items. Technology has grown rapidly over the past several years and as a result, new ways of thinking and teaching (or facilitating) for organizations and new styles of learning for their employees have been discovered. These innovations provide opportunities for interesting and useful approaches to learner-centered interventions.

The media and materials that are available to the instructional designer and developer will significantly impact the choice of the learning strategies and how the selected ones will be implemented for the intervention. Media and materials should be used with care, and attention must be given to ensure that the appropriate uses of them are made in a competency-based format. I recommend combining and maintaining a balance between the use of emerging learning technologies that emphasize self-learning and the use of other strategies that afford employees with opportunities to learn with and from others by using face-to-face learning strategies. The nature of the subject matter and the job performance required will suggest the combinations of strategies that should be used on a case-by-case basis.

"Make-or-Buy" Decisions

Designers and developers are often faced with making decisions on when the organization should internally create (i.e., "make") rather than purchase (i.e., "buy") their media or materials for an instructional program. Although these can be complex decisions, here are two sets of general guidelines you can follow:

1. You should probably "make" (or contract to make) your media or materials when:

   - The contents of the applications or the competencies and performance objectives are highly specific (or specialized) to the training or education needs

   - The cost of the materials needed is prohibitively expensive or otherwise not within your budget, and an adequate substitute is needed. (Of course, there are also costs associated with internal development. These costs must be weighed against the cost of *not* having the materials.)

   - The materials you need are not available on the market

2. You should probably "buy" your materials or media when:

   - Highly sensitive competence or other assessment instrumentation is needed, and especially when assurance that the results will have high validity and reliability is needed

   - A vendor product can satisfactorily constitute a total instructional approach to competence acquisition and assessment as it is envisioned within the organization

- It is more cost-effective to purchase the items than to develop them internally

- The internal resources or expertise are not available for completing the development work

- Quality is a serious concern of the client and/or the HRD staff for the particular application and the resources are not available to produce them internally at the required quality level

- "Making" and "buying" cost the same but "buying" frees up internal resources for work on priorities whose value will more than make up for the "buying" cost

- The materials are ideal for the application and there are no constraints on their purchase

Emerging Training Technologies

Emerging training technologies play a significant role in training and education opportunities in organizations today and may play an even more significant role in the future. They are discussed next.

HRD professionals report finding it difficult to remain current on the latest technologies available for training or educating adults. Wallace Hannum's (1990) book, *The Application of Emerging Training Technologies*, is a good place to start whether you need an in-depth description of a new technology and its applications or general information on the current and future applications of technologies. Hannum's categories of emerging training technologies provide a useful framework for understanding the types of new technologies currently available.

Hannum categorized emerging training technologies by focusing on the three main technological areas: computer technology (computer-delivery), communications technology (conferencing), and optical disc technology. Hannum defines each of the categories as follows:

> Computer delivery refers to the use of a computer to deliver training materials directly to learners; conferencing refers to the use of communication technology, satellite or broadcast television, and telephone lines to allow people at different locations to confer with each other; optical disc technology refers to storing and retrieving sounds, images, and programs on laser-read discs. (p. 19)

The three categories include delivery systems, storage media, and applications. He also observes that it is impossible to clearly isolate these three technologies from one another because they are interrelated in what they can do and how they are used. For example, "many interactive delivery systems link optical technology and computer technology. This begins to erase the distinction between computer-based training (CBT) and interactive videodisc (IVD)" (p. 19). Nonetheless, these categories provide us with a fundamental group of what can seem a chaotic assortment of new technological possibilities.

When it comes time to design and deliver a competency-based curriculum, you will want to consider the new technologies available to you. The application of any one of these technologies (as with other media) will require certain front-end investments in hardware and/or software, and possibly other resources. You should look at start-up and immediate costs as well as the longer term costs of maintaining the system, amortizing the capital equipment investment and upgrading the technology. A considerable portion of the following information on emerging technologies was abstracted from Hannum (1990) and is included as a courtesy to the reader from the American Society for Training and Development.

Computer Delivery

The mention of computers in training or education brings to mind their most straightforward application: the learner interacting with program content while sitting at a computer workstation. In this mode, the lesson content is ordered into a sequential pathway and the achievement of most of the program contents can be assessed by computers. The learner completes the various learning paths and performance is assessed at critical path points. The learner receives immediate evaluative feedback from these assessment exercises. Three forms of technology are used: artificial intelligence, hypermedia, and embedded/concurrent programming.

Artificial intelligence techniques are being introduced to supplement CBT programs. These techniques are structured to detect how the learner is thinking and allows the program to make path decisions based on intermediate actions by the learner. Artificial intelligence is a particularly important technology for the competency-based movement since it can be used to replicate the way the "expert" or exemplary performers do their job. This technology complements the concept of competency-based performance improvement. The computer program uses an expert model and "organizes the human expert's knowledge base into problem-solving approaches or ways of thinking about the topic" (Hannum, 1990, p. 26). However, only certain types of competencies are appropriate for development into expert systems at this time. These include "models of good performance; clearly identifiable and visible data and/or decision-making strategies; and tasks requiring repetitive cognitive practice" (p. 27).

A second form of technology in the computer-based training category is the use of *hypertext* or, in the broader sense, *hypermedia.* In this application, learners can pick and choose the pathways they will take to pursue the content stored in the computer.

The third form of computer-based delivery methods is *embedded* and/or *concurrent* training. When the training material is placed inside another application computer program (e.g., a word processing program), it is referred to as "embedded." When it is run parallel to one or more other application programs, it is considered "concurrent." The availability of embedded or concurrent training allows the learner to immediately acquire learning assistance on the use of the subject application program by inputting one or more simple commands. Help is an instant away by simply touching the keys on the keyboard.

For further information in this category, you might care to refer to Gery (1987), Hannum (1988), or Ofiesh (1989).

Conferencing

The second category of technology is *conferencing.* Through this highly advanced mode of communication, the trainee can interact with other trainees across thousands of miles. This category includes these forms:

- Asynchronous computer conferencing

- One-way video teleconferencing

- Two-way digital teleconferencing

In an *asynchronous computer conferencing* setting, the instructor (or instructors) and the students are connected in several remote or scattered locations by individual computers. All persons who are on-line can interact with each other. This is a useful form of learner-centered instruction which allows the learner time to stratify the learning experience without time constraints (unless, of course, time constraints are deliberately placed on the learning process).

One-way video teleconferencing is a way of presenting "live" instruction to a range of remote locations with the added advantage of two-way audio, which allows remote-location participants the ability to call in questions or have a discussion with the presenter. The video/audio technology interface has recently been improved and, consequently, has made this a very attractive training technology.

Two-way digital video teleconferencing allows users on both ends to see *and* talk to each other and exchange information. Cost and its interface with the state-of-the-art remains a major issue with this form of conferencing.

Optical Disc Technology

The third category of training technology, optical disc technology, is based on this hardware's capability for storing and retrieving very large amounts of data. Hannum (1990) comments:

> Advances in optical storage will further enhance the design and delivery of interactive learning materials. The distinction between video-based and computer-based training will further blur as optical drives become common storage devices for personal computers. By combining the decision-making capabilities of computers, the vast storage capacity of optical discs, and digital video display technology, means are available to support powerful training approaches. (p. 47)

Let's look more closely at the forms of optical disc technology.

Compact disc read-only memory (CD/ROM) technology uses a compact optical disc as a storage medium for preserving audio, text, graphics, and photographic images in digital form. The CD/ROM storage capability is then matched with the power of a personal computer for applications in the training or education environment. One of the major attributes of CD/ROM is the volume of its storage capacity. For example, up to 270,000 pages of text or the equivalent of 1,500 floppy disks can be stored on a single CD/ROM.

Interactive videodisc (IVD) technology has all the advantages of computer-based instruction, but with the added dimensions of sound, graphics, and full-motion video. The computer's microprocessor controls access to the information on the videodisc. The learner can access information from a keyboard, lightpen, or touchscreen. Hannum (1990) informs us that "IVD provides multiple branching capability, immediate feedback, a one-on-one student-instructor ratio, and engagement of the learner through sight, hearing, and touch" (p. 48). IVD is highly learner-centered and is especially useful for administering performance simulations.

Digital video-interactive (DVI) technology allows a learner to participate in the training process through the use of full-motion video, high-resolution images, high-speed graphics, and high-quality audio and textual materials. This technology makes it possible for a learner to interact with full-scale models. At present, DVI technology is just beginning to be developed and used.

Compact disc-interactive (CD-I) technology uses a compact disc to achieve full-motion video. CD-I is a form of interactive multi-media that can display text and both still and moving images. A CD-I player, which is a self-contained piece of hardware, consists of a CD/ROM drive and a microprocessor. Although CD-I was developed as a commercially marketed product, it has training applications, especially for simulations. At present, however, CD-I is incompatible with personal computers. We can probably expect to see the emergence of training applications of CD-I, especially in the commercial or the consumer market.

Comments

A wealth of learning strategies and emerging technologies are influencing the delivery of training and education. These tools help the practitioner accomplish the objective of having learner-centered, competency-based performance improvement opportunities. Some forms of the technology might be used to develop whole competencies, or must be used for only certain dimensions of a competency whose remaining components are developed through the use of other, nontechnological approaches. At the risk of oversimplification, what is important is to ensure that the application achieves *maximum* learning at *minimum* cost.

Decisions regarding the appropriate and most *cost-effective* use of technology are nearly as complex as the technology itself. One training executive reported that "training has suddenly become so capital intensive, that it has put us in the hot seat. We must choose between alternate modes and models of equipment and risk recommending investments that prove to be unwise—in equipment and systems that quickly become obsolete—or we must recommend against all of them" (Lusterman, 1985, p. 15). Also, the new technologies tend to become obsolete very quickly as they are replaced with either enhancements to hardware or software, or are altogether replaced with different hardware or software.

A partial solution would be to select those technologies that allow for flexible modification of the courseware as job competency demands change, therefore accommodating modifications to the content of the intervention or the strategy used without frequent hardware changes. The advent of new technologies has impacted HRD and their managers' decisions on the most advantageous applications of a given technology to the development of the competence needs of their employees, consistent with available resources, organization factors, and the most advantageous HRD practices. The challenges are predicted to continue for some time.

For an informative review and discussion of performance improvement technology, consult Gayeski (1991a, 1991b, 1991c).

SUMMARY

In this chapter, select learning or instructional strategies and their use in a competency-based framework were presented and discussed. The advantages and disadvantages of using mediated strategies and emerging technologies in the design and development of competency-based learning interventions were also discussed.

REFERENCES

Argyris, C. (1980). Some limitations of the case method: Experiences in a management development program. *Academy of Management Review, 5* (2), pp. 291-298.

Armistead, C. (1984, February). How useful are case studies? *Training and Development Journal, 38*(2), pp. 75-77.

Berger, M. A. (1983). In defense of the case method: A reply to Argyris. *Academy of Management Review, 8* (2), pp. 329-333.

Craig, R. L. (Ed.). (1976). *Training and Development Handbook* (2nd ed.). New York: McGraw-Hill, 1976.

Craig, R. L. (Ed.). (1987). *Training and development handbook: A guide to HRD.* New York: McGraw-Hill.

Derven, M. G. (1989, March). Fail-safe pilot programs. *Training and Development Journal, 43* (3), pp. 63-64.

Eitington, J. E. (1984). *The winning trainer: Winning ways to involve people in learning.* Houston: Gulf Publishing Co.

Frantzreb, R. B. (Ed.). (1991). *Training and development yearbook: 1991.* Englewood Cliffs, NJ: Prentice Hall.

Gagne, R. M. (1977). *The conditions of learning* (3rd ed.). New York: Holt, Rinehart and Winston.

Gagne, R. M. (1985). *The conditions of learning and theory of instruction* (4th ed.). New York: Holt, Rinehart and Winston.

Gagne, R. M., & Briggs, L. J. (1979). *Principles of instructional design* (2nd ed.). New York: Holt, Rinehart, and Winston.

Gagne, R. M., Briggs, L. J., & Wager, W. W. (1988). *Principles of instructional design* (3rd ed.). New York: Holt, Rinehart and Winston.

Gayeski, D. M. (1991a, January). What we can learn from our past mistakes. *Performance and Instruction, 30* (1), pp. 1-4.

Gayeski, D. M. (1991b, February). PT in emerging organizations. *Performance and Instruction, 30* (2), pp. 45-47.

Gayeski, D. M. (1991c, March). Tools and technologies. *Performance and Instruction, 30* (3), pp. 35-40.

Gentry, J. W. (Ed.). (1990). *Guide to business gaming and experiential learning* (for the Association for Business Simulation and Experiential Learning). East Brunswick, NJ: Nichols/GP Publishing Co.

Gery, G. (1987). *Making CBT happen*. Boston, MA: Weingarten Publications.

Gray, J., & Constable, J. (1983). Case method in management training. In B. Taylor & G. Lippitt (Eds.), *Management development and training handbook*. London, UK: McGraw-Hill Book Co., Ltd.

Hannum, W. (1988). Designing courseware to fit subject matter structure. In D. J. Jonassen (Ed.), *Instructional designs for microcomputer courseware*. Hillsdale, NJ: Lawrence Erlbaum Assoc., Publishers.

Hannum, W. (1990). *The application of emerging training technology*. Alexandria, VA: American Society for Training and Development.

Hannum, W., & Hansen, C. (1989). *Instructional systems development in large organizations*. Englewood Cliffs, NJ: Educational Technology Publications.

Haslam, E. L. (1990, September). The case for simulation. *CBT Directions*, pp. 10-16.

Hendrickson, J. (1990, March). Training in context. *Training*, pp. 65-70.

Hudspeth, D. R., & Knirk, F. (Guest Ed.). (1991). A series of related articles found in *Performance Improvement Quarterly*, *4* (1), pp. 2-87.

Kelly, H. (1983, February). Case method training: What it is, how it works. *Training*, pp. 446-449.

Keys, B., & Wolfe, J. (1990). The role of management games and simulations in education and research. *Journal of Management*, *16* (2), pp. 307-336.

Knowles, M. S. (1980). *The modern practice of adult education: From pedagogy to andragogy*. New York: Cambridge Book Co.

Knowles, M. S. (1984). *Andragogy in action*. San Francisco: Jossey-Bass.

Knox, A. B. (1986). *Helping adults learn*. San Francisco: Jossey Bass.

Lusterman, S. (1985). *Trends in corporate education and training* (Conference Board Report No. 870). New York: The Conference Board.

Nadler, L. (1982). *Designing training programs: The critical events model*. Reading, MA: Addison-Wesley.

Newstrom, J., & Scannell, E. (1990, January). Games to train by. *Training and Development Journal*, *44* (1), pp. 227-228.

Ofiesh, G. S. (1989, January). Emerging technologies of information and their potential impact on education, training and human productivity. *Business Economics*, *24* (1), pp. 36-41.

Pigors, P., & Pigors, F. (1987). Case method. In R. L. Craig (Ed.), *Training and development handbook: A guide to HRD*. New York: McGraw-Hill.

Pike, R. W. (1990). *Creative training techniques handbook: Tips, tactics, and how-to's for delivering effective training*. Minneapolis, MN: Lakewood Books.

Silberman, M. (1990). *Active training: A handbook of techniques, case examples, and tips*. San Diego, CA: University Associates.

Spruell, G. (Ed.). (1987). *Getting results with the case method.* Alexandria, VA: American Society for Training and Development.

Trollip, S. R. (1990, 2nd Quarter). Simulations: Back to the basics. *Authorware Magazine*, pp. 6-9.

Chapter 7

TRACKING THE PERFORMANCE OF THE SUBSYSTEMS: THE EVALUATION SUBSYSTEM

In this chapter, you will learn how to conceptualize an evaluation subsystem that is appropriate for your application and developed with available resources. Evaluation and its role in HRD are discussed. A comprehensive view of the practice of evaluation in HRD is presented, along with some resources that are particularly useful for evaluating a competency-based performance improvement program or learning intervention.

IN RELATION TO THE STRATEGIC SYSTEMS MODEL

The Evaluation Subsystem is the central monitoring subsystem for the other subsystems included in the competency-based performance improvement system. Development of the Evaluation Subsystem is Step 5 of the Strategic Systems Model.

A review of Figure 7.1 (on the following page) reveals the critically important role of the evaluation subsystem within the Strategic Systems Model. Notice that the outputs of the evaluation subsystem impact the operation of all of the earlier subsystems. Because of evaluation's critical position in the Strategic Systems Model, we will return to this subject shortly, in the context of accountability and evaluation goals.

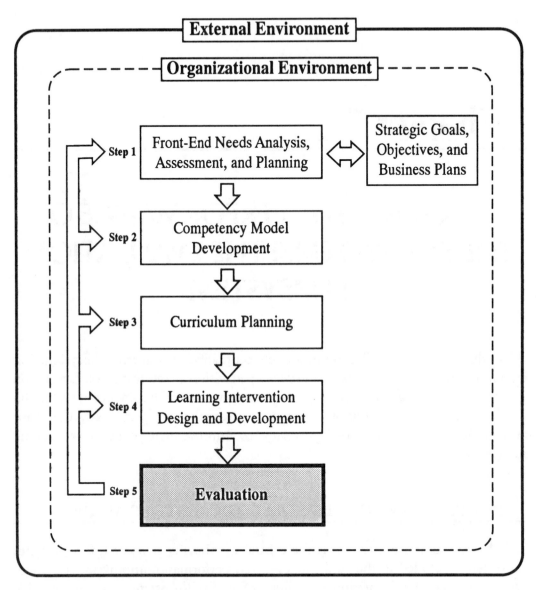

Figure 7.1: The Evaluation Subsystem of the Strategic Model

EVALUATION AND HRD

Organizations invest literally millions of dollars each year in training or educating their employees. They make the bulk of this investment in HRD on the premise that training or education will enhance their employees' job performance and therefore, ultimately contribute to the achievement of the organizations' strategic objectives.

The underlying assumption of this view is that these training or education interventions are organization results-oriented. In this context, any evaluation of organization training or education should (1) verify the direct relationship between the program(s) and intervention(s) to the achievement of the job outputs expected of employees and (2) verify that those outputs contribute to the accomplishment of the organization's strategic objectives. Specifically, the following evaluation questions at the job performance and organization levels must be answered:

- Have the employee competencies that most significantly contribute to achieving their job outputs been identified?

- Are program participants acquiring the competencies (singly and in combination with each other) included in the instructional program(s) or intervention(s)?

- Are the program(s) or intervention(s) contributing to improved job performance? That is, can employees correctly apply the competencies on the job, within the constraints of the workplace climate?

- What are the contributions of the training or education program to the achievement of strategic organization goals?

In order to affirmatively answer each of the questions above, there must be internal accountability within the HRD function. Positive answers to the questions below are essential for achieving the job outputs and organization strategic goals outcomes noted above. Therefore, HRD leaders need answers to these "grass-roots" evaluation questions:

- How comprehensive and useful are the front-end needs analysis, assessment, and planning procedures and processes? Are the procedures and processes capturing true profiles of organization needs? Are the front-end analyses, assessment, and planning techniques appropriate? Are the mechanisms used to meet performance improvement needs the most appropriate and cost-effective ones? What areas need improvement?

• Do the identified competencies address the targeted employees' performance requirements and needs? Are competency models (or menus) comprehensive?

• Is there a curriculum subsystem, and if so, is it efficient and effective in addressing the identified needs?

• Are the program or intervention designs effective and efficient, given available resources and organization constraints? Are learning assessments appropriate, reliable, and valid?

• Are existing performance improvement systems appropriate for the application environment? Are they effective and efficient?

• Is the evaluation subsystem comprehensive, given available resources? (Yes, even the evaluation system should be evaluated!)

Let's review these items in light of the Strategic Systems Model. Notice that in Figure 7.1 the Evaluation Subsystem receives its inputs from the following steps:

Step 1. The front-end needs analysis, assessment, and planning subsystem (What are the needs, their priorities, and how can, or will, they be met?)

Step 2. The competency menus or models subsystem (What are the job performance requirements?)

Step 3. The curriculum plan (What is included in the performance improvement curriculum, and how are the curriculum components organized?)

Step 4. The program or intervention design and its learning events (How are the programs or interventions structured and what learning processes, procedures, and media are used?)

Notice also that the outputs of the evaluation subsystem in the Strategic Systems Model are fed back to any or all of the earlier subsystems, depending upon individual situations. It is this feedback and revision process that helps maintain the stability, balance, and consistency of the entire competency-based performance improvement system over its life span. Imbalance in any subsystem signals a need for modifications or adjustments to any (or all) of the subsystems. In other words, information flows in several directions within the total system.

The outputs of the Evaluation Subsystem could include a wide variety of information and evaluation results for the system's products and services. For example:

- An assessment of day-to-day logistical operations

- Assessments of the employees' achievement of the learning objectives and competency acquisition

- The effectiveness of the learning strategies for employees' achievement

- The effectiveness of the instructional staff or facilitators

- The importance and usefulness of the competencies included in the performance improvement program or those acquired by the employees as a result of their participation in the intervention

The evaluation subsystem, then, is a "leading indicator" that reveals successes and that also warns when corrections in any of the subsystems are needed to bring the performance improvement subsystem into proper balance.

USEFUL MODELS FOR EVALUATING A COMPETENCY-BASED SYSTEM

There are two evaluation models for conceptualizing and planning evaluation activities that will answer important questions about competency-based performance improvement systems: the CIPP Model and the Kirkpatrick Model.

The CIPP Model is useful for conceptualizing the evaluation of education or training systems that are focused on bringing about needed change. The systems described in this book are meant to create change in organizations through improved employee performance.

When the Strategic Systems Model is appropriately applied, tremendous benefits result for the evaluator. These are discussed next.

Advantages of a Competency-based System for Evaluations

To achieve their mission, evaluators require a number of sources for information and data on the performance improvement system they are evaluating. Those who evaluate performance improvement programs or interventions for the types of competency-based systems described in this book are fortunate because they have a rich supporting data base for designing and completing the evaluation tasks. As you read about the two models later, keep in mind that the following information on the subsystem components is immediately available for use by an evaluator:

- Macro-level needs analysis, assessment, and planning information for the system, including alternatives, strategies, options, and the possible choices for the program or learning intervention(s)

- Macro-level assessments of employees' competence needs

- Job competency model(s) that include the environmental conditions, job outputs, key competencies and excellence factors, and the behavioral indicators for the job and its performance within the organization context

- Micro-level assessments of employees' needs, based upon the competency model elements

- Program or learning intervention designs and implementation approaches

- Evaluation requirements, options, or an evaluation plan

These basic raw materials are often missing or otherwise unavailable to those responsible for planning and completing evaluations. Taking a competency-based approach from the conceptual stage of the performance improvement system design lays the foundation for having a comprehensive evaluation subsystem later on. As you learn about the two models for evaluation and the information required to use them, keep in mind the availability of the items above and how they will support the evaluation work.

The CIPP Evaluation Model

The CIPP (Context, Input, Process, Product) Evaluation model is useful for designing evaluation studies for decision-making purposes (i.e., formative evaluation), and also for accountability (i.e., summative evaluation) purposes. Performance improvement systems of the type described in this book require both types of evaluation; the CIPP was chosen because it differentiates the two types of evaluation and establishes a framework for conceptualizing each type of evaluation.

The CIPP had its origins in 1970 through the work of the members of the Phi Delta Kappa National Study Committee on Evaluation (Stufflebeam et al., 1971). In the CIPP Evaluation Model, "Evaluation is the process of delineating, obtaining, and providing useful information for judging decision alternatives" (Stufflebeam, 1974, p. 121). There are four basic classes of decisions in this evaluation model (adapted from Stufflebeam, 1974, p. 121):

1. *Planning*—includes the choices of the program or training system objectives

2. *Structuring*—decisions made during the design stage for the training or education system

3. *Implementing*—decisions needed to implement and execute a training or education system design

4. *Recycling*—judgments of the results realized from the training or education system

Associated with the four types of decisions are four kinds of evaluation (Stufflebeam, 1974):

1. *Context (C) evaluation* serves *planning* decisions by identifying unmet needs, unused opportunities, and underlying problems.

2. *Input (I) evaluation* serves *structuring* decisions by projecting and analyzing alternative procedural designs.

3. *Process (P) evaluation* serves *implementing* decisions by monitoring project operations.

4. *Product (P) evaluation* serves *recycling* decisions by identifying and assessing project results.

The CIPP Evaluation Model prompts the evaluator to provide the information needed for maintaining HRD program accountability. Stufflebeam (1974) describes this application in the following manner:

1. *Context (C) evaluation* provides a record of [program or project] objectives chosen, those rejected, and the relation of chosen and rejected objectives to information about needs, opportunities, and problems.

2. *Input (I) evaluation* provides a record of the chosen and rejected procedural designs and data concerning the strengths and weaknesses of alternative designs.

3. *Process (P) evaluation* provides a record of the actual implementation process.

4. *Product (P) evaluation* records project attainments and decisions concerning the continuation, modification, or termination of the project.

Maintaining program or project accountability requires having records of decisions and actions for each of the CIPP components.

When the CIPP is used for decision-making purposes, the four evaluation processes are referred to as *proactive* or *"formative"* evaluation. When the use of the CIPP is accountability-driven, the evaluation processes are referred to as *retroactive* or *"summative"* evaluation (Stufflebeam, 1974, p. 122). Figure 7.2 illustrates a framework that relates the CIPP Evaluation Model to the formative-summative concept of evaluation.

TYPES OF EVALUATION

ROLES OF EVALUATION		Context	Input	Process	Product
	Decision Making		Proactive (formative) evaluation		
	Accountability		Retroactive (summative) evaluation		

Figure 7.2: A Framework that Relates the CIPP Model to the Formative-Summative Concept of Evaluation

Source: Popham, 1974, p. 122. Reprinted with permission.

Utilizing the CIPP requires an evaluator to complete three actions: delineating, obtaining, and providing. First, the evaluator must delineate the questions to be answered and provide information for decision-makers. This requires collaboration between the evaluator and the decision-maker(s). Obtaining the information requires the completion of a technical set of activities that usually includes measurement, data processing, and statistical applications by the evaluator. The "providing" step includes, in general, reporting out the information obtained by the evaluator (Stufflebeam, 1974, p. 122).

Figure 7.3 illustrates a composite framework for conceptualizing and designing CIPP evaluation projects. Since each organization training or education program has its own unique qualities, characteristics, and constraints, decisions must be made regarding the evaluation objectives, how those objectives will be met, and for which program purposes or objectives. Each application within an organization setting could be quite different from any other application.

TYPES OF EVALUATION

		Context Role		Input Role		Process Role		Product Role	
		Decision making	Account-ability	Decision making	Account-ability	Decision making	Account-ability	Decision making	Account-ability
S T E P S I N	E V A L U A T I O N	Delineating	(What questions will be addressed?)						
		Obtaining	(How will the needed information be obtained?)						
		Providing	(How will the obtained information be reported?)						

Figure 7.3: A Framework for Designing CIPP Evaluation Studies

Source: Popham, 1974, p. 122. Reprinted with permission.

Evaluation designs and outputs that result from an application of the CIPP are judged in terms of three standards, according to Stufflebeam: technical adequacy, utility, and cost-effectiveness. "Technical adequacy concerns validity, reliability, and objectivity; utility involves the relevance, scope, timeliness, importance, pervasiveness, and credibility of the evaluation; cost-effectiveness constitutes the final standard" (Stufflebeam 1974, p. 123).

Based upon his review of the CIPP Model, Galvin (1983, p. 52) concluded that the CIPP is particularly valuable for evaluating management training and development because, in addition to being effective, it is also efficient, comprehensive, balanced, and useful. This is positive testimony of the value of the CIPP Model for evaluating management training and development. Moreover, the CIPP model is particularly suitable for our purposes because it is useful for conceptualizing the evaluation of both soft and hard competence training or education systems.

Galvin (1983. p. 52) observed that the model:

- Supports the use of simple evaluation procedures rather than the use of more complex ones that might not be fully understood

- Is easily understood by nontraining professionals

- Provides a foundation for improving program effectiveness

- Gives the evaluator a framework for determining the type of evaluation data that are needed

- Includes both formative and summative evaluation tracks

- Takes a balanced view of evaluation relative to research, measurement, and judgment

- Is helpful because it can be used to evaluate the full scope of programs or interventions within an organization

The use of the CIPP Evaluation Model helps the evaluator identify the evaluation "pieces" and how those pieces fit together to compose a total plan. If preferred, the evaluator can conceptualize two separate yet integrated evaluation subsystems: one for decision-making purposes and the other for accountability purposes. The matrix included in Figure 7.3 provides clues for designing the subsystems. Each subsystem (e.g., the formative or summative subsystems) is conceptualized by answering each of the three questions (found in the body of the matrix) across twelve cells of the matrix for "Decision making."

For example, let's examine how a plan could be designed for a "Context" evaluation. You will find it helpful to refer to Figure 7.3. First the evaluator states the evaluation questions to be addressed (i.e., the "Delineating" action) for the context role. Next, the evaluator states how the needed information will be obtained (the "Obtaining" action). Finally, the evaluator describes how the obtained information (i.e., the evaluation outputs) will be reported to the client or client group (the "Providing" action).

In-depth information on the CIPP Evaluation Model can be found in Stufflebeam et al. (1971). Trapnell (1984) describes and discusses the major attributes of the CIPP Model and its application to the evaluation of training at various levels of an organization.

The Kirkpatrick Model

The second useful evaluation model is attributed to Donald L. Kirkpatrick (Kirkpatrick, 1975, 1978). The Kirkpatrick model is popular with HRD practitioners, and it is oftentimes referred to in the HRD literature. The CIPP and Kirkpatrick models complement each other in the overall practice of evaluation for competency-based performance improvement systems. The CIPP Model is useful for identifying what aspects of a program or intervention will be evaluated and how the evaluation will proceed. The Kirkpatrick Model provides a framework for evaluating training or education programs or interventions at four levels of a hierarchy of evaluation results. Once the overall conceptual plan for an evaluation is complete (i.e., as a result of an application of the CIPP Model), the Kirkpatrick Model helps the evaluator describe evaluation activities for answering the evaluation questions relative to the program or intervention impacts.

Kirkpatrick's model describes evaluation that can occur within four levels of a hierarchy of evaluation results (Phillips, 1983, pp. 36-37):

1. *Reaction Level*—Evaluates the reactions of the participants to a program or intervention, including such items as its content, instructional design, the media used, the instructor's peformance, and so forth.

2. *Learning Level*—Measures the learning achievement realized by the participants

3. *Behavior Level*—Measures changes in job performance, such as the adoption of new or changed behaviors by the participants on the job

4. *Results Level*—Evaluates the strategic impacts of the program or learning intervention on the total organization and seeks findings that illustrate how the acquired competencies worked, either singly or in combination, to achieve theorganization's strategic goals. These results could include, but not necessarily be limited to, cost savings, improvements in productivity, and quality improvements.

The Kirkpatrick Model emphasizes the *learner*, the learner's reactions to the program or learning intervention, the degree to which the competencies were acquired, the changes in job behavior that resulted following the program or intervention, and the strategic organization impacts of the new or changed employee behaviors.

Further information on the Kirkpatrick model can be found in Kirkpatrick (1975, 1978), Eitington (1984), and Birnbrauer (1987a, 1987b).

HRD Practitioners' Preferences

James Galvin (1983) conducted and reported the results of a survey of the preferences and practices of HRD persons who use the CIPP and Kirkpatrick evaluations models for evaluating management training and development curricula. The survey questionnaire provided data that was used to ascertain respondents' preferences between the two evaluation models and also to determine a measure of the respondents' attitudes toward evaluation. The survey respondents consisted of 300 members of the American Society for Training and Development; an 80 percent response rate to the survey was achieved.

A statistically significant number of the survey respondents indicated their preference for the CIPP Model over the Kirkpatrick Model. The survey also revealed that the higher the respondents scored on their preference for the Kirkpatrick Model, the higher they tended to score on the scale of their attitudes toward the evaluation of management education.

As a result of his findings, Galvin (1983, pp. 55-57) reached the following conclusions:

1. The CIPP model was preferred by significantly more training specialists when evaluating management training and development programs.

2. Kirkpatrick's model may be more appropriate for evaluating manual and technical skills training, but it is too narrow for evaluating management training.

3. Implementing an evaluation model requires examining the "fit" that exists between the larger curriculum development process and the model that is chosen. If a broad approach to curriculum development was used, then a model with a broad view of evaluation should be used.

In summary, the CIPP Evaluation Model offers a conceptual framework for designing and organizing two very different yet equally important types of evaluation subsystems for performance improvement systems that evolve from an application of the Strategic Systems Model. A contribution of Kirkpatrick's model is that it suggests useful ways for examining the outcomes of a training or education system at four levels of specificity and importance within an organization context. The fact that these training or education systems are competency-based improves the application of the Kirkpatrick model, since the employee performance improvement outputs and indicators of them are clear very early in system design.

Once the overall evaluation subsystem has been designed, the evaluator must plan for, and collect, the data needed to answer the evaluation questions included in the plan. Depending upon the evaluation questions, the evaluator will probably need to collect the following data at one or more levels within the Kirkpatrick hierarchy: the participants reactions, the learning achievements realized by participants, changes in the participants' job behavior as a result of the performance improvement experience, and the organization impacts of the performance improvement system. HRD practitioners often have critical information needs in this area. They must know what evaluation activities can be used to collect the data they need to answer evaluation questions at each of the Kirkpatrick levels. The next four sections of this chapter address that need for information.

Evaluation Activities at the Reaction Level

Among evaluation activities at the "reaction" level are the design, collection, analysis, and reporting of data or other information from participants during or shortly after a training or education program or intervention has been completed. In current practice, this involves collecting data on the participants' reactions to the training or education experience, in the form of perceptions, feelings, impressions, or comparative associations with other factors relevant to the HRD experience (e.g., the job requirements, outputs, work climate, organization environment or culture, and so forth).

Reaction data can be collected from group-oriented interventions or programs (i.e., where groups of learners are assembled for the learning activities) or from participants who complete learning experiences singularly (e.g., using a computer-based training module).

Pros and Cons

Professionals in HRD are prone to criticizing the value or usefulness of participant reaction data, regardless of how well the surveys were designed or how systematically the data were collected, analyzed, and reported. Many believe that the social aspects of the programs or learning interventions interfere with a participant's ability to constructively evaluate their learning experience. Eitington (1984) summarized the critics quite well when he stated: "Enthusiasm, they say, is almost certain, given an adequately interesting and active program, hotel/motel food, a friendly trainer, a chance to get away from the usual office routines (and even the family in some cases), and a chance to have a few drinks with old buddies" (p. 245).

Nonetheless, others such as Kirkpatrick, Phillips, and Connolly, either fully support or recognize the value of collecting, analyzing, and using reaction data from participants. Kirkpatrick believes that "evaluators miss valuable information when they dismiss reaction evaluation as merely 'happiness surveys,'"—and warns, "We'd better start looking at it as measuring customer satisfaction, and considering participants and companies as customers or we're in trouble" (Callahan, 1986, p. 10).

Recent empirical findings support the value of evaluation outputs at the Reaction Level. After voicing some of the common criticisms of reaction data, Phillips (1983) states:

> Possibly the criticism is unjustified. Recent research conducted by Aaron Elkins (1977) shows a direct correlation between positive comments at the end of a program and the actual improved performance on the job. Elkins' research was based on 90 government supervisors and managers who completed a basic management course. In all the variables examined, trainee reaction was the strongest determinant of on-the-job application of the new management principles. Those participants who enjoyed the program most were the ones who achieved the most on the job. Those who did not like it apparently did not bother to do too much of anything with it. (p. 132)

Connolly (1983) reports that "[participant evaluation] has . . . proven to be a reliable assessment method. Research has shown that participants' evaluations of the effectiveness of training programs are at least as valid as those of their subordinates or managers. These results were confirmed in a 1981 study I conducted at Eastman Kodak Company" (p. 92).

Regardless of one's position on this issue, this form of evaluation is a highly popular, if not one of the most popular, forms of evaluation for training or education programs and interventions. In a more positive framework, participants' reactions have many benefits and uses *if the reaction questions request specific, pointed information on the intervention attributes, and if they are collected, analyzed, and reported in a technically sound manner.* I agree that responses to an item such as "Agree or disagree: The course materials were satisfactory" provides little useful information to the developer for improving or enhancing the course materials. Instead, when the question is specifically referenced to individual elements of materials that were used, useful information will be collected. Question construction is a technical area of survey design that must be carefully completed if evaluators are to obtain information that will be immediately useful for making the judgments needed to implement program improvements.

Several sections follow that describe different types of data collection activities that can be used to evaluate programs or interventions at the Reaction Level. They include pilot testing, group-based techniques, and an intervention-based technique.

Pilot Testing

When a new competency-based performance improvement system is created, the programs or interventions must be pilot tested before they are fully implemented. All elements of the programs or interventions need to be subjected to actual use before you can conclude that they are working properly. Pilot tests can reveal deficiencies in the design, implementation mechanisms, the learning materials or media, the learning assessment processes, and any other subsystem elements which should be corrected before a program or intervention is fully implemented. And when performance improvement systems are involved, if something *can* go wrong, it *will* go wrong, usually at the early stages of system design and implementation!

Dick and Carey (1985) suggest that Reaction Level data for a pilot test should be collected in three stages. Keep in mind that although an underlying assumption of this process is that many programs or interventions will eventually be completed by groups of participants, rather than by learners in a one-on-one format, this does not diminish the usefulness of the technique. The technique has the advantage that the evaluator has access to a wide variety of employee opinions on the new intervention, because three separate samples are drawn from the target population in order to collect data for the pilot test. The three pilot test stages or steps recommended by Dick and Carey are as follows:

- One-on-one testing

- Small-group testing

- A full-fledged field trial

Step 1. One-on-one testing. During the one-on-one testing phase, a learner from the target population is given the instruction or participates in the learning intervention with close observation from an evaluator. Several attributes are examined during this and later stages. A subject-matter expert becomes familiar with the lesson or module performance expectations and its instructional elements. The subject-matter expert looks at the validity of the performance objectives relative to the competencies, the accuracy and clarity of the instructional materials, and any student assessment items or materials. During this one-on-one testing phase, the evaluator or observer has an opportunity to:

- Clarify estimates of the participants' prerequisite competencies

- Identify gaps in the meaningfulness or usefulness of the instructional presentation

- Modify inappropriate expectations of the number and types of competencies that can realistically be achieved by the target population

- Improve any learner assessment activities that lack specific directions or verbiage

Step 2. Small-group testing. To conduct small-group testing, a small group of learners is selected from the target population to conduct the test. Usually, an "attitude" or opinion assessment, a pretest, and a posttest on the content are given. The opinion survey could cover a wide variety of topics of importance to the success of the program or intervention once it is implemented. The pre and posttests on the program or intervention content help determine whether learning has occurred, and at what level.

Step 3. Field trial. The third and final stage of pilot testing is the field trial. A regular offering of the program or intervention is presented to a larger sample of the target population. The learners take a pretest on the performance of the competency, instruction is provided, and a posttest follows. The opinions of the participants and all instructors who participated in the field trial are solicited. All aspects of the instructional program are examined in detail. The instructors' performance is also reviewed. This is the final tryout of the materials and the learning strategies prior to full implementation of the program or learning intervention. Once the information is collected and analyzed, revisions are made to the program or intervention, and full implementation begins.

Additional information on pilot testing methods can be found in Chernick (1992) and Smith & Wedman (1988).

Group-in-Action Techniques

Julius Eitington (1984) offers an interesting assortment of methods for collecting and using participant reaction data, which he refers to as "group-in-action" techniques. These techniques have numerous advantages, according to Eitington (p. 246):

- They stimulate thinking about personal learning. Group interaction provides the learner with new avenues of thought about the experience and need for growth and improvement.

- The participants' questions about the intervention can be "reality tested" within the group.

- Ideas for program improvement (methods, administration, or facilities issues) can be obtained.

- If the program or intervention is a highly participative one, the evaluation process is simply an extension of the program or intervention, and a logical way to conclude the experience.

Eitington recommends that the use of any group-in-action activities should precede the use of questionnaires (p. 246).

Several of Eitington's activities are particularly appropriate in the context of this book, including *Self-appraisal, Circular Whip, Fishbowl,* the *Individual Course Cri-*

tique, and the *Small-group Course Critique*. These techniques are briefly described below, in a synopsis of the details found in his book (pp. 246-248).

Self-appraisal is a process in which the participants are assigned to dyads, triads, or some other small group configuration. This subgroup is a forum for the participants to describe and discuss their learning. The participants can be given an open-end assignment, they can discuss their expectations for the intervention or program and whether those expectations were met, and they can be asked to assess and discuss their acquisition of the competencies relative to the learning strategies that were used. If individual goal-setting for the program or intervention was done at the outset of the experience, the learners can be asked to discuss the degree to which their goals were met. Finally, a "sentence completion" format can be used. An example of this is, "In applying the time management competency, I found it difficult to . . . ." The impacts of these techniques are enhanced when the findings discovered in the small groups are shared with the whole group, at which time in-depth clarifications can be obtained.

The *Circular Whip* technique is completed by having the participants form a circle of no more than fifteen persons. Each participant, in turn, is asked to share what the most significant learning results were for her or him. The open-ended sentence completion technique can be used to encourage a lively response. Subsequent "whips" around the circle can be used to answer additional questions about the participants' assessments.

The *Fishbowl*, or group-on-group, observation activity affords an opportunity for all participants to become involved in the group assessment process. First, clearly state the evaluation issues you want discussed. Divide the entire group into teams of 6-8 participants; you must have an even number of teams, thereby allowing several fishbowls to operate simultaneously. Assign the groups either letter A or B. Pair the A and B teams. Let Group A be the inner group that responds to the evaluation issues while Group B observes. Next, Groups A and B change places, with Group B as the discussants. Group B now comments on the observations of Group A. Group B also responds to the evaluation questions. A reporter for each subgroup will then report out the results of each subgroup to the total group.

The *Individual Course Critique* includes the "posting technique." To use the "posting technique," you ask the participants to write out on a sheet of paper their ideas about three dimensions of the program or intervention: its content, methods, and administration. They post their ideas collectively on flip charts and a general group discussion follows, in which the contents under each category are examined.

To use the *Small Group Course Critique* activity, you divide the group into three smaller critique teams. Give each group one aspect of the program or intervention to critique. Stimulate and direct their thinking by asking questions such as:

1. How can the program or intervention content be improved? (List several suggestions.)

2. How could the program or intervention instructional methods be improved?

3. How can aspects of the intervention or program other than the contents and instructional methods be improved?

You can add in other questions that would yield information you might particularly need. Once the small groups have completed their critiques, the main ideas are posted on flip charts in the total group. The facilitator, or a group member, should facilitate a collective, summarizing discussion on the findings. Eitington includes other variations on the small-group course critique in his book.

An Intervention-Based Process

This intervention-based process for collecting, analyzing, and utilizing participant reaction data is used to monitor the moment-to-moment reactions of the participants during an intervention. It provides literally hundreds of "snapshots" of the performance of the intervention(s) for which data are being collected. You can perform data analyses that will suggest hypotheses for higher level evaluation studies of participants' learning levels, changes in their behavior while on the job, and the impacts of the program or intervention on the achievement of organization objectives. The evaluation process relies on the systematic collection, analysis, and reporting of data from participants during a competency-based program or intervention. The collected data extend well beyond the information provided by items on a traditional "smile" or "happiness" sheet filled out at the close of a training or education event.

This evaluation mechanism is administered during the intervention(s) by the event facilitator, administrator, or instructor at key stages of the learning process. It can be automated and administered by using computer-driven data collection systems, if that is preferred. Rather than asking participants the typical "Did this event make you feel good?" questions, this evaluation mechanism includes the collection of data representing the participants' perceptions of:

> • The importance of each competency (and consequently, each of the performance objectives) included in the learning event for their successful job performance

- The degree to which their work environment will (or can) support the application of the acquired competencies

- The frequency with which each competency will be used on the job

- A summary assessment of the collective value of the competencies for effective job performance

- The value added by the learning strategies which were used for the learning event

- The quality of the services provided by the instructor, facilitator, or administrator relative to the learning strategies

- Any additional items of particular interest to the program sponsor(s), designers, instructors, or facilitators

Some comments on the items above are in order.

"Importance" ratings are meaningful only when the participants have had some experience with the competencies in the job context or in a highly related job or setting. Otherwise, the participants may not be able to realistically rate the importance of the competencies for the work situation until they have gained some experience on the job. Each situation will need to be treated on its own merits. Overall or average importance ratings outside a predefined range can be a signal that the curriculum subsystem or the job competency model elements should be examined in light of the contemporary job realities. The individual importance ratings for a competency, in conjunction with other types of ratings, are a rich source of hypotheses about the value of the competencies for successful job performance.

The ratings participants assign to their perceived levels of achievement for a competency prior to and following the program or intervention provides *clues* (*not* hard facts) about the elements of the curriculum and the quality of the instructional program. These ratings estimate the participants' perceptions of how well the competence acquisition process went for them. In effect, they form an opinion of the "learning value" to them. When employees return to their job, they carry these perceptions with them. These opinions or perceptions of how much (or little) they learned are usually reported to others in the workplace, including their immediate manager. Low levels of perceived achievement or ratings that suggest the learners were already competent in one or more dimensions of the program or intervention prior to their participation send a message to the HRD staff *and to the client* that a content or other type of review is in order. There can be, of course, many explanations for observing anomalies of this type. One way to investigate the underlying meanings of these ratings is to interview the respondents (or a subgroup of them) and the instructor or facilitator for the program or intervention. Reviews of pre- and posttest data are also a useful source of information. It is best to have multiple measures of these perceptions when possible.

The "before-and-after" achievement rating process discussed above is most useful for gaining insight on the participants' perceived achievement of soft competencies. Certainly when the competencies included in the program or intervention are concrete, observable, and measurable, then you will most likely administer paper-and-pencil tests, skill demonstration exercises, or similar exercises to determine the learners' level of competence.

Most of the ratings should be completed by the participants at selected intervals during, rather than at, the conclusion of the entire program or intervention. The optimal time to have the participants rate the competencies and certain other items in the list above is immediately following the close of a learning module, or following the completion of a conceptual cluster of learning modules that represent a principal competency. This is a decision that must be made according to each program or intervention.

The ratings are easy for the participants to complete. They can be recorded on a mark-sense answer sheet (that can be interpreted by a scanner) with little or no prompting by the instructor, facilitator, or administrator. After they have completed two or three ratings and, as a result, understand the rating system, they can usually complete the remaining ratings during the event on their own, without prompting. If the learning event is highly structured, usually the facilitator or instructor only has to remind the participants that it is time (during the event) to provide the ratings. The type of intervention (e.g., computer-based learning, classroom instruction) only very minimally impacts the completion of the assessment process. Rating cues, which alert the learner to complete the rating(s) at the appropriate times, can be built into virtually any intervention or program.

The overall administration of an assessment system of this type can be totally or partially automated. A totally automated system allows the participant to input their ratings at a computer workstation by using a menu-driven program and a keyboard, lightpen, touchscreen or similar device to respond to the items. This allows for a paper-free operation. This approach is especially easy to integrate with automated instructional media because it can be integrated into the design of the learning system components.

A semi-automated system, on the other hand, requires a minimum investment in hard-copy components, computer hardware, and software. The hard-copy components include, but are not necessarily limited to, the following:

- Assessment booklets for the participants' use while completing the event

- Response sheets for recording the participants' ratings, which can be interpreted by an optical scanner

- Identification cover pages for each set of response sheets

- A competency list that describes the contents of the program or intervention

- Internal record-keeping system

The assessment booklets used by the participants, include:

- The instructions for completing the data collection forms and providing the ratings

- The scales they are to use for each type of requested rating

- A competency list for the particular intervention or program

The response sheets are used by the participants to report their ratings. The assessment book can be designed so that it is generic and modularized, therefore making it useful for a wide variety of evaluation applications.

The response sheets can be either hand-scored or machine-scored by using an optical mark reader (OMR) scanner interfaced with a personal or a mainframe computer. Hand-scoring is *NOT* recommended. This decision will be driven by the availability of the resources and equipment within the organization. If a system is to receive anything more than minimal application, it is strongly recommended that the investment in an automated operation be made.

The required technology includes:

- An OMR scanner

- A high-quality personal (or other) computer system

- Interface software for the scanner-to-computer connection

- Statistical software

• A moderately sophisticated laser printer with full graphics capabilities

A color printer is not really needed, yet it is nice to have. The system should be able to receive commands or messages from external computer systems and to send specific data analyses and reports to workstations in remote places. Access to these data should be provided to individuals in the organization with a "need and right to know." This includes, but is not limited to, the client or client organization, the facilitator or instructor, the HRD manager, and the intervention or program developers. These persons should have immediate access to menu-driven, interactive computer programs that support the analysis and reporting of the data using a wide variety of analysis procedures or techniques. If pre-formatted analysis reports are used, they must include a set of " flags" that will alert the users to review data for areas of the program or intervention that warrant attention. Another option is to construct a "relational data base," which provides the users with various analysis configurations for the data.

A system of this sort can include data for literally hundreds of programs, interventions, or courses. Depending upon how complex the system is and the volume of the data that must be processed, a certain amount of support will be required to maintain the system. Overall, the data and their analyses can make significant contributions to maintaining the optimal functioning of a competency-based training or education system. This requires, of course, that decision-makers value the system, regularly review the data, use it to conduct further program or intervention reviews, and make modifications to the total performance improvement system, as warranted by the findings.

Summary

In summary, reaction data are useful, and I believe they are a very necessary component—though not the *only* necessary component—of a comprehensive, systematic evaluation subsystem for a competency-based HRD program or intervention. There are several reasons for collecting and using participant reaction data:

1. If your evaluation resources are limited, reaction data systematically collected in a sophisticated manner are better than having *no* evaluation data.

2. They are immediately available and can alert the trainer, HRD management, and the client(s) to trends in the program or intervention. These trends can alert key persons to changes in policy, opera-

tions, and so forth that have occurred since the program or intervention was implemented and that affect the messages presented in the performance improvement opportunity.

3. They alert the HRD department to the perceptions of who is perhaps the "real client"—those being trained or educated. These persons carry perceptions of the HRD investment to the workplace—and subsequently to their immediate managers. These managers are a critical element of the HRD-client relationship. What the participants report to their immediate managers can enhance, as well as detract from, the support the HRD department receives from the client or client group. Many examples can be cited where a high-investment HRD intervention has been terminated as a result of negative perceptions that were reported to senior management by one, two, or three "strategically placed" individuals in the organization hierarchy. As Donald Kirkpatrick was quoted as saying, "Decisions [on programs or learning interventions] by top management are frequently made on the basis of one or two comments . . . from people who have attended" (Callahan, 1986, p. 10). In these cases, a broad base of reaction data were probably never collected, and the outcomes reported to senior management. Kirkpatrick and other practitioners argue for the collection and reporting of reaction data as a way of addressing this problem. When criticisms are lodged and reaction data are not available, the defendants have no supporting evidence for asserting the value of the intervention— although possibly dozens of other participants praised the experience.

4. In the event that the training or education opportunity is *not* at the quality level it should be, the probability is high that the competencies upon which the program was designed will not be transferred to the job. If asked the correct questions with the correct posture, employees can, and will, express their honest opinions about the training or education event and its applicability to their job. (This makes an assumption, of course, that they have a relatively clear picture of the job requirements.)

Participant reactions to a program or intervention can be, and will be, useful if they are designed, collected, analyzed, and reported in a systematic manner. Short of meeting those requirements, it is probably not worth the investment required to have participant reaction data.

Additional viewpoints on the topics in this section can be found in Carlisle (1984); Newstrom (1987); and Komras (1985).

Assessing Participants' Learning Achievement

The second level of the Kirkpatrick model is the "Learning" level. This level of evaluation relies on obtaining data about, and assessing, the participants' learning or changes in target performance during the program or intervention. Its objective is to determine what the participant can now do, or can now do differently, as a result of his or her participation in the competence acquisition program or intervention.

Testing

One of the more popular assessment forms for determining performance changes is the administration of pre- and posttests on the competency. If the competency and its performance are concretely defined and can be directly measured by a test item or set of test items, then a pre- and posttest method can be a useful learning evaluation measure. This approach is appropriate when assessments of many psychomotor or cognitive competencies are needed. However, when the acquisition of interpersonal or intrapersonal competence is to be assessed, written test items will often reach only a limited dimension of the performance. Certain intellectual or cognitive components embedded in interpersonal and intrapersonal skills can be tested using paper-and-pencil tests. However, the total assessment of these skills comes when one can observe their demonstration in the context of job performance. In a formal learning environment, the use of a simulated job environment and the replication of situations from that environment can be used for assessment purposes. Under these conditions, you can observe the application of the competency and can infer the job outputs or results that will be realized. You also have the advantage of observing the use (or lack of use) of subordinate or allied competencies.

The design, development, and use of performance tests is a discipline unto itself. Numerous books have been written on this subject. Research on testing methods and techniques abounds, and dozens of articles on the nature of tests and their appropriate uses can be found in professional journals. If the HRD professional plans to design, develop, and use competency-based performance tests to measure participants' achievement or to conduct other forms of program or intervention evaluations, then some preparation on the design and use of tests will be essential. The following three articles from the recent literature might be a useful place to start:

- Cantor (1988) discusses how to design, develop, and use performance tests. The introductory comments are useful for focusing on the scope of testing. Cantor emphasizes test validity, but leaves issues of statistical reliability to other sources on the subject.

- Smith and Merchant (1990) discuss the use of competency exams for evaluating training. The writers include discussions on written items (paper-and-pencil tests) and also practical items (work samples and simulations). They include a discussion of test issues for both hard and soft competencies. A case report on competency testing at General Dynamics is provided. This article is very comprehensive. Once again, statistical issues are left for other books or materials.

- Alliger and Horowitz (1989) provide a report on an innovative way to assess training courses which results in assessments of not only the participants' knowledge, but also their levels of confidence in their answers. One attribute of the program was the inclusion of questions that were "mini-case studies." These questions required a participant to use situational analysis in conjunction with their knowledge of a principle or idea in order to respond. The methods used and how the results of the tests were used within the organization are presented.

Once you have reviewed these articles, you will find it easier to refer to books or other opportunities for additional help on the subject.

Learning Strategies Used As Assessment Mechanisms

A powerful assessment mechanism for competency-based programs or interventions is the use of job simulations. A simulation exercise can focus on the application of a single competency or on the use of several competencies in conjunction with each other. Critical path assessments of the subordinate competencies to the principal competency(-ies) can also be completed. Simulations used for assessment purposes can be as simple or as complex as you care for them to be. What must always be clear are the performance expectations, activities, and the conditions for successful performance. In general, when you design an instructional or assessment simulation, it should replicate—as nearly as possible—the manner in which the competency is used on the job.

Other learning strategies (see chapter 6) that can also be used as assessment mechanisms are role-plays, case method exercises, and games. If they were used as a learning strategy, they can be used again (using new data or circumstances) for the assessment of competence acquisition. When used properly, these strategies allow for direct observations of employees' performance as it might be exhibited while they are applying the competencies in the job context.

Surveys

In general, the same technical requirements for attitude surveys also apply to surveys that are used for competence assessment purposes. They must be carefully designed, and the items must precisely address the dimensions of the competencies and the issues internal to them. They must always be pilot tested. The survey contents must be integrated with the program or intervention contents, and the data or information analysis and interpretation guidelines must be precise and clear to the users.

Action Plans

Action plans developed by the participants in a program or intervention are a common form of encouraging transfer of the competencies to job performance. They can also be used to estimate the probability of how an employee's newly acquired competencies might be applied on the job. This is a measure of the degree to which competency acquisition has been internalized (Eitington, 1984, pp. 248-249).

Behavior Change Assessments

Kirkpatrick's third level of evaluation is an assessment of the degree to which competence acquisition has been transferred to the job. It is well accepted that an employee's ability to demonstrate competent performance in a formal or planned learning situation does not guarantee the same performance level on the job. The employee's supervisor, and in a larger context, the organization itself, must support the implementation of the employee's changed performance. The work environment must support the application of the competencies.

In order to assess the degree to which competency acquisition has been transferred to the job, inquiries regarding the subject employees' specific job performance must be made. There are several ways to research changes in performance, including the use of:

- Self-and-others pre- and post-intervention performance assessments and individualized performance planning mechanisms

- Achievement measures of the accomplishment of action-plan objectives

- Training impact assessment

Let's examine each of these in greater detail, then we will consider some alternative research-based approaches and other information at this evaluation level.

Self-and-Others Pre- and Post-Intervention Assessment

A "self-and-others competency assessment" process is a technique that some organizations use to help employees assess their strengths, identify their competency development needs, and develop personal training plans to meet those needs. The critical elements of the instrument include the competencies that are taken from a competency model that the organization has identified or researched for the targeted job. Employees identify their pre-training needs by asking others (including, for example, their peers, immediate supervisor, or subordinates) to assess the degree to which they believe the employee has acquired and has used each of the critical job competencies. An analysis and interpretation of the responses results in the identification of critical needs for growth relative to the competencies included in the assessment instrument.

Once an employee completes the training plan that was developed according to the identified competency needs, the assessment process is administered once again, usually six months or more following the completion of the items in the employee's personal plan. The difference between each pair of pre- and post-intervention scores for each competency reveals the perceived change in performance that occurred over the interval of time between the administrations of the instrument. The scores reflect the degree of growth or change, if any, that has occurred.

These types of data can be used for program or intervention evaluation purposes, and for individualized planning by employees. However, you will need to treat the collection, analyses, and reporting of the data as a research project if they are to be used as program evaluations. For example, you must be able to rule out the possibility that factors *other than* the competence-acquisition activities that were completed by the employees were responsible for any of the observed changes in job performance that were reflected in the pre- and post-intervention scores. These factors can include changes in organization policy, management personnel, ways of doing the work, and many other factors too numerous to mention. The evaluator proceeds to analyze the data in light of the factors that affect performance within the context of the organization. These analyses result in confirming or denying hypotheses about the overall effects of a competence acquisition process on day-to-day job performance.

An application of a self-and-others assessment process is very useful tool for measuring affective or "soft" competencies. However, if it is necessary to measure concrete knowledge or functional skills competencies, then work sampling or observation methods would be more useful. Those techniques and others are more appropriate for assessing the application of concrete, well-defined competencies.

Action Plans Assessment

A second way the effects of a competence acquisition process can be measured is by tracking employees' progress on the completion of any action plans for performance improvement that were developed in advance of, or during, the program or intervention. An initial action plan should be developed in cooperation with the employee's immediate supervisor. The action plan items must have measurable and observable criteria for determining when the performance objectives or requirements have been achieved. Verification that the performance objectives were achieved must usually be obtained from an employee's supervisor. Using an action plan approach as a program or intervention assessment tool requires considerable advanced planning by the evaluator.

Training Impact Assessment

Linn Coffman (1990) describes the Training Impact Assessment (TIA) as a "process that requires managers to look collectively at what happens to their employees as a result of training. .... TIA helps eliminate managers' uncertainties about the effectiveness of training programs" (pp. 77-78). The TIA, according to Coffman, is a high-impact evaluation process.

A synopsis of the six steps an evaluator follows to complete the TIA is included below:

Step 1. Invite key clients to participate in the assessment sessions.

Step 2. At the first session, the key clients are charged with data gathering on the training effectiveness.

Step 3. At the second session, subgroups share the positive effects of training.

Step 4. The subgroups enumerate the negative or unachieved results.

Step 5. The entire group shares the overall results, positive and negative.

Step 6. The lists are consolidated, an action plan is decided and agreed upon, and a follow-up date is set.

Coffman shares numerous suggestions for ensuring the success of the project. She also discusses validity issues for the evaluations that result from an application of the process. "The TIA approach," says Coffman, "also results in managers supporting and committing to effective training. By communicating their support to higher management, they can influence executives who may not recognize effective training programs" (p. 78). The chapter references include two additional items by Coffman (1979, 1980) that you might care to review.

Other Assessment Methods

Although the three methods discussed above are highly effective tools for behavior change assessment, a number of practitioners in the field have suggested additional methods that may answer more specifically your assessment needs. These practitioners include:

- *Paul Erickson.* His evaluation approach includes measuring and determining whether participants remember what they were supposed to have learned and how to apply it on the job. Erickson (1990) conceived and applied this process while at the Navy Research and Development Center (San Diego, CA). The approach is competency-based and involves having a group of trained employees respond to several competency-based cases when they return to their job following the training. The process provides evaluation data useful for course revision and for overall program or learning intervention evaluation.

- *Robert Brinkerhoff.* Brinkerhoff (1983) refers to his approach to job performance evaluation as the success-case approach. The process involves identifying, interviewing, and documenting the results achieved by several employees for whom the training or education was highly beneficial. The results of success-case analyses are particularly appealing because they can lead to "building broad-scale data collection methods to determine the extent of training impact" (p. 58). The results can also contribute to demonstrating the worth of training, designing a broad-scale quantitative survey, promoting and supporting the benefits of training, and redesigning training. The author provides the steps for designing the evaluation study.

- *Roger Poulet and Gerry Moult.* Poulet and Moult (1987) describe how to evaluate the impacts of values in a program or intervention and the roadblocks that the employee confronts when attempts are made to apply the competencies on the job. They explain how corporate values are adapted and converted into action at British Airways. The authors illustrate their analysis approach with a model. You will recall my concerns expressed in chapter 5 that HRD professionals must make a paradigm shift that will lead them to place additional emphases on the inclusion of affective competencies within many more of the formal competency-based training and education opportunities offered by their organizations. Poulet and Moult discuss (pp. 62-63) how the evaluation process can proceed when affective competencies are at issue.

• *Elizabeth Moore.* Moore (1984, p. 92) describes a before-and-after approach to performance appraisal based on competence factors that concurrently measured the impact of a training program at the Massachusetts Mutual Life Insurance Company. Moore includes very specific details of her methodology, explains the results that were achieved, and describes their significance.

• *Susan Connolly.* Connolly (1983) describes a procedure she used to verify participants' reactions to the effectiveness of a training program by conducting post-training interviews with the people trained, their superiors, and their subordinates. She also includes the major requirements for determining evaluation needs and an evaluation design, and the critical elements needed for an evaluation proposal that can be used to effectively communicate with a client on the parameters and structure of the evaluation.

Organization Impact Evaluation

The fourth, and possibly the most sophisticated, evaluation level of the Kirkpatrick model is that which judges the effects that training or education programs or interventions have had on the achievement of an organization's strategic goals. These are called organization impact evaluations. An example of typical "accounting language" questions that are oftentimes asked are, "Does investing in corporate training add enough value to our human resources asset to make it a priority investment? . . . Does capital spent on training have a high return on investment and a short payback period, coupled with high present value?" (Godkewitsch, 1987, p. 79)

Unfortunately, training or education impact evaluations are not frequently done in organizations. Lookatch (1991) stated that "in almost 15 years' experience in the HRD field, I've observed that barely one in ten HRD professionals ever produces a bottom-line measure of training's impact—either in dollars or improved skills" (p. 47). Lookatch's statement is verified time and time again by HRD practitioners.

Nevertheless, a number of impact evaluation approaches have evolved in response to a recent interest in documenting the impact of training or education programs or interventions in the face of shrinking resources. These approaches have a wide range of sophistication and complexity, and they can be quite rigorous.

Describing a more rigorous side of impact evaluations, Hunter and Schmidt (1983) state: "Quantification of the economic impact of psychological programs [e.g., training or education] in organizations requires a determination of (a) the size and variability of the resulting increase in job performance, and (b) the economic value of the increase in job performance. The new methods of meta-analysis allow attainment of the first of these, and in relation to the second, utility analysis methods enable us to translate job performance increases into estimates of the economic value of the program" (p. 473). In a 1987 article, Godkewitsch (pp. 79-81) provided an overview of the approach, including some typical examples of the application of the techniques. Procedures and details for determining training impacts are also described in depth by Robinson and Robinson (1989a, 1989b).

Requirements for Organization Impact Evaluation

The determination of organization impacts that result from training or education programs or interventions requires having—in most situations—the following:

- An organization climate of acceptance for the use of organization impact evaluation techniques, methodologies, and the outcomes that result from their application

- A committed interest and the cooperation of the client or client group

- A commitment to invest in work of this type from senior management in the HRD function (or its parent function)

- High-quality front-end analysis results and well-formulated plans that include impact evaluation as an essential project component

- Internal or external evaluation resources (human resources, hardware, software, and so forth) for completing impact-level evaluations

- Cooperation within the organization for the collection, analysis, interpretation, and reporting of evaluation results

Let's briefly review three of these points.

First, the initial item above states the requirement for a climate of acceptance for the techniques, methodologies, and the outcomes that result from their application. At times, the results of impact studies are not readily or widely accepted as realistic estimates. Even with the most rigorously conducted analysis projects, it is sometimes difficult to illustrate dollar-savings in strict accounting terms. It is probably more advantageous to document the outputs employees are achieving relative to the competencies they have acquired and are using, and how those competencies were acquired.

It is also important to focus on how the program contributed to meeting strategic objectives. Sometimes HRD contributions do not have a direct link to larger organization outputs, and these linkages must be illustrated. The size of the organization, the nature of the organization's products or services, the simplicity or complexity of the organization structure, and so forth impact how these relationships are established. Additionally, causal relationships between results achieved and the contributing factors for those results are, at times, difficult to establish. When these causal relationships are cloudy or are not clearly established, it is difficult to defend statements that organization outputs are directly attributable to employee competence acquisition. When the relationships are based on assumptions, these assumptions must be clearly cited and understood by the client and other recipients of the analysis results.

Second, impact evaluation studies require a considerable amount of early, front-end planning and other work in order for them to be successful. This is especially the case for obtaining and using evaluation resources. Impact evaluation projects are usually organization-based research projects. Therefore, the planning is essentially the same as that which is required for any large-scale research project. Competency-based approaches establish relationships between critical HRD components and organization components from the moment work begins. These components and relationships are some of the most crucially needed elements for doing impact evaluations. Therefore, by applying the steps of the strategic model for training or education system development, support for doing impact evaluation studies naturally follows.

Third, in addition to the planning which is essential, impact evaluation projects can require a considerable amount of time and resources to complete. Organization principals must decide just how valuable and useful the results will be and how the results will be used once they are available. These decisions will drive several downstream decisions regarding the work and just how detailed it will be, and, consequently, the time and resources that will be needed to realize those results.

Evaluation Design

When a front-end planning decision has been made to pursue the completion of an organization impact evaluation, the evaluator and the client or client group need to make several critical decisions regarding the evaluation approach and its costs. Each project has its own requirements, opportunities, and challenges. Therefore, the evaluator must account for these items in any design that is constructed. The evaluation design can take several forms, using either a wide or a narrow focus and a variety of procedures and analysis complexities. For this reason, it is very difficult to prescribe a methodology or an approach that you should take to design an organization impact project. Two points on this are made below:

1. Many evaluations, and nearly all organization impact studies, are dependent on the use of research designs and statistical data analysis techniques. Numerous printed resources are available on these topics. Some helpful references to review include Phillips (1983, 1991); Campbell & Stanley (1966); Kearsley (1982); Popham (1974); Robinson & Robinson (1989a, 1989b); and Brinkerhoff (1987). These sources will lead you to other resources that you might find necessary as you proceed.

2. If you are inexperienced in this area, you might want to first review some reports of impact evaluation projects which have been reported in the literature. Interestingly, few impact evaluation reports have been published in the training and development literature. Bell and Kerr (1987) observed: " The concept of evaluation has received widespread recognition as beneficial, but the practice of evaluation has lagged behind. Few reports of actual program evaluations have been published; compared to the number of training programs, few evaluations have been conducted." They also stated: "According to the report of one study [Smeltzer, 1979], less than 12 percent of 285 companies studied evaluated the results of supervisory training programs in management" (pp. 70-73). Several studies were selected from the literature and brief descriptions are provided below to help you understand the nature of this work.

- Bell and Kerr (1987) report on an evaluation project that was completed for all levels of the Kirkpatrick model. The evaluation design, according to the authors, " demonstrated that effective and economical evaluation is possible" (p. 70). The article includes several tips that the HRD professional staff can use to strengthen management's support for the practice of evaluation.

- Paquet, Kasl, Weinstein, and Waite (1987) reported on extensive details of an evaluation study that was completed on CIGNA's management training program. The study concentrated on how managers used their training to improve productivity and to measure a return on the investment. Tips are included for planning and designing an evaluation project of this type. References to two articles for collecting training cost data are included.

- Sauter (1980) discusses a cost-benefits review process relative to tracking the development of executives in the federal service. The evaluation methods, including the costing procedures and the algorithms that were used, are provided in the article. The author also provides references of potential interest.

Using Evaluation Results to Advantage

Once an investment in evaluating a program or intervention has been made, there should be a return on the evaluation investment itself. There are at least three objectives associated with any major investment in evaluation:

1. Determine the strengths, contributions, and areas of improvement that are needed for the subject of the evaluation.

2. Provide information for generating or considering options, or for decision-making purposes.

3. Illustrate and promote the value of HRD products as services within the organization.

It is axiomatic that evaluation results must be provided to the client and human resources professionals who are responsible for the program or intervention if the results are to be used to identify and make improvements. It's important to establish a time frame when results will be available to decision-makers and other persons who are in a position to effectively use the results. Evaluation results that reach critical persons in the organization too late to be useful represent a waste of resources.

Evaluation results need not be employed in an adversarial manner within the organization. They can be used to effectively market and promote HRD products and services within the organization. Richard Lookatch (1991, p. 50) provided some tips on how to do this. Here are his suggestions:

1. Hold a meeting with line-level and higher level managers. Express the evaluation results in terms of the bottom line when possible.

2. Publish evaluation results in internal publications of the organization.

3. Use the results of evaluations to justify additional HRD expenditures.

4. Formally share the results with trainees to reinforce their progress and contributions.

5. Develop a "bottom-line file." This file should contain materials that justify the HRD function within the organization.

6. Prepare and distribute an annual report to senior managers that includes HRD's contributions in terms of dollars saved and earned.

Evaluation need not be, and should not be, an adversarial activity which an organization's players must tolerate. Systems improvement is a major use of evaluation results by HRD and their clients. Understanding the contributions of HRD to the health and well-being of the at-large organization is an equally important contribution in the longer term.

IN CONCLUSION

Positive organization change can result in the achievement of a wide variety of organization objectives, such as increased market share, lower operating costs, enhanced profits, improved services to clients and customers, and others. Improved employee performance is frequently (although not always) a key change factor in achieving these organization objectives. The Strategic Systems Model, which is the foundation for this book, teaches that in order to have lasting change in employee performance, every element of the immediate organization system must be impacted as a result of the change mechanism(s). Appropriate organization processes, and their successful interface and operation, are critical to the achievement of improved performance, and subsequently, to organization change itself. The next three chapters portray the experience of three medium-to-large organizations and the "total organization" change results they achieved from an application of the Strategic Systems Model. Each application is different in certain ways from the others. They all share the attribute that large-scale organization change was realized as a result of the emphasis they placed upon systematic, competency-based performance improvement for their employees.

REFERENCES

Alliger, G. M., & Horowitz, H. M. (1989, April). IBM takes the guessing out of testing. *Training and Development Journal, 43* (4), pp. 69-73.

Bell, J. D., & Kerr, D. L. (1987, January). Measuring training results: Key to managerial commitment. *Training and Development Journal, 41* (1), pp. 70-73.

Birnbrauer, H. (1987a, July). Evaluation techniques that work. *Training and Development Journal, 41* (7), pp. 53-55.

Birnbrauer, H. (1987b, December). Trouble-shooting your training program. *Training and Development Journal, 41* (9), pp. 18-20.

Brinkerhoff, R. O. (1981, December). Making evaluation more useful. *Training and Development Journal, 35* (12), pp. 66-70.

Brinkerhoff, R. O. (1983, August). The success case: A low-cost, high-yield evaluation. *Training and Development Journal, 37* (8), pp. 58-61.

Brinkerhoff, R. O. (1987). *Achieving results from training.* San Francisco, CA: Jossey-Bass.

Callahan, M. (Managing Ed.). (1986). *Essentials for evaluation.* Alexandria, VA: American Society for Training and Development.

Campbell, D. T., & Stanley, J. C. (1966). *Experimental and quasi-experimental designs for research.* Chicago, IL: Rand McNally Co.

Cantor, J. A. (1988, September). How to design, develop, and use performance tests. *Training and Development Journal, 42* (9), pp. 72-75.

Carlisle, K. E. (1984, August). Why your training-evaluation system doesn't work. *Training,* pp. 37-40.

Carnevale, A. P., & Schulz, E. R. (1990, July). Return on investment: Accounting for training. *Training and Development* (Supplement), *44* (7), pp. 1-32.

Chernick, J. (1982, April). Keeping your pilots on course. *Training and Development*, *46* (4), pp. 69-73.

Clegg, W. H. (1987, February). Management training evaluation: An update. *Training and Development Journal*, *41* (2), pp. 65-71.

Coffman, L. (1979, August). An easy way to effectively evaluate program results. *Training and Development Journal*, *33* (8), pp. 28-32.

Coffman, L. (1980, October). Successful training program evaluation. *Training and Development Journal*, *34* (10), pp. 84-87.

Coffman, L. (1990, June). Involving managers in training evaluation. *Training and Development Journal*, *44* (6), pp. 77-80.

Connolly, S. (1983, October). Participant evaluation: Finding out how well training worked. *Training and Development Journal*, *37* (10), pp. 92-96.

Dick, W., & Carey, L. (1985). *The systematic design of instruction* (2nd ed.). Glenview, IL: Scott, Foresman and Co.

Dunn, S., & Thomas, K. (1955, April). Surpassing the 'smile sheet' approach to evaluation. *Training*, pp. 65-71.

Eitington, J. E. (1984). *The winning trainer: Winning ways to involve people in learning*. Houston, TX: Gulf Publishing Co.

Elkins, A. (1977, June). Some views on management training. *Personnel Journal*, pp. 305-311.

Erickson, P. R. (1990, January). Evaluating training results. *Training and Development Journal*, *44* (1), pp. 57-59.

Gagne, R. M., Briggs, L. J., & Wager, W. W. (1988). *Principles of instructional design* (3rd ed.). New York: Holt, Rinehart and Winston.

Galvin, J. C. (1983, August). What can trainers learn from educators about evaluating management training? *Training and Development Journal*, *37* (8), pp. 52-57.

Godkewitsch, M. (1987, May). The dollars and sense of corporate training. *Training*, pp. 79-81.

Hunter, J. E., & Schmidt, F. L. (1983, April). Quantifying the effects of psychological interventions on employee job performance and work-force productivity. *American Psychologist*, pp. 473-478.

Isaac, S., & Michael, W. B. (1971). *Handbook in research and evaluation.* San Diego: Edits Publishers.

Kearsley, G. (1982). *Costs, benefits, and productivity in training systems.* Reading, MA: Addison-Wesley.

Kirkpatrick, D. L. (1975). *Evaluating training programs.* Madison, WI: American Society for Training and Development.

Kirkpatrick, D. L. (1978). Evaluation of training. In R. L. Craig (Ed.), *The training and development handbook,* New York: McGraw-Hill.

Komras, H. (1985, September). Evaluating your training programs. *Training and Development Journal, 39* (9), pp. 87-88.

Lookatch, R. P. (1991, July). HRD's failure to sell itself. *Training and Development, 45* (7), pp. 47-50.

Lyne, G. E. (1989, December). How to measure employee attitudes. *Training and Development Journal, 43* (12), pp. 40-43.

McCullough, J. M. (1984, June). To measure a vacuum. *Training and Development Journal, 38* (6), pp. 68-70.

McEvoy, G. M., & Buller, P. F. (1990, August). Five uneasy pieces in the training evaluation puzzle. *Training and Development Journal, 44* (8), pp. 39-42.

Maher, J. H., & Kur, C. E. (1983, June). Constructing good questionnaires. *Training and Development Journal, 37* (6), pp. 100-110.

Moore, E. R. (1984, November). Competency-based training evaluation. *Training and Development Journal, 38* (11), pp. 92-94.

Newstrom, J. W. (1987, July). Confronting anomalies in evaluation. *Training and Development Journal, 41*(7), pp. 56-60.

Paquet, B., Kasl, E., Weinstein, L., & Waite, W. (1987, May). The bottom line. *Training and Development Journal, 41*(5), pp. 27-33.

Phillips, J. J. (1983). *Handbook of training evaluation and measurement methods.* Houston, TX: Gulf Publishing Co.

Phillips, J. J. (1991). *Handbook of training evaluation and measurement methods* (2nd ed.). Houston, TX: Gulf Publishing Co.

Popham, W. J. (Ed.). (1974). *Evaluation in education.* Berkeley, CA: McCutchan.

Poulet, R., & Moult, G. (1987, July). Putting values into evaluation. *Training and Development Journal, 41* (7), pp. 62-66.

Robinson, D. G., & Robinson, J. (1989). *Training for impact.* San Francisco: Jossey-Bass.

Robinson, D. G., & Robinson, J. (1989, August). Training for impact. *Training and Development Journal, 43* (8), pp. 34-42.

Sauter, J. (1980, April). Purchasing public sector executive development. *Training and Development Journal, 34* (4), pp. 92-98.

Sheppeck, M. A., & Cohen, S. L. (1985, November). Put a dollar value on your training programs. *Training and Development Journal, 39* (11), pp. 59-62.

Smeltzer, L. R. (1979, August). Do you really evaluate, or just talk about it?" *Training,* pp. 6-8.

Smith, J. E., & Merchant, S. (1990, January). Using competency exams for evaluating training. *Training and Development Journal, 44* (1), pp. 65-71.

Smith, P. L., & Wedman, J. F. (1988, Summer). Read-think-aloud protocols: A new data-source for formative evaluation. *Performance Improvement Quarterly, 1* (27), pp. 13-22.

Stufflebeam, D. L. (1974). Evaluation perspectives and procedures. In W. J. Popham (Ed.), _Evaluation in education._ Berkeley, CA: McCutchan.

Stufflebeam, D. L. (1974). Alternative approaches to educational evaluation: A self-study guide for educators. In W. J. Popham (Ed.), _Evaluation in education: Current applications._ Berkeley, CA: McCutchan.

Stufflebeam, D. L., Foley, W. J., Gephart, W.R., Guba, E. G., Hammond, R. L., Merriman, H. O., & Provus, M. M. (1971). _Educational evaluation and decision making._ Itasca, IL: Peacock.

Trapnell, G. (1984, May). Putting the evaluation puzzle together. _Training and Development Journal, 38_ (5), pp. 90-93.

Chapter 8

COMPETENCY-BASED TRAINING AT TEKTRONIX, INC.: THE MANAGERS-OF-MANAGERS PROGRAM

ORGANIZATION PROFILE

Tektronix (Tek), Inc., based in Beaverton, Oregon, was founded in 1946 by two Oregonians, Howard Vollum and Jack Murdock. They wanted to make an oscilloscope that could measure electrical signals rather than just display a signal, which was the state-of-the-art for such electrical test and measurement equipment at that time.

Starting with that one product, Tek has grown to a Fortune 500 company with annual sales of $1.3 billion and a catalog of more than 3,000 products. The company is among the major U.S. exporters, with about half of its sales going to international markets. There are about 11,000 employees worldwide; about 7,000 of them are based in Oregon.

Tek's goal is to apply its technologies to customer needs. Its technologies are focused in the areas of the acquisition, processing, and display of signals and images. Tek products are used in the research, design, production, testing, and service of electronics-based products and systems. The company has more than 50,000 customers, none of which commands more than 4 percent of its total sales. Manufacturers of electronic equipment make up the largest customer segment, followed by the computer industry and the government.

Tek has three core businesses: the Test and Measurement Group (Test and Measurement Tools), the Computer Graphics Group, and the Television Systems Group. The three core businesses are supported by centralized research and development and international operations through Tek Labs. Tek Labs is responsible for long-range applied research in key technical areas vital to Tek's future. Research and development are also carried out in the product divisions, but on a more product-focused and market-oriented basis. Tek Labs maintain close working relationships with the various divisions to sustain a synergy of research resources. Tek's founders were committed to excellence in its products and service and to its people. These commitments remain at Tek today.

PROGRAM OVERVIEW

Tektronix, like many of its competitors, was faced with new pressures—and new opportunities. Tek's markets were in a state of flux, competition was increasing, and profitability was under growing pressure. The Manager-of-Managers Program (MMP), which is described and discussed here, was created to address these and other issues by training a corps of highly skilled, knowledgeable, and already competent managers-of-managers. The MMP was not to be a traditional management training program, based on management principles which could apply to any one of a hundred industries. To the contrary, the MMP was designed to focus on the real problems and opportunities that Tek managers faced, and that they anticipated facing in the future of the company. The driving mechanism was a focus on the creation of the specific competence required of Tek managers-of-managers to meet and to successfully address challenges both internal and external to Tek.

FRONT-END NEEDS ANALYSIS, ASSESSMENT, AND PLANNING

Tek had been operating a multi-week management development program for middle managers that was widely believed to have outlived its usefulness. This program was based on the generic functions of management that one would typically find in a stable management environment where the job of managing remained virtually consistent from day to day. This clearly did not reflect the current business environment at Tek. A cross-organizational focus group was formed, an all-encompassing evaluation of the existing program for managers-of-managers was conducted, and a Tektronix-specific, competency-based management development effort was recommended. McLagan International, Inc., was contracted to drive the competency model process as well as to provide macro- and micro-design program expertise. A cross-organization executive level Management Steering Group initiated work on the competency model.

DEVELOPMENT OF THE COMPETENCY MODEL

The competence foundations for the MMP consisted of researching a company-wide competency model which was eventually to be known as the Model of Excellence for Managers-of-Managers (MEM). The competency model was developed with input from multiple levels and divisions.

Tek's MEM described a manager-of-manager's role in forwarding the Tek mission and strategy. It was created to:

1. Help guide the management performance, training, education, and development of all Tek employees who manage other managers in the company worldwide

2. Provide a common language and partial focus for the activities and systems that support management performance and development in the company, including management goal-setting, management performance appraisal, individual management development and career planning, management learning and development programs, and management promotions

3. Help influence the culture of Tektronix to support the organization's needs for the future

The MEM addressed three questions:

1. What projections can we make about Tek's future internal and external environments?

2. Given the internal and external environments, what results do managers-of-managers need to produce?

3. What knowledge, skills, and convictions do managers-of-managers need to develop over both the near- and long-term futures?

The resulting MEM consisted of three parts:

1. A list of assumptions about Tek's business context

2. Eleven key outputs that Tek managers-of-managers must consistently produce to fulfill their responsibility as key enablers of results in the business

3. Fifteen knowledge and skill areas (i.e., competencies) which analyses have identified as key to producing the eleven management outputs

The outputs and competencies were designed to be used as a frame of reference to help all of Tek's managers-of-managers and their superior managers to better discuss, support, improve and develop managerial performance. They are tools to be thoughtfully and constructively used as helpful bases for, but not as substitutes for, judgment and communication. In this manner, the MEM could be used to help focus management performance and training on behaviors and results that have high value for Tek's business success and for individual development.

The outputs managers were expected to produce included:

1. Business results: The work unit's products, services and technical/financial contributions to the organization

2. Unit plans: The strategic and operational plans

3. Work Environment: The psychological climate around and among workers, and the manager

4. Objectives: Individual employee goals and targets

5. Assessment of Intangibles: The recognition of critical factors, issues, trends, and opportunities before they are obvious to others

6. Leadership: Vision, purpose, and meaning for others

7. Managerial Talent: Managerial talent to staff the organization

8. Communication Linkage: The relationships and information channels that carry important information

9. Sense of Urgency: Effective influence over others' priorities

10. Feedback: Information to others about performance issues

11. Customer Relations: Ongoing trust and goodwill between Tektronix and its customers

Several assumptions about Tek over the five years subsequent to implementation of the MMP were identified. These assumptions included the following:

1. Emphasis on short- and long-term business results and accountability will increase the needs for business discipline and bottom-line orientation.

2. Decentralization and organization structure changes will bring accountability to lower levels.

3. It will be harder to retain key people due to competitive and entrepreneurial pull.

4. Managers will be called on to manage both rapid change and maturity.

5. Increased global competitive pressure and expanded international business will require Tektronix managers to expand capabilities.

6. Individual employee work values and priorities shifts will require greater flexibility for job satisfaction.

7. The economic environment will be an increasingly challenging force.

8. Increased worker participation and emphasis on flexible work designs will require different management interactions with workers.

9. Managers will need to embrace information technology both as an internal resource and as a means for achieving competitive advantage.

10. Competition and customer expectation will exert pressure on all Tek businesses to reduce cost and increase value added.

11. Technological change will accelerate.

To achieve the business output expectations (given the assumptions about the Tek management context), it was determined that managers-of-managers required conceptual, business, interpersonal, and technical competence. This conclusion was reached as a result of the research process, which is described later.

The conceptual competencies that resulted included strategic thinking, observation skill, problem analysis skill, risk assessment skill, and alternative generation. The business competencies featured Tektronix understanding, organizing skill, planning, business financial knowledge, and customer/market understanding. The interpersonal competencies included responsive communication skill, speaking skill, and influencing skill. Product knowledge and manufacturing/engineering understanding were the technical competencies. The fifteen competencies found in the MEM were defined in the language of the corporate culture and its environments. For each competency, behavior descriptions, or "action examples," of each competency for three levels of expertise and performance were included in order to make the meaning of the competency explicit to the users. The elements of the MEM are illustrated in Figure 8.1.

In the MEM, the levels of expertise are defined as follows:

1. *Basic:* The manager-of-managers will have a general understanding of the key competencies and will be able to function in simple, repetitive situations.

2. *Intermediate:* The manager-of-managers will have a deep understanding of the job dimensions and competencies; they will be able to function in a broad range of moderately difficult situations.

3. *Advanced:* The manager-of-managers will have a broad understanding of the job dimensions and competencies; they will be able to function in complex, varied situations. The manager-of-managers will be a model of subject-matter mastery and competence.

The MEM was developed using the following process:

1. *Environmental Analysis.* Using the judgment and collective experience of the Management Steering Group, a list of assumptions about the future context of management work at Tek was defined. These assumptions served as the backdrop for the remaining elements of the competency model. It was firmly believed that the model must be future-oriented. It was to reflect not only the current competencies needed by the target population, but also other competencies that were based upon the strategic directions of the company and management's best guesses about future challenges.

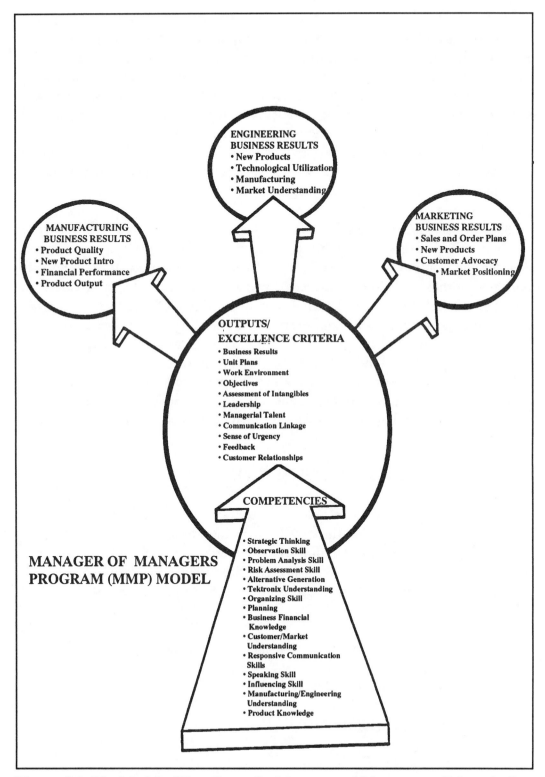

Figure 8.1: The Model of Excellence for Managers-of-Managers at Tektronix, Inc.

2. *Job Outputs or Results Analysis.* The management Steering Group was additionally tasked to define the results or "outputs" expected from managers-of-managers. In a facilitated brainstorming session, senior managers on the Steering Group were asked to list the results that were expected of managers-of-managers. Once an initial draft of the results was obtained, the Steering Group reviewed and added missing elements. Following completion of the list, once again using a process of facilitated brainstorming, the Steering Group identified the quality requirements or "excellence criteria" for each job output or result. The question "When this output is produced in an excellent manner, what is present?" was repeatedly asked until the excellence criteria for each output were identified.

3. *Competency Identification.* With the job results or outputs and their quality or excellence criteria defined, the Steering Group was asked to identify, for each output area, ten high-output or exemplary producers among the ranks of managers-of-managers, or those individual manager-of-managers who consistently produced an output in an excellent fashion. The high-output managers-of-managers were asked to write stories containing behavioral examples of when they had produced an output. The stories were content-analyzed and a list of competencies was developed. The Steering Group reviewed the emergent list of competencies and reflected that some key competencies needed for the future had not been reflected in the behavioral examples of the exemplary managers. Thus, a few future-oriented competencies were added to the list, based on the judgment of the members of the Steering Group.

PLANNING THE MMP CURRICULUM

Once the competency model was developed and endorsed by Tek's operating units and senior management, the MMP curriculum design process was initiated. Throughout the process of building the competency model and working in a collaborative fashion with the Management Steering Group, a number of key business themes emerged. These business themes became the foci for the MMP curriculum:

- The Tek Manager-of-Managers as a Change Agent

- Managing for Profitability

- Managing for the Market

- Managing Technology

- Leadership and Influence

- Managing for Manufacturing Excellence

- Managing People, Organization, and Work Environment

- Managing for the Future; Integration

Training for the specific competencies contained in the MEM was embedded in each of the modules. At the front-end stage of the design for each module, a cross-organizational design team, which was composed of subject-matter experts and key members of the senior management team, identified highly specific results which were expected of managers-of-managers and the competencies they needed in order to produce those results. Thus, for each module centered around a key business or functional focus, a subset of the MEM was identified to guide the development of specific elements within the module.

CURRICULUM INTEGRATION WITHIN THE ORGANIZATION

Top-level executive support for the curriculum and the MMP was achieved through the design and implementation of an overview of each of the manager-of-managers program modules. More than 50 of Tek's top executives were invited to participate in a one-day executive overview of the MMP. This overview included a detailed review of the critical content of each module, and senior executives were provided an exposure to a few of the key conviction-shaping sessions.

Curriculum integration within the organization below the manager-of-managers level was not attempted until some time after the implementation of the MMP. This was due, in part, to resource constraints and prevailing business conditions. About four years following implementation of the MMP, a Leadership Development Process (LDP) for first-level managers was conceived and implemented. Some competencies included in the MMP were also included in the LDP. The competencies included in the LDP were, of course, interpreted relative to the role and responsibilities of first-level managers. The leadership model used in the MMP was also used in the LDP.

INSTRUCTIONAL DESIGN STRATEGY

The MMP successfully integrated management training with business needs and results using a strategy of high involvement of people throughout Tek. Each instructional module was designed and continuously updated by a separate team made up of Tek line managers, staff designers, the best external subject-matter experts available, and a Tek executive sponsor. This group of persons was called the "Module Design Team."

The executive sponsor for each module was also present each time the module was delivered. This design strategy resulted in executive support for and input into the MMP while these activities simultaneously educated Tek executives in state-of-the-art research and thought on the module topics. This meant that both the trainees and the trainers were jointly involved in real-time, mutual competence development.

Virtually every Tek executive at the vice president level and above has participated on a design team, including the Tek President/Chief Executive Officer and Tek's Executive Vice President. Module Design Teams not only created the initial module designs, but the Design Teams also met after the delivery of each of the modules to formatively evaluate it and to create updates and changes for subsequent deliveries of the module. An important result was that a dynamic, rather than a static or once-and-forever, design approach was successfully adopted. As a result, MMP training was always up-to-date.

IMPLEMENTATION ACTIVITIES

The MMP was administered at the time by Tek's Corporate Human Resources Planning and Development Department. Between 180 and 200 managers-of-managers participated in the program at a given time. Participants attended eight, one-week sessions over a two-year period.

During the sessions, competence acquisition occurred in a wide variety of ways. The instructional activities included a high level of learner participation and experiences. Cases, simulations, exercises, and discussions focusing on actual Tek businesses and issues were used. The training delivery strategy also incorporated the use of discussions with Tek executives on critical Tek issues. A team approach was used for planning and interpreting ideas and information from an individual manager's situation. Computer-based simulations provided the participating managers an opportunity to examine their individual strengths and areas where improvement was needed.

Participants were required to complete pre-training work and post-session activities. This strategy was used to establish strong linkages between a manager's work setting and competence acquisition during the formal training experience. Pre-training work included personal development tasks such as individual assessments, reading, case studies, "shadowing" an executive for a day, and meetings with a participant's staff to work on real Tek problems and projects. The MMP faculty included experts from inside and outside Tek. The sessions also included videotaped interviews with Tek executives and managers. The instructional activities incorporated the use of speakers from other successful companies who shared their experiences and insights. The external speakers also included visiting customers and suppliers. This provided a unique opportunity for MMP participants to interact directly with persons whose input, feedback, and satisfaction were crucial to Tek's business success.

Action-oriented assignments were made during each session. These assignments were implemented by the managers-of-managers between the MMP sessions over a two-year period. Each session ended with goal-setting and developmental planning by each participant. The program developers and managers noted that this strategy resulted in breaking down distinctions and barriers which are frequently drawn between "work" and "training." Participants saw the MMP as "work," and as a place where they could bring problems, and receive advice and help from their peers, executives, and external experts. In turn, Tek management clearly observed the transfer of the training results to a manager's job. The pre-training work and the post-session module meetings and assessments resulted in the entire Tek organization "going to school" with the MMP participants.

Beginning in the fourth module, and continuing through the end of the program, the instructional strategy required the MMP participants to complete a Business Impact Project (BIP). BIPs required General Manager approval and work on real Tek business issues generally beyond the participants' regular job expectations. Examples of BIPs that were undertaken include creating a Tek Labs European Design Center, the development of an information/control system for a start-up environment, the development of alternative distribution methods, and a project to reduce time-to-market for products containing software. Positive business results that would not have otherwise occurred were realized in many areas of Tek's business, and these ranged from marketing to technical improvements. The BIP instructional strategy both developed and reinforced participants' competence, and it brought timely business issues to the MMP. Tek executives could see real impacts of the MMP on Tek's businesses.

Finally, the instructional design included a "wellness" program that was integrated with other topics. Wellness was integrated into each MMP module through stretch and relaxation breaks and informative presentations on personal health and wellness topics. An external health maintenance organization was used to deliver this component of the MMP. Assessments and personal consultations on a variety of health issues—including risk factors, nutrition, exercise, and stress—were offered. As a result, the participants exhibited enhanced awareness of the importance of personal health issues, and they made personal commitments to health maintenance action plans.

EVALUATION OF THE MMP

Multiple levels of evaluation of the MMP were undertaken. A version of Kirkpatrick's four-level evaluation model (see chapter 7) was used to conceptualize an MMP evaluation plan. The formal strategies that were used are described below.

Reactions to the MMP. Participant feedback on each instructional segment was collected by using a format called "Notes in Brief." Additionally, each instructional week had its own participant reaction questionnaire, which was completed by the participating managers at the end of the week. The feedback was consolidated and discussed by the instructional design team, and adjustments were made to the instructional program prior to the next offering of the intervention.

Achievement of the competencies. A management competence assessment process was constructed and administered at several stages of each manager's participation in the MMP. The competence assessment process included collecting data for each manager from the participating manager as a self-assessment, a group of the manager's peers, a group of subordinates, and the manager's boss. This process was administered prior to a manager's participation (in order to establish a competency baseline for the participant), again halfway through the MMP, at the end of the program, and six months following a manager's completion of the MMP. Early in the implementation of the MMP, significant performance improvements were evident in three areas: competence in developing a customer and market focus, financial competence, and competence in product knowledge.

Application of the competencies. As part of the pre-training work prior to each module, the participants were asked to think through and remember any applications they had made of the competencies that had been acquired from previously completed module(s). The MMP participants discussed the key learning points and what application they had made of them.

Organization impacts of competency acquisition. As described earlier, a Business Impact Project was required of all MMP participants. These projects were intended to have significant impacts on the Tek businesses which were represented by the MMP participants and, in some cases, by the entire Tek organization. In order to ensure maximum organization impact, each project required approval by a General Manager. Business Impact Project reports included cost/benefit analyses of the project's impacts on Tek businesses.

In addition to the evaluation approaches discussed above, periodic interviews of the MMP participants, their bosses, and their subordinates were conducted throughout the life of the MMP. These interviews served as data collection opportunities on the learning that resulted from the managers' participation, the applications of the competencies that were included in the program, and the organization impacts that were realized.

Overall, the evaluation results for the MMP strongly supported the statement that the program achieved its objectives. It was also determined that significant organization impacts were realized Tek-wide.

ACKNOWLEDGEMENT

This chapter was coauthored by Karin Kolodziejski and David D. Dubois. Karin Kolodziejski is the Director, Strategic Human Resource Programs, Tektronix, Inc., Wilsonville, Oregon.

Chapter 9

COMPETENCY-BASED LEADERSHIP DEVELOPMENT AT THE DEFENSE MAPPING AGENCY: U.S. DEPARTMENT OF DEFENSE

ORGANIZATION PROFILE

This chapter describes an exemplary competency-based leadership development program for supervisors, managers, and executives at the Defense Mapping Agency (DMA). The program is a key element of a long-range effort to enhance leadership competence at the DMA. The DMA is an independent agency of the U.S. Department of Defense (DOD). DMA's mission is to provide support on matters concerning mapping, charting, and geodesy to the Office of the Secretary of Defense; the Military Departments, the Chairman, Joint Chiefs of Staff and Joint Staff; the Unified and Specified Command; the Defense Agencies, and other Federal Government Departments and Agencies.

The DMA, which is headquartered in Fairfax, Virginia, is a single-mission organization committed to providing mapping, geodetic, and cartographic products and services in support of national defense and other U.S. interests, treaties, and international agreements. DMA employs 8,000 military and civilian career employees. Its principal production facilities include field units located in Brookmont, Maryland; Reston, Virginia; and St. Louis, Missouri. Three strategic factors that contribute significantly to DMA's success are its responsiveness to diverse customer requirements throughout the world, its overall productivity, and the timeliness of its products and services.

PROGRAM OVERVIEW

The events surrounding the conceptualization, design, development, and implementation of the program will be described. At the time of publication, the final stages of the integrated leadership curriculum were being implemented Agency-wide within DMA. The authors will describe the current state-of-the-practice with the project products and will present preliminary results. Additional program components planned for the near-term future will also be discussed.

The project products were conceptualized and developed as a partnership among DMA senior, mid-level managers, and first-level supervisors and the Agency's Human Resources Directorate. Technical and program development support were provided by Human Technology, Inc. (HT). The DMA Project Leader was Edmund R. Karoly, the Agency's Chief of Training, and Alex Douds was the Project Director for HT.

Work on the leadership development training program was initiated at a time of tremendous change for DMA. The rapid pace of change under which DMA operates is illustrated by the following:

- Implementation of a state-of-the-art hardware and software Digital Production System (DPS), bringing far-reaching changes in production equipment, procedures, and facilities. These changes necessitated a comprehensive DPS training program inventory in the early stages of implementation.

- Organization downsizing throughout DMA as a part of the overall DOD realignment resulting from changes in the former Soviet and Eastern European theaters

- The unexpected requirement to provide support for the Persian Gulf war. This support was unprecedented in scope and quantity of the products required. Thousands of products were produced in a round-the-clock, multi-shift operation. The Agency received special recognition from the Secretary of Defense and other senior DOD officials, including the Chairman of the Joint Chiefs of Staff, General Colin Powell

- DMA's continuing requirement to support the drug interdiction effort

Given the rapid changes evident in the DMA environment, the Agency intended at the outset that its subsequent efforts to address agency leadership needs would achieve the following objectives:

1. Establish and maintain a climate of continuous improvement and responsiveness to customer requirements through effective leadership at all levels of the DMA, conducive to achieving a high level of individual, team, and organization productivity

2. Enhance individual leadership competencies to facilitate execution of the Agency's mission and goals, with maximum concern for product and service quality

3. Ensure a rapid and effective transition to new DMA production technology and to ensure optimal support to DMA military customers during times of war and peace

4. Ensure effective transition to new leadership in the decade ahead

Given this climate, DMA leaders focused their attention more on the leadership requirements than on the management attributes of their supervisors, managers, and executives. They placed their emphases on the identification of a set of future-oriented leadership competencies that would help their Agency develop leaders who could meet both present and future leadership challenges.

The overall plan for the design, development, and implementation of the DMA leadership development agenda concurs with the Strategic Systems Model on which this book is based. That is, they conducted front-end macro-level needs analysis, assessment, and planning; competency model development and a micro-level assessment of employees' needs, based upon the model; curriculum planning; design, development and implementation of the instructional program; and formative and summative evaluations. The next section of this chapter includes a summary of the front-end macro-needs analysis, assessment, and planning process employed by the DMA.

FRONT-END NEEDS ANALYSIS, ASSESSMENT, AND PLANNING

Prior to conducting a needs assessment, a review of existing DMA supervisory and management training was conducted. The results were typical of many private and public sector organizations. Below is a summary characterization of training prior to the development of the DMA Leadership Development Program:

- There was no DMA-wide, integrated training and development effort for Agency supervisors, managers, and executives. Some organizations supported management and supervisory training more actively than others.

- Supervisors and managers generally participated in training sporadically, beyond an initial introduction to personnel management training courses. One organization center offered a course to their supervisors on managing for productivity. Some individuals had attended a number of courses during their careers, while others had attended none or only one course.

- Timing of training was generally linked to new responsibilities, but some did not attend training other than selected courses to maintain state-of-the-art technical knowledge and skills. On occasion, individuals on their own initiative obtained Agency support to participate in special graduate-level executive programs at local universities.

- Training was focused on traditional supervisory and managerial topics, with limited focus on leadership areas. Selected mid-level and senior managers participated in U.S. Office of Personnel Management courses at its Federal Executive Institute and Executive Seminar Centers, and in other courses.

- Training was offered by numerous vendors, each reflecting different models, principles, and philosophy. Training of supervisors and managers had no apparent linkage to Agency corporate values and priorities.

- Application of learning on the job was not monitored closely, making impact of training difficult to ascertain. There was no evidence of a work-culture impact or lasting behavioral change as a result of training.

In summary, there was no planned, integrated training program for DMA leaders, and courses focused more on supervision and managerial concepts than on leadership. There was no corporate plan of training for Agency leadership.

Four significant events at the DMA are critical to understanding the evolution of the leadership development training program.

First, DMA recognized a need for, and consequently established, a strategic human resources plan with extensive input from senior leaders within the organization. DMA conducted an Agency-wide work force climate survey. The response rate was significant (93% responded). Two areas that were identified for improvement included Leadership Development and Career Management. A separate but integrated program to improve career management in the Agency is also underway.

Second, a planning meeting was held in the Summer of 1989 involving key leaders in the Agency, including the Director of the Systems Center, all production organization technical directors, and the Agency Deputy Director for Human Resources (Director of Personnel at the time). This meeting resulted in the first Agency-wide strategic plan for the development of DMA's human resources. The plan was quickly codified as a DMA policy statement, and it was endorsed by DMA's Director. The policy outlined Agency philosophy and priorities on the training, education, and career development of DMA employees. It delineated, for the first time, the principle of priority training as a "necessary cost of doing business." This policy served as the framework for establishing a new training, budgeting, and funding system which protects nondiscretionary (Priority One) Agency training requirements, including Leadership Development.

Third, early and continuous support from the Director and Deputy Director of the Agency was secured. They have demonstrated their support visibly and often throughout the design, development, and early implementation process of the leadership initiative.

Fourth, virtually every other key DMA senior leader has contributed prominently to ensure a fully relevant, responsive program. Prior to 1989, as indicated earlier, DMA did not have an integrated leadership training program. Management training courses did not adequately convey DMA leadership values and, consequently, they did not prepare DMA leaders for the future challenges confronting the Agency. Consequently, DMA created the Leadership Development Program (LDP) to address this shortfall, as well as to respond to employee concerns expressed in the work force survey. The goal of the LDP, in short, is to develop and retain top-quality leaders into the next century.

As you read subsequent portions of this chapter, you should recall that the DMA top leadership planned, *from project inception*, to design and develop a conceptually- and content-integrated leadership development curriculum *across all management levels of the DMA*. All DMA leaders were to be given training drawn from a single DMA-endorsed model for Agency leadership. This deliberate attention to vertical curriculum integration significantly contributed to the ultimate efficiency and overall design effectiveness of the LDP.

In summary, a front-end needs analysis, a well-defined concept of what leadership meant within the strategic emphases of the DMA (projected over a realistic time frame), a thoroughly researched competency model, competence and needs assessments of the target populations, and unconditional support from senior DMA leaders rank high among the remaining critical keys to the success of the LDP. Although not specifically analyzed in the program's research, it is also reasonable to assume that external and internal macro- change prompted the need to ensure a highly competent leadership to guide the Agency through difficult and challenging times.

The competency, or leadership, performance model was the first major product that was needed for creating the remaining elements of the LDP. Figure 9.1 includes the principal leadership competencies from the model, and a sample of the subordinate competencies and the job behaviors and activities that further define each of the principal competencies.

The research process and the elements of the leadership competency (or performance) model are described below.

DEVELOPMENT OF THE DMA LEADERSHIP COMPETENCY MODEL

The Agency named its leadership competency model the "DMA Leadership Framework (LF)." The LF describes what leaders (in the collective sense) should do and the knowledge, skills, and other personal characteristics they need to effectively lead within the DMA organization. DMA senior leaders defined leadership as "the ability to create a vision for the organization and to inspire in others the trust and commitment to work together to accomplish it." In this sense, "leaders" are distinguished from "managers," yet they are complementary roles. Organizations need both to flourish.

Managers concentrate on making sure that day-to-day operations run smoothly. Leaders, on the other hand, provide vision to the organization, and they show its workers how what they do contributes to achieving the organization's strategic goals. The LF, or the leadership competency model, which resulted from extensive research, specified the dimensions (i.e., principal competencies), subdimensions (i.e., subordinate competencies), and the actions (i.e., the behaviors and activities) of leadership at the DMA.

LF "dimensions" are the principal competencies needed for exemplary leadership performance, and they are critical for success in management positions at *all* levels of the DMA organization. Certain principal competencies are more critical in some managerial levels than in others. Overall, however, all of the principal competencies are essential to success. The LF, or DMA, competency model which resulted from

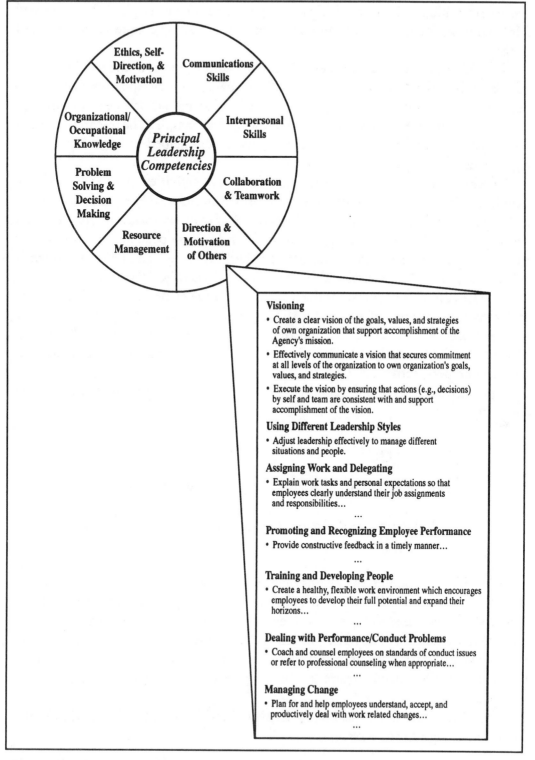

Figure 9.1: DMA Leadership Competency Model with an Illustrated Competency

the research included eight principal competencies. For example, "Direction and Motivation of Others" is one of the eight principal leadership competencies included in the LF.

LF "subdimensions" are the key subordinate competencies of the eight principal competencies (the "dimensions") that DMA managers must possess in order to demonstrate effective leadership performance. "Visioning" is a competency subordinate to the "Direction and Motivation of Others," for example. The research revealed there were a total of 42 subordinate competencies that helped to further define the eight principal competencies within the LF.

"Actions" are the specific job behaviors and activities that elaborate the "subdimensions" or subordinate competencies within the LF. For example, "Create a clear vision of the goals, values, and strategies of own organization that supports accomplishment of the Agency's mission" is a leadership action that would be expected when the manager demonstrated the "Visioning" competency, which is subordinate to the "Direction and Motivation of Others" Competency.

The LF, therefore, represents the leadership competencies and the job behaviors and activities required of successful supervisors, mid-level managers, and senior managers DMA-wide. The LF, and the methods which were used to develop it, provide a mechanism to have "ONE DMA" (as the senior managers mentioned) from a leadership perspective.

The methodology for developing the DMA/LF required completion of the following steps:

1. Development of a preliminary leadership framework

2. Refinement of the preliminary leadership framework

3. Validation of the revised leadership framework with DMA senior management

We will now examine the details of each action step.

The U.S. Office of Personnel Management's "Management Excellence Framework (MEF)" was used as one source document for the development of a preliminary leadership framework. The MEF, which spells out the behaviors and characteristics of effective Federal managers, was itself based on ten years of research in the Federal environment. Exemplary private and other public sector programs were also researched.

The preliminary DMA leadership framework which resulted departed from the MEF in two significant ways:

1. It was enhanced to reflect state-of-the-art leadership concepts, based on a review of selected current leadership literature and an analysis of outstanding private sector leadership development programs.

2. It was developed to specifically address the DMA environment, factors, and needs. It was also based upon senior DMA leader interviews and a review of DMA documents. Existing DMA courses, the DMA work force survey, and DMA's current succession planning guidance all offered useful data on the leadership demands described by DMA leaders.

The books that were reviewed for the leadership literature review process met three criteria: They were all written by nationally-recognized leadership experts, were considered state-of-the-art in the leadership field, and were published within three years of DMA project inception. The authors included Gary Yukl, Paul Hersey and Kenneth Blanchard, Warren Bennis, James Kouzes and Barry Posner, Robert Waterman, and Noel Tichy and Mary Anne Devanna.

Interviews were conducted with representatives of selected private sector organizations with outstanding leadership development programs. These are programs business leaders recognized as exemplary. The private sector organizations included General Electric, IBM, Xerox, Center for Creative Leadership (University of Maryland office), and Ford Motor Company. These telephone interviews revealed that different private sector organizations have their own unique way of developing leaders and that there is a wide degree of diversity among these leadership programs. The contractor, with specific guidance from the DMA program manager and the Agency's Deputy Director for Human Resources, conducted thirteen interviews with twenty-six key DMA senior managers. The senior managers offered their views on the leadership values and behaviors needed now and in the future at DMA. They focused on what values and behaviors they wished to see addressed in the DMA LDP. The interview was carefully structured to ensure consistency in its protocol and outcomes.

Specifically, they considered:

• Current and future changes at DMA

• How those changes will affect first-level supervisors, mid-level managers, and senior managers

• Leadership values and behaviors needed at DMA

- Possible seminar topics for senior management training

- The possible impact of a LDP at DMA

In brief, the senior managers who were interviewed portrayed the changes occurring at DMA as massive and revolutionary. These changes included a revolutionized production system and processes; abrupt transition from decentralized to centralized functional organization alignments; resource constraints; increased external competition (e.g., companies are appearing that can do the work only DMA could once do); future changes in the mix of products DMA deals with; current change in the nature of the work, with less exercise of cartographic judgment and a more workstation operator mode; and finally, a trend toward increased diversity of the work force. Senior managers indicated that DMA's current environment of rapid change would require that its supervisors and mid-level managers possess leadership as well as technical skills at all organization levels. Senior managers also indicated that their challenge would be to work together to create a corporate approach to cope with constant change, and to provide leadership under those conditions.

The major points made by senior managers about differences which could be anticipated in DMA as a result of the LDP included:

- It will contribute to building one DMA; managers will work more as a team with a common set of interests and goals; everyone will understand the direction DMA is going and why.

- There will be agreement and consensus on core values at the top of the organization and senior managers will be modeling those values.

- There will be recognition that paying attention to people and to production are not incompatible and that, while both are required of supervisors and mid-level managers, results come from taking care of people.

- Leadership skills will be rewarded as well as technical skills.

- A content-integrated program of courses will be provided for supervisors, managers, and executives.

- Initial supervisory training will be provided to non-supervisors.

These expectations could also serve as research hypotheses to be tested and reported at a later time when an overall evaluation of the LDP would be completed.

The second step above included the refinement of the preliminary framework to reflect the DMA environment more concretely. To accomplish this, four panels of DMA first-level supervisors and mid-level managers (42 persons in all) reviewed and suggested changes to the preliminary framework. These panels represented all major headquarter elements and all DMA Components. Based upon the work of these panels, the framework was revised.

The third step was the validation of the revised framework with DMA senior management. DMA senior managers met twice to review the revised version. Their charge was to make sure that the framework accurately reflected all the leadership values and concepts they consider desirable for DMA. Based on the first meeting, the framework was revised and was then circulated among the same group. A second meeting was held to review the revised version as a final check.

CURRICULUM PLANNING

In order to complete the curriculum design and planning phase of the work, DMA and HT first conducted a training needs survey. The survey enabled DMA managers at all levels to indicate where leadership requirements and needs were greatest at DMA. The survey items included the 42 subdimensions (or subordinate-level competencies) that were included in the LF. Based on the results, analysis identified which of the 42 leadership competencies were the most critical to address in what later became the core courses and topical workshops in the curriculum. Thus, a curriculum plan was developed by directly using the survey analysis results. The leadership competencies selected for inclusion in the curriculum were the basis for what eventually became DMA's training model for the LDP.

All 42 leadership competencies, of course, have value for DMA managers. The survey results made it possible to identify the leadership competencies where training had the greatest potential to improve DMA leadership effectiveness.

Three groups of DMA managers were surveyed: first-level supervisors; mid-level managers; and senior or executive managers.

In the survey, supervisors, mid-level managers, and senior executives rated each leadership competency on:

- Its importance for success in their jobs, and the

- Level of skill needed compared to the level of skill they currently possessed.

Senior executives not only rated the leadership competencies in terms of their own job demands, but they also gave their assessment of the job requirements and needs of supervisors and mid-level managers across DMA. As a result, two different perspectives on the skill levels of supervisors and mid-level managers were obtained: the self-assessments at each level, and the opinions of the senior executives regarding their subordinate managers' and supervisors' levels of skill.

Top-level support is critical to the success of any leadership development program; organizations with outstanding leadership programs consistently identify this as an essential element. Top management needs to be actively involved in developing the program and in defining its focus and its aims. And senior managers need to exemplify the leadership qualities the program addresses.

As a result, the survey analysis focused on the perspective of senior managers and their assessment of the significance, required skill level, and mid- and first-level managers' training needs, in each leadership area. The leadership areas selected for training were those identified by senior managers as top or mid-priority. Where the "self" reports differed, senior manager assessments prevailed. However, during design and development of training, special emphasis was given to those competencies that both the senior manager and subordinate manager agreed were top priority.

As a result of the analysis, the curriculum plan for DMA's LDP contained two major components:

- Three core leadership courses, one for each level of management, and

- A series of topical workshops. (One- or two-day seminars offering in-depth study of a specific leadership topic focused on special interests and needs of DMA leaders. Topical workshops are intended to supplement the core courses.)

The three core courses would be designed to address the competencies identified as highest priority for the particular level of management. For example, twelve top-priority competencies were identified on which to base the core course for first-level supervisors:

- Accepting the Leadership Role

- Being Action-Oriented and Results-Focused

- Keeping Employees Informed

- Keeping Higher Level Management Informed

- Listening

- Being Sensitive to Others

- Team Building

- Empowering Employees through Participation

- Assigning Work and Delegating

- Promoting and Recognizing Employee Performance

- Dealing with Performance/Conduct Problems

- Training and Developing People

The curriculum plan also called for a series of topical workshops for the three levels of DMA managers. Each workshop is built around one or more competencies identified as middle priority by DMA senior managers.

Workshops designed for each level are presented as separate interventions. However, some topics are presented for more than one management level. Figure 9.2 shows which topical workshops will be offered to which level of manager. In some cases (Time Management, for example) the same workshop may be appropriate for all three levels. In others, material may need to be tailored to a management level because of the unique requirements of that management level. For example, a quick review of the table in Figure 9.2 (on the following page) reveals that the topical workshop on "Persuasive Speaking" is a mid-priority need for all three levels of management. This suggests that a workshop will be designed, developed, delivered, and evaluated which addresses this perceived need for all management levels. Several curriculum issues immediately surface: How similar will the content be across the three subpopulations of DMA management? To what degree should the content be integrated across the subpopulations? What perspective should be taken for each level of management? Do we need one, two, or three separate topical workshops to satisfy this need? Similar analyses can and are being performed for the competencies identified for the core courses.

On the other hand, you will note that the "Writing" competency was identified as a mid-priority need for only the mid-level managers. This implies that a topical workshop on competence in writing appropriate for the demands of mid-level managers within the DMA environment would satisfy the organization need. Curriculum analyses of this type help in creating curriculum and course content alternatives that maximize both their efficiency and effectiveness. A major result, among several others, is cost savings.

Topical Workshop	First-Level Supervisor	Mid-Level Manager	Senior Manager
Quality Leadership Skills	√	√	
Conflict Management	√		√
Managing Change	√		√
Time Management	√	√	√
Persuasive Speaking	√	√	√
Managing Technological Change		√	
Program Management		√	
Visionary Leadership		√	√
Writing		√	
Performance Management		√	
Self-Development		√	
DMA's External Environment			√

Figure 9.2: DMA Topical Workshops by Management Level

When the curriculum plan was completed, the core courses for supervisors and mid-level managers were developed and implemented. At publication, 75% of the supervisors and nearly 50% of the mid-level managers target groups had attended training.

Criteria for the selection of employees who would attend training were specifically linked to the needs assessment process. Supervisors were identified as only those individuals who had direct supervisory responsibility (including performance review) over subordinate employees or direct reports, regardless of grade level; Senior Executive Service employees were not included.

On the other hand, the selection criteria for the mid-level managers course went beyond admitting those persons traditionally defined as mid-level managers (i.e., leaders who supervise subordinate supervisors). The course also included program managers who do not have direct report supervisors, but who occupy key leadership positions. These individuals manage major Agency programs involving oversight and technical direction of extensive resources.

The inclusion of program managers in this category is consistent with the Agency's goal of establishing leadership awareness at all levels. DMA plans to initiate individualized training to all employees to enhance self-awareness, to build strong interpersonal skills, and to empower them to accept personal responsibility for leadership on the job.

The core course for executives is in the early stages of design. In the next section you will learn about the design and development techniques that were used to translate the curriculum plan into learner-centered, competency-based learning interventions.

TRAINING DESIGN, DEVELOPMENT, IMPLEMENTATION, AND TRAINING TRANSFER STRATEGIES

In order to translate the leadership competencies to competency-based learning interventions, the following steps were completed for each course:

1. Conduct an organization context analysis for each of the competencies.

2. Organize the top-priority competencies into major topics (content clusters).

3. Prepare a design guide.

4. Develop instructional materials (e.g. videotapes, instructor's guide, participant course book, etc.).

5. Preview course with senior leadership.

6. Conduct pilot tests of instructional materials.

7. Develop the final version of the instructional materials.

8. Develop and implement a strategy to reinforce transfer of the leadership skills to the job.

For illustrative purposes, we will briefly discuss how each step was implemented in the design and development of the core course for first-level supervisors. The first activity, context analyses, involves collecting data from the target population on how each competency is actually applied in the day-to-day job. In the DMA case, interviews were conducted with a representative group of DMA first-level supervisors to determine answers to questions such as:

• What are the job situations in which the competency is used?

• What are the difficult aspects of applying this competency?

• How do you know that you are performing this competency well?

Such job-specific data enables the instructional designer to target the learning toward what's really important to the target population. This information is used to translate the competency to specific performance objectives—relevant to a competency—for the participants. It also provides valuable data useful for creating context-specific examples, case studies, and other items that are useful in the instructional process.

The next activity organized the top-priority competencies into major topics, based on what was learned from the context analysis process. It involved organizing the principal or top-priority competencies into logical, topical groupings for the purposes of training design.

Figure 9.3 includes a section from the instructional content design document that was prepared for the first-level supervisor core course. This example illustrates the design concept for the "Team Development" content cluster, and the "Interpersonal Communication Skills" topic within that content cluster. The leadership competencies that will be developed for this topic are identified first. For this instructional segment, the competencies "Being Sensitive to Others" and "Listening" are critical prerequisite or foundation competencies that must be acquired by the participants before they can acquire the process competencies:

• Empowering Others Through Participation

• Keeping Employees Informed

• Keeping Higher Level Management Informed

This particular document also includes a discussion of the content for which instruction will be developed, and how that content is related to competency acquisition.

The next step involved preparing a detailed instructional design guide. The DMA design guide described how each major topic is broken down into instructional modules. Each module describes the training outcome, the performance objectives (which were derived from the context analyses), and the learning activities that would ensure the learner achieves the performance objectives and subsequently acquires the leadership competencies.

Instructional Content Design

Content Cluster: **Team Development**

Topics: **Interpersonal Communication Skills**

Leadership Competencies to be Developed

- **Listening**
- **Being sensitive to others**
- **Empowering others through participation**
- **Keeping employees informed**
- **Keeping higher level management informed**

Supervisors must be aware of, and respond to, the needs of people who work for them. They must understand individual perferences and how those preferences affect the way people communicate, resolve problems, and organize their work. . .

Figure 9.3: Excerpt from the Instructional Content Design for the First-Level Supervisor Intervention

The learning activities for the DMA first-level supervisor core course encompassed a full array of learner-centered instructional techniques: videotape exercises, self-assessment questionnaires, role-play, case study, practical exercises, simulations, and critical incidents. The instructional strategies emphasized a highly interactive, action-oriented approach to competency acquisition.

Next, the instructional materials were developed consistent with the design guide specifications. Once the materials were ready, the course was reviewed with senior DMA leaders. This consisted of a one-day overview of the significant instructional components of the course.

Two pilot test offerings of the course were completed. The course contents, the emphases which were given to each course element, and the materials were evaluated. Needed revisions were made, and the delivery of the course was implemented.

The designers created and implemented a training transfer strategy for the core courses. The objective of the strategy was to reinforce the transfer of the leadership competencies acquired during the training experience to the job. For example, for the first-level supervisor core course, those who attended the course and their managers completed a leadership self-assessment prior to the class. On the first day of class, participating supervisors reviewed these data and identified their priority leadership developmental needs. These needs represented areas of focus during and following the class. Consulting with their managers about these development needs following the class was encouraged.

The training transfer strategy also included the delivery of a half-day orientation for the participating supervisor's managers (i.e., DMA mid-level managers) regarding the leadership competencies that would be acquired by the first-level supervisors. The mid-level managers were directed on the numerous ways they could positively support the competency transfer process on the job. Finally, on the last day of class, participating supervisors developed specific action plans to describe how they wanted to apply the skills back on the job.

Similarly, a training transfer strategy was developed for the Mid-level Managers Course. Senior leaders play a much more active, hands-on role in the Mid-level Managers Course. Key leaders from production and mission support (i.e., Acquisition, Human Resources) organizations compose a senior panel on the first night of the one-week residential course. These leaders provide insight into macro-changes confronting the Agency, share information on DMA Quality Program values and goals, and discuss their perspective of an informal "leadership covenant." The covenant focuses on key elements of the Leadership Framework, which are considered most essential for success.

During the course, the mid-level managers—in addition to building leadership skills—reflect on this covenant in their core leadership teams (CLTs). On the final day of the course, the teams make final presentations to the Director of the Agency, making commitments to honor the "contract" and to surface obstacles to attaining its terms.

The Director not only responds to these concerns, but also prepares them in hard-copy form, including the question-and-answer exchanges. Once prepared, they are presented by the Director to the Agency's top leaders. This complete cycling-through of the communication process and subsequent corrective actions have served to put "teeth" in the principles of the course.

EVALUATION OF THE LDP

A plan was prepared to evaluate the LDP. The plan was based upon the four-level Kirkpatrick evaluation model (see chapter 7) for its design. The first level that was planned required obtaining the participants' reactions to the training experience; data were collected using a detailed end-of-course questionnaire. At the second level, an evaluation of the learning that occurred during the course was also measured by the end-of-course instrument. The third level of evaluation specified the collection of data relative to the changes in the trainees' behavior while on the job. A post-training questionnaire completed by the trainees and their immediate supervisors was used to collect these data, in addition to interviews conducted with a sample of trainees and their immediate supervisors. At the fourth level, measuring organization impacts, the evaluation was completed using the post-training questionnaire data and economic data provided by the agency.

All levels of evaluation were completed. For the first level of evaluation—the participants' initial reactions to the first-level supervisor core course—an end-of-course questionnaire was used to ascertain the participants' perceptions of the following elements:

- Overall satisfaction with the core course

- Contribution of the course to professional development

- Course costs versus benefits

- General comments about the course

The Level I evaluation data base included responses from 373 graduates of the first seventeen offerings of the course. The findings were as follows:

1. An overwhelming majority of the participants were very satisfied with the course.

2. A majority of the participants felt the course made a significant contribution to their professional development and felt the course benefits far outweighed its costs.

3. The participants' written comments about the course were extremely positive with regard to the personal learning and value of the course, and with regard to the quality of instruction.

Level II evaluation data—participant learning that occurred during the course—was also measured via the end-of-course questionnaire. Participants were asked their perceptions of the following:

- Knowledge and skill gains, by topic

- Value of each topic to job performance

Again, based on the 373 responses across seventeen course offerings, the findings showed that:

1. The participants reported substantial perceived learning gains in all topic areas.

2. The perceived value of the course content to job success was very high.

Level III evaluation data—changes in trainees' on-the-job behavior—was collected using two methods. First, a post-training questionnaire asked trainees and their immediate supervisors to provide their perceptions of the following for each of the leadership areas addressed by the core course:

• The level of skill the trainee's job requires for success

• The trainee's level of skill prior to taking the course

• The trainee's level of skill following the course

Respondents also answered questions to assess their perception of the effectiveness of the leadership program.

Analysis revealed that the training did indeed translate into improvements in on-the-job performance in all leadership areas. Both trainees and their immediate supervisors reported statistically significant increases in on-the-job skill levels in all twelve leadership areas following the course ($p < = .05$). Furthermore, the vast majority of trainees and their supervisors felt that:

1. The course contributed to the trainee's job satisfaction and personal growth

2. They would recommend the course to other supervisors

3. DMA should continue its investment in the course

Second, interviews were conducted with a random sample of trainees and their immediate supervisors to obtain specific illustrations of how the leadership behaviors covered in the course were being used on the job. The nearly 100 examples cited by 35 interviewees provided clear anecdotal evidence that trainees were successfully applying the leadership behaviors and skills on the job.

The fourth and final level of evaluation—organizational impact of the course—was determined using the data obtained from the post-training questionnaire along with economic data provided by DMA's training staff. Together, these data provided an indication of the value of the course in relation to its cost; that is, the return on investment (ROI) to DMA.

To calculate the ROI, a methodology was adapted from research conducted at the U. S. Naval Ordnance Station in 1989-1990 (Wright, 1990). The approach called for first assessing the overall degree of job success attributable to a given set of competencies and assigning a dollar value to them based on average salary and benefits of the trainees. This information was then used along with job requirements ratings and pre- and post-course skill ratings to translate course benefits into dollars.

Computations took into account the costs associated with designing, developing, and delivering the training, including administrative and staff costs. The results of this analysis pointed to a return on investment of $2.32 for every dollar invested by DMA in the course for the first year.

One aspect of the course, in particular, should be mentioned. As noted earlier, the early plans for the LDP included an intention to have heavy involvement and the endorsement of senior leaders at the DMA. This involvement continued into each offering of the first-level supervisor core course. Senior DMA managers had a role and actively participated in a portion of the delivery of every offering. The participants' comments on the evaluation reflected the benefits of this practice relative to transmitting a unified DMA message throughout the organization.

Although the LDP is in its early stages of assessment, the DMA LDP is impacting the Agency beyond the anticipated improvement of individual leadership skills. The program, in particular the Mid-level Managers Course, is serving as a principal vehicle for bringing about a significant cultural change in the Agency.

The Mid-level Managers Course has established the first forum for direct dialogue between mid-level leaders (generally GM-14s and GM-15s and equivalent military officers who direct division-level staffs) and senior leaders in the Agency. The CLTs, formed early in the course, exchange viewpoints with senior leaders on issues affecting DMA and their ability to function effectively as leaders and as a team. Obstacles to sound leadership practices are identified in this exchange, and responsibility and ownership are determined.

This open dialogue between groups of leaders in a learning environment is a "first" for the Agency, and is culminated in presentations and discussions with the Director, DMA, on the final day of the course. The Director freely discusses issues raised by the CLTs. Key issues, obstacles, and possible solutions are captured in writing and are shared by the Director with his senior staff in meetings held during the week following the course. This often leads to decisions and actions that impact specific concerns and problems identified in the course.

This closed-loop activity results in a reinforcement of principles taught in class with regard to openness, empowerment, team action, and visionary leadership. As the Agency moves toward the next phase of its evaluation of the LDP, there may be an opportunity to assess results both individually and organizationally.

FUTURE ACTIVITIES

As a continuing development process, the following initiatives are planned or are in process at the time of publication:

1. Design, develop, and implement an executive leadership skills workshop specifically designed for DMA senior executives, candidates for senior executive positions, and equivalent military officers.

2. Design, develop and implement a pre-supervisory leadership skills training course for selected employees who are in non-supervisory positions and who aspire to, and exhibit high potential for, leadership in the Agency.

3. Create a team development program for titled and non-titled leaders throughout the Agency.

4. Conduct near- and long-term evaluation processes to ascertain the LDP's return on investment to the Agency.

SUMMARY

In summary, DMA has made significant progress in addressing identified shortcomings in the development and training of its leaders. It's near-future plans for focused programs for executives and for those aspiring to entry-level leadership positions will ensure a complete, integrated leadership development program. Of equal significance are the dynamic paradigm shifts occurring in DMA's internal communication and decision-making practices.

These changes, embodied by the DMA's active and visible leadership, reinforce the core principles and competencies imparted in the DMA LDP. The LDP has also been integrated with the DMA's Total Quality Management Program. This combination of planned, just-in-time leadership and process-skills performance improvement activities for its employees provides a powerful program of change to help meet the massive challenges confronted by DMA beyond the year 2000.

REFERENCE

Wright, C. (1990, June). *Research report: Return on investment and learning transfer.* Indian Head, MD: U.S. Naval Ordnance Station.

ACKNOWLEDGEMENTS

The overall success of the LDP was due, in large measure, to the personal involvement, commitment and support of a large number of DMA persons. The following persons were highly influential in contributing to this success: Major General William F. James, (USAF), Director, DMA; Penman ("Red") Gilliam, Deputy Director, DMA (formerly Deputy Director for Management and Technology); Kenneth Daugherty, Senior Scientist, Headquarters - DMA (formerly Director, Systems Center); William Hogan, Deputy Director, DMA, for Programs, Production and Operations; Curt Dierdorff, Deputy Director, Human Resources, DMA; James Skidmore, Technical Director, Aerospace Center, St. Louis, MO; Lon Smith, Director, Systems Center (formerly Technical Director, Hydrographic/ Topographic Center, Brookmont, MD); Paul Peeler, Director, Technical Services Center (formerly Technical Director, Reston Center, Reston, VA); and Chuck Hall, Technical Director, Hydrographic/Topographic Center.

The coauthors for this chapter included Edmund R. Karoly (Chief, Human Resource Development and Career Development, Defense Mapping Agency), Alex F. Douds (Project Director, Human Technology, Inc.), and David D. Dubois.

Chapter 10

COMPETENCY-BASED MANAGEMENT DEVELOPMENT FOR SENIOR MANAGERS AT THE NEW ENGLAND TELEPHONE COMPANY

OVERVIEW

The contents of this chapter describe an application of competency model technology that is somewhat different from the applications included in the last two chapters.What is described here is the history, planning, development, and implementation of a competency-based executive leadership development program at the New England Telephone Company (NET), headquartered in Boston, Massachusetts. The Human Resources Department of NET has developed and used competency models for a number of jobs within the organization. In a later section of the chapter, NET's positive and negative experiences with the use of competency model technology are shared.

There was one central question that needed answering: What competencies do NET executives need to lead the organization into the future? NET insisted on ensuring that the competency foundations they chose for the development of their executives were rooted in the strategic plans, directions, and needs of the corporation. This also included a need to ensure that the target population would be convinced that the competencies represented their job requirements.

The research was completed by a team consisting of professional persons internal to NET and external consultants from McLagan, International, Inc. The processes that were used incorporated a variety of information sources—both internal and external to NET. They included the participation of literally hundreds of corporate executives and mid-level managers. The research emphasized concentration on future business conditions, both within and external to the NET environment. Let's examine how this was accomplished.

THE FRONT-END MACRO-NEEDS ANALYSIS AND PLANNING PHASE

The needs analysis and planning stages of the project were initiated shortly after the break-up of the Bell Telephone system. The newly formed New England Telephone Company, a local exchange telephone company, was an outgrowth of the Bell System break-up.

The break-up of the Bell System catapulted the local exchange telephone companies into a sea of changes in technology, competition rather than monopoly, new customer expectations, governmental regulation, organization structure, and the impacts of work force demographics.

Within the context of these factors, an organization climate survey was conducted with the work force. A sample of employees reported that, in their opinion, the existing management team was less than fully capable of leading a healthy new business. At the same time, middle managers voiced their concerns that the management style which was prevalent in the organization at the time was inconsistent with the new business environment. Corporate officers responded by making the development of managers and executives a corporate strategy, as one way of dealing with these problems. A task force was organized to identify the educational and developmental needs of more than 500 middle and executive managers and to formulate ways to address those needs. At NET, this target population included all managers above the first two levels of management. The management development program that resulted from the research served the needs of both executives and middle managers.

Since broad-based ownership of the project results was a project objective from the outset, a large number of persons was involved in product development. First, and most important, an Advisory Committee of 16 middle managers who were "opinion leaders" was formed. The members of this committee had extraordinary responsibilities for this project, which included work on the development of the competency model, providing advice on the data collection protocols, interpretations of the data, and, in general, providing advice and recommendations.

The project resources (people and funding) were provided by two senior executives from the Human Resources Department. They also recruited the Advisory Committee, reviewed project recommendations, and represented the project to the corporate officers, including the president.

An inter-departmental committee, the Human Resources Council, was formed, which consisted of persons who were organizationally one level below the corporate officers. These persons provided guidance for, and endorsement of, the project at critical path points of its development. This Council acted in an advisory capacity to the Human Resources Department.

Finally, a Project Team, which consisted of three Human Resources managers and members of an external consulting firm, planned the project and collected, analyzed, and reported the data. The Project Team worked closely with the Advisory Committee.

As an initial major action, it was necessary to develop a clear set of expectations or parameters for the project. This was done by the senior Human Resource executives and the Project Team. They agreed that, at a minimum, the project results would:

- Address both the present and future needs of the target population

- Verify an alignment of the corporate business strategy with these managers' development

- Emphasize the target managers' job results or outputs rather than the tasks or activities that they performed

- Emphasize the target managers' generic needs across the management levels, and the departments and functional specialties represented by them

- Guarantee ownership by the target population

The project expectations provided a firm foundation for making the following decisions on how the project would be designed and managed:

- The needs of the target population would be determined by completing an empirical study.

- Three project products would result: (1) a job performance model for executives and middle managers, (2) an assessment of these managers' strengths and needs for improvement, and (3) the expectations held by potential participants for a "developmental process."

• The project would involve as broad a base of persons in the planning and conduct of the research as possible.

Next, the job competency model was developed.

DEVELOPMENT OF THE COMPETENCY MODEL

The job competency model research was designed to reveal and describe in generic terms the ideal performance of an NET executive and middle manager. When it was completed, the competency model included a statement of the job competencies and their behavioral indicators for executive and middle managers, the job outputs or results expected of these managers, and the conditions of their performance.

The critical competencies in this case were the broad knowledge and skills that would enable these managers to produce the expected job outputs. The job outputs were the "deliverables" of executive and middle-manager performance to internal and external customers. These outputs could be represented as products, services, information, decisions, and so forth. The criteria were used to judge the excellence or quality of a manager's delivery of each job output from the customers' perspective. The conditions included the environmental factors that were predicted to have the greatest impact upon NET executives' and middle managers' competencies. In order to further define and clarify the elements included in the model, each competency included a sample of behavioral indicators relative to each competency. A sample segment from the competency model that resulted from the research process is included as Figure 10.1.

The primary source of information on the conditions, job outputs, and criteria components of the competency model resulted from brainstorming sessions with the Advisory Committee. Additional surveys and interviews were conducted with other sources to confirm, deny, or enhance the initial findings of the Advisory Committee. The Project Team interviewed fifty-two middle and executive managers (i.e., members of the target population) on the dimensions above. They also interviewed nine of the ten NET corporate officers to verify and expand the model.

Next, the Human Resources Council reviewed the conditions, outputs, and criteria. They recommended that the findings be verified through additional research with external NET stakeholders from several sources. A panel consisting of the following persons was chosen for interviews by the Project Team: two stock brokerage firms, the chairs of two state utility commissions, utilities analysts from two bond-rating companies, four strategic and marketing planners at the holding company that owns NET, a recognized telecommunications consultant, and communications managers from three NET customers. In addition, two focus groups of small business customers and two focus groups of residence customers were conducted.

FUTURE CONDITIONS AFFECTING MANAGEMENT REQUIREMENTS (1990-1994)

Many conditions—technological, competitive, societal, political, financial, organizational—impact our business and, consequently, determine the skills needed to manage the business. The following conditions are predicted to have the biggest impact.

1. *Quality Service* is essential for business success.

2. Competition is *proliferating* and *intensifying*.

3. Customers are demanding *unique communications solutions* and *pricing options*.

4. *Competitors understand* our customers' needs, know how to market and provide service to them.
. . . .

CONTRIBUTIONS OF MIDDLE MANAGERS AND EXECUTIVES

The top 350 managers of NET serve many constituencies: customers, employees, NYNEX management, regulators—to name just a few stakeholder groups. Our service can be described in terms of the the contributions (output) we give to these stakeholders. Our outputs can be decisions, plans, strategies, policies, information, advice, solutions to problems, etc. The lefthand column lists the most critical contributions for 1990-1994, and the right column lists the criteria that make each output excellent from the stakeholders' perspective.

CONTRIBUTIONS AND DEFINITION:	QUALITY REQUIREMENTS: This contribution will be considered excellent when:
1. **STRATEGIC VISION:** Articulation of the long-range direction, goals, and image of the Company	a. Decisions reflect long-term focus rather than short-term issues. b. It reflects an understanding of the market place. . . . .

COMPETENCIES

In order to provide the contributions, managers need to possess expertise in the following eighteen skill and knowledge areas. The relative importance and depth of experience depends on the unique requirements of individual jobs. Generally, various contributions require the use of a mix of knowledge and skills. In order to illustrate what each competency might look like in a general way, sample behavioral indicators are listed for each knowledge and skill area.

BUSINESS/TECHNICAL KNOWLEDGE

1. *Understanding of Business Planning:* Knowing how to assess the internal and external business environment, and to develop strategic, operational, and tactical plans

Develops plans that clearly reflect corporate and departmental priorities

Changes plans based on new data

Figure 10.1: Illustrative Elements of the Management Performance Model (MPM) for Senior Managers at New England Telephone Company

The conditions, outputs, and criteria were also reviewed against NET business plans. The following plans were included for analysis: the current NET Business Plan, the current NET holding company Marketing Plan, and a position paper that was prepared by the NET holding company to stimulate strategic planning by its subsidiaries.

The revisions that were based on the research findings noted above were first provided to the Advisory Committee for approval. Next, the document received review and approval from the Human Resources Council. Following these reviews and approvals, it was determined that the job conditions, outputs, and the criteria were known for NET's executive and middle managers. The next step taken for the completion of the model was the development of the competencies and their behavioral indicators.

The Advisory Committee met and developed a list of job competencies and definitions of them. Next, a survey was designed and conducted whose purpose was to identify NET's outstanding or exemplary managers. These persons were used to identify the most critical job competencies. The entire target population was surveyed. Fifty-two percent of those contacted responded; 100 exemplary managers were identified.

The pool of 100 managers identified above was assigned to one or more of the job outputs. Some managers, by virtue of their responsibilities, were assigned to more than one job output. In general, eight to fourteen managers were assigned to each job output.

The managers identified the most critical job competencies for each of the job outputs. To accomplish this, a checklist of 35 competencies (i.e., those competencies generated by the Advisory Committee) was provided to the respondents. A survey response rate in excess of 80% was achieved. A competency was considered to be critical for job performance when it was checked by at least 50% of the respondents *and* for at least three job outputs. The final list that resulted from these data analyses consisted of fifteen competencies.

The list of fifteen competencies was reviewed by the Advisory Committee. The members of the committee compared these findings with those from earlier research with persons and groups external to NET. This resulted in the addition of three competencies to the list: Regulatory Knowledge, Financial Understanding, and Market Understanding. The Advisory Committee believed the exemplary managers attributed lower values to these competencies than should have been assigned to them. Accordingly, the final competency list consisted of eighteen competency statements.

The remaining (and final) elements of the executive competency model that was to be developed were the behavioral indicators for each of the competencies. Since the elements of the final competency model were to be used to assess managers' strengths and needs for development at a later project stage, a questionnaire was constructed. The questionnaire consisted of behavioral statements derived from the consultants' records, brainstorming products by the Project Team, and individual interviews with three of the exemplary executive managers. Five behavioral indicators were associated with each competency statement in the questionnaire.

Two trials of the questionnaire were completed. The questionnaire was revised based on those trials. Nine managers from the target population sorted the behavioral statements by competency in order to eliminate behaviors that were linked with more than one competency. The questionnaire was revised. Two additional trials of the questionnaire were completed. A principal components factor analysis, using a varimax rotation, confirmed the correlations of the behavioral indicators with the competency statements.

The competencies, their behavioral indicators, the job conditions, outputs, and excellence criteria were completed to form the Management Performance Model (MPM) or competency model. The MPM described what executive performance should be. Next, the model was used to do a micro-needs assessment of middle managers and executives.

THE MICRO-NEEDS ASSESSMENT FOR EXECUTIVES

Two purposes were established for this phase of the project:

1. Verify the need for management competency development.

2. Identify the design priorities.

In order to complete these objectives, data were collected and analyzed from the internal and external sources used to develop the competency model.

Pairs of interviewers met with, and questioned, several persons external to NET. These interviews included the following topics: current problems, future conditions, management's response to these problems and conditions, ways of developing management's capabilities, and the consequences of not coping with the issues. Interview summaries were prepared and those who were interviewed edited the summaries if they felt it was needed. The summaries were content-analyzed for themes and issues. Specific statements in the summaries were identified for the themes and issues. Five topics resulted from the analyses.

Internal to NET, a mail questionnaire survey of sixty corporate executives, representing all levels and departments in the target population, was conducted. The sixty managers were identified by Human Resources Executives as "opinion leaders."

The questionnaire included ninety-five statements about the NET management team. These statements were derived from the excellence criteria included in the competency model. The respondents were directed to make two judgments about each statement:

- The extent to which performance needed improvement

- The changes that could bring about improvement

An 83% response rate was realized for the survey.

The internal survey data were summarized for each item across levels of management and by the job outputs from the competency model. This constituted the internal data base on the target population's performance needs.

The data from the internal and external respondents regarding the development needs of NET executives and middle managers were analyzed. Both the internal and external respondents most often attributed deficiencies to "culture and management style." External sources next cited "management skills" as the reason for organizational deficiencies. On the other hand, internal respondents (and especially those from the middle levels) attributed the deficiencies to "organizational structure." A set of management development needs, relative to the elements of the MPM, was constructed.

The final phase of the micro-needs assessment process was to determine the expectations of the target population regarding the manner in which their development would occur. The product was a list of features that would increase the probability of managers taking advantage of any development process that was researched and created. Ideas were obtained from the managers who were interviewed earlier, and from brainstorming sessions with the Advisory Committee and the Human Resources Council. The middle managers and executives expressed an interest in having an individualized approach to their development. Other suggestions included having a broad range of development resources, the use of reward systems, a focus on individual needs, the use of coaching, and a focus on impacts rather than activities.

APPLICATION OF THE MANAGEMENT COMPETENCY MODEL

In order to align any proposed executive development program with other human resources subsystems, two linkages were identified. The development subsystem was included in NET's strategic planning. Also, the NET "reward system" was aligned so that it supported development. These were both accomplished. In addition, NET human resources managers have aligned systems and policies to support executive manager performance consistent with the elements of the competency model.

Consistent with the findings and actions described above, an approach was adopted that would require executives to manage their own development. This application of competency model technology differs from other applications found in this book in that the competency model was not used to create a training curriculum, courses, or so forth. In this case, NET believed that they should adopt a human resource development *process* rather than a specified *training program* for their executives. Their rationale for this was that they wanted these managers to adopt and maintain the mindset that they should update and expand their competence on a continuous basis throughout their career, rather than feel that they had developmentally "arrived" upon completion of an organizationally endorsed curriculum.

The objective of the Management Development System (MDS), as the process was called, was to help executive and middle level managers develop those competencies critical to NET's business. Essentially, the MDS was designed as a consulting service of the Human Resources Department to NET executives and middle managers. The major goals of MDS were to:

- Help managers understand the performance and contribution that was expected of them

- Help managers determine their strengths and developmental needs

- Help managers locate learning resources

- Teach managers to maximize their learning skills

- Provide guidance on how to informally network and encourage the use of this practice as a means of development

The nine components of the MDS are listed and briefly described below.

- *The "Management Performance Model."* This is the executive and middle manager competency, or performance model, whose development was described earlier.

- *The seminar, "Introduction to Management Development."* This is a half-day session designed to introduce the MDS to the target audience.

- *A diagnostic process.* This is a process designed to provide feedback to managers on their strengths and developmental needs. An instrument is used which is keyed to the job competencies listed in the competency model. Statements of behavior are included for each competency; ratings of the importance of the behavior for a person's job and a rating of the person's expertise in that behavior are included. A manager uses the instrument to collect ratings from their boss, peers, and subordinates; a self-rating is also made.

- *The "Development Planning Workshop."* The manager creates a personalized performance model from the Management Performance Model, analyzes the diagnostic data, creates a self-development plan, and develops a commitment to follow through with the plan. Other topics include coaching and planning developmental discussions with the boss. Networking is done.

- *The Learning Resource Guide.* This is a catalog of learning resources which are organized around each of the competencies. Resource examples include courses, workshops, publications, computer software, audio and videotapes, and so forth. The Guide includes over 250 references.

- *Guide for Development Partners.* This is a booklet that lists ideas on how to give and receive coaching. The common theme of this booklet is "partnership."

- *Support Services.* The executive can request support services from the Human Resources Department. Examples of the services that were provided included resource searches, additional diagnostic surveys, assistance in finding networking contacts, counseling for making changes to the development plan, and consulting in team development with an executive and their reporting managers.

- *The "Benchmarks" instrument.* This commercial instrument was included in MDS due to requests from managers who especially wanted information useful for analyzing the reasons for roadblocks to their careers.

- *"Leadership Development" Workshop.* This two-day workshop, conducted by an external consultant, helps managers examine roadblocks to their careers. A private counseling session is a feature of the workshop, as well as a two-hour discussion with an NET officer.

As noted earlier, MDS was included in the NET Business Plan and was aligned with other NET human resources systems in mutual support of each other. In addition, top-level support for the MDS was realized, and MDS was introduced to the target population in a systematic manner. Deliberate attempts were made to track early experiences with the MDS. A synopsis of the evaluation plan and results follows.

EVALUATION OF THE MDS

Several evaluation projects were completed to determine the effectiveness of the MDS. These seven studies were conducted over a five-year history of the MDS. The primary purpose of these ongoing evaluations was to provide the information needed to maintain and evolve the management development process within NET.

The first study was conducted in order to learn about the overall level of functioning for the management development process. Telephone interviews were conducted with several managers following the first few sessions of the "Development Planning Workshop." It was learned that the managers' use of internal NET courses (i.e., training) and personal reading were the most-used development mechanisms. It was also learned that none of the managers were able to maintain the schedule that was established for completing their development plan. Accordingly, a decision was made to include support services as a major component of the MDS.

In the second study, the demand for various support services was examined. To gather information, participants were contacted six to eight weeks after the "Development Planning Workshop" to review their progress and to offer assistance. Once again, internal training courses and personal reading were the most frequently mentioned development mechanisms that were utilized. In addition, coaching contacts appeared to have a significant effect on the learning experience. Based on this finding, coaching activities were given more attention in the workshop.

The third study examined the potential impact of the MDS on NET training statistics. The early participants reported a deliberate use of NET training resources, and MDS was a part of NET strategy to increase investment in the training and development of employees. The MDS was only one of numerous factors which stimulated an impressive gain in the use of formal training from the 1983-1985 to the 1986-1988 time frame. However, the gain at NET could not be attributed only to the implementation and delivery of the MDS.

The fourth study examined the impact of the MDS experience upon managers' self-development. To gain information on the impact, two groups of randomly selected managers were interviewed. Two groups were contacted: those who had chosen to complete the diagnostic work and the "Development Planning Workshop," and a second group who had completed the orientation portion of the MDS, but who had not taken advantage of the MDS process itself. The subjects in both groups were asked to describe their personal development over the prior twelve months. The following development opportunity categories were used for the analyses: seminars, reading, tapes, partnerships, and job moves. The categories that showed the largest quantitative differences between the two groups of managers were "reading" and "partnerships," which represents networking with colleagues around a developmental issue.

The fifth study attempted to determine indications of the impact of a manager's personal development as a result of participation in the MDS on job performance. A randomized experimental-control-group design was used to examine the impact issue. Although it was acknowledged that the study included measurement difficulties inherent to evaluation projects of this sort, several findings resulted. It was determined that career move recommendations by the manager's boss supported the expectation that MDS participants would be recommended more frequently for promotion or transfer. Another finding was that the MDS seems to have attracted ambitious, upwardly mobile managers.

The sixth study had two related objectives. The first objective was to repeat the executive and middle manager competency model-building process and to document any changes to the job requirements and, therefore, to the development needs of the target population. The second objective was to obtain ideas for improving the MDS. The competency model was then five years old. In brief, a highly similar research methodology and the same target population (executives and middle managers) were used to develop the new MPM.

An advisory group of middle and executive managers developed candidate assumptions about future business conditions affecting NET, and they defined the "contributions" (called "outputs" in the earlier model) expected of NET middle managers and executives. They also identified what they believed were the critical competencies. Interviews with the president, four vice-presidents, and 21 middle and executive managers were conducted, and a draft competency model was prepared, using all of the information then available. The draft competency model was tested with executives in affiliated companies, with communications managers of four large NET customers, industry analysts with two bond-rating services, and two telecommunications consultants. A final executive competency model was prepared.

The contents of the former and new competency models were compared in order to determine differences that might have occurred in the performance expectations of the target population over the five-year period. It must be said, however, that it was not clear just how much of the change that was observed can be attributed to actual changes in the business, as opposed to changes in how the stakeholders perceived the business. The degree of change was found to have been uniform across the three model components (i.e., the future conditions, contributions, and competencies). Changes from the 1985 model were observed in the behavioral indicators included in the 1990 model. These changes were attributed to a change in methodology. The indicators found in the 1985 model resulted from three sources: the Project Team, the consultants' files, and interviews with several managers. By comparison, the indicators in the 1990 model resulted from a brainstorming session with the managers. A richer quantity of results was realized by using the latter method.

Under the "conditions" section, issues of competition replaced earlier concerns about internal organization and technology from the earlier model. In the "contributions" portion of the new (1990) model, there was a shift from getting things done within micro-work units to achieving accomplishments across organizational and corporate boundaries. The trend in changes to the job competencies across the two models was a movement away from a need for traditional forms of "business knowledge" toward a need for skills for successfully coping with change, and especially organization change. The 1990 model placed more emphasis on interpersonal skills, such as influencing skills. These changes appeared to be consistent with a shift toward cooperation across organization boundaries and away from earlier emphases on getting work accomplished within the hierarchy. Overall, the 1990 model reflected changes from the 1985 model that appear to be reasonable for the recent history of American business.

The second study objective was to obtain suggestions about the MDS process. Two suggestions were frequently observed:

- Simplify the diagnostic questionnaire.

- Provide another group experience similar to the "Development Planning Workshop." This reflected an interest by the participants to obtain additional feedback and to interact with other managers around career issues.

The seventh evaluation project examined the relationship of executives' investment in their personal development and the development activities reported by their subordinate employees. The study was conducted in conjunction with a routine NET-wide survey of employee development practices. Analyses revealed that employee development activities were greater in NET organizations that were managed by managers who were involved in their own self-development. The observed increased participation in development tended to be in favor of self-initiated development rather than of management-sponsored development.

Although these studies were conducted in an "action research" environment, where it is typically very difficult to maintain a high level of control over factors that might influence the findings, those responsible for the MDS and the evaluations and the results that are reported above are reasonably confident in the research implications for the MDS. The completion of these studies renewed an awareness of the numerous measurement challenges and problematic areas which are inherent in studying the dimensions and impacts of "soft" processes or programs in a dynamic organization context.

NET's experience in this regard revealed that, in order to accomplish high-quality results from such projects, two resources are needed. First, there must be a long-term commitment to do this type of evaluation work. And second, the evaluation principals must have a knowledge of the organization context in which the evaluation processes, activities, and results occur.

LESSONS LEARNED

Over the past several years, NET's Human Resources Department has applied competency model technology to at least twenty projects; the applications were in the "soft" competencies occupations. Several important lessons were learned from these experiences, which could be of assistance to others who are using, or considering the use of, a competency model (or menu) approach to human resource development. These lessons are by no means exhaustive. As others use the technology and the information in this book, new findings are sure to follow. Until then, the suggestions which follow will lead the way to these new opportunities.

- The MDS process revealed a need to include multiple perspectives on the needs of any target population. Internal and external sources can often have a wide variance in their perspective of the target population's needs.

- The needs analysis, assessment, and planning processes, and the competency model development process (as they were used in the MDS) served as a political process aimed at building support for the eventual outcomes.

- A major problem, recognized very early in the project, was persuading executives to take their development seriously. The project design and activities built awareness and ownership by the target population.

- A clear, well-defined project plan is essential before work is started on the project. This should include the use of a memorandum of understanding and the agreement of all the project partners on elements of the project.

- A group brainstorming approach produces a better quality and quantity of ideas when compared with other practices for determining the behavioral indicators needed for the competency model.

- The greater the level of organization support, the more likely it is that the project will be successful. This is an application of the well-known and often-applied "involvement buys commitment" concept. When the human resources development project leader either fails to obtain or loses support from the client and/or senior management once the project begins, the project will likely fail.

- Competency models require periodic validations over their lifespan in order to ensure that they accurately reflect the job conditions of the subject employees' work situation. One way to view this with regard to management and models for other types of jobs is to link the revision schedule with parallels in the business planning update cycle.

- When commercial or published competency models are used, whether or not they are supplemented by competencies peculiar to the application environment, they must be validated within the context of the application environment.

- Other reasons for a failure to successfully complete a competency model project can also be associated with one or more of the following factors:

    — failure to locate a committed organization sponsor

    — the departure of an otherwise committed sponsor before the project is completed or the results are "institutionalized"

    — an inability of the staff to complete one or more critical tasks that affect project success (e.g., due to a lack of access to a population from which data are required)

    — the unavailability of technical resources

    — other work priorities overshadowing the project or detracting needed resources from the project

— organization realignments or work processes interrupting the model-building processes

— labor disruptions interfering with project completion

— an organization liaison that is critical to project success collapsing for any one of a number of several possible reasons

As increased use is made of competency model technology, new or different techniques and processes will be discovered and perfected. New research results should also enlighten the process. This should reduce or eliminate the potency of some of the current threats to successful use of the approach.

In summary, the case described in this chapter illustrates a successful application of competency model technology to human resource development. Due to the extreme generosity of NET staff, several important lessons they learned during their work were shared. The hope is that others will be inspired to openly share their experiences and suggestions.

REFERENCES

McLagan, P.A. (1989). The Models. In *Models in HRD practice.* Alexandria, VA: American Society for Training and Development.

Rothwell, W.J., & Sredl, H.J. (1992). *The ASDT guide to professional human resource development roles and competencies, Volume II* (2nd ed.). Amherst, MA: HRD Press

ACKNOWLEDGEMENTS

This chapter was coauthored by Martin E. Smith and David D. Dubois. Mr. Smith is currently the Director-Quality, New England Telephone Company, Boston, Massachusetts. He was the Director-Employee Development when the work described in this chapter was completed.

Information included in this chapter was also reported in an article authored by Mr. Smith, entitled " The Search for Executive Skills," that was recently published in *Training and Development* (September, 1992, pp. 88-95). The authors acknowledge, with appreciation, the cooperation of the American Society for Training and Development for their permission to jointly publish a portion of that information in this chapter.

GLOSSARY

Affective Domain. The affective domain of learning outcomes includes learning objectives that emphasize a feeling tone, an emotion, or a degree of acceptance or rejection (Krathwohl, Bloom, & Masia, 1964).

Attitudes. An attitude is a persistent state that modifies an individual's choice of action with regard to objects, persons, or events (Gagne & Briggs, 1979).

Behavior Level Evaluation. Behavior level evaluation, from the Kirkpatrick Evaluation Model, measures changes in job performance, such as the adoption of new or changed behaviors by the participants on the job (Kirkpatrick, 1975).

Boundary Competency. A boundary competency is a competency that shares a relationship with the competency requirements for a job that is either higher or lower in a hierarchy of jobs.

CIPP Evaluation Model. The CIPP (Context, Input, Process, Product) Evaluation Model is a multi-dimensional evaluation model that is useful for designing evaluation studies for decision-making purposes (i.e., formative evaluation), and also for accountability (i.e., summative evaluation) purposes (Stufflebeam, 1974).

Cognitive Domain. The cognitive domain of learning outcomes includes learning objectives which emphasize remembering or reproducing something which has presumably been learned. It also includes learning objectives which involve the solving of some intellectual task for which the individual has to determine the essential problem and then reorder given material or combine it with ideas, methods, or procedures previously learned (Krathwohl et al., 1964).

Cognitive Strategies. Cognitive strategies govern an individual's learning, remembering, and thinking behaviors. The individual solves a variety of practical problems by efficient means. Creative problem solving is an example of a cognitive strategy (Gagne & Briggs, 1979).

Competency-based Curriculum. A competency-based curriculum is one whose content specifications are defined in competence terms, consistent with the definitions above.

Competency Model. A competency model includes those competencies required for satisfactory or exemplary job performance within the context of a person's job roles, responsibilities, and relationships in an organization and its internal and external environments (adapted from Boyatzis, 1982).

Computer Delivery. Computer delivery refers to the delivery of a learning intervention or opportunity which is supported, either in part or wholly, by computer technology.

Concentration Umbrella Strategy. When an organization uses a "Concentration Umbrella Strategy," it concentrates on its recognized strengths—whether in its products or services—within its markets. The strategy is to invest its resources in its current initiatives (Pearce & Robinson, 1985).

Context (C) Evaluation. Context (C) evaluation, from the CIPP Evaluation Model, serves planning decisions by identifying unmet needs, unused opportunities, and underlying problems (Stufflebeam, 1974).

Core Competency. A core competency is one that is a principal or critically essential competency for successful job performance for a given job at a given level in an organization hierarchy.

Core Intervention. A core intervention refers to a performance improvement opportunity whose subject-matter contents are based on one or more core competencies at a given level of an organization hierarchy.

Curriculum. A curriculum consists of a system of performance improvement opportunities (such as courses, programs, learning interventions, or other performance improvement opportunities), the content specifications for them, and a conceptual framework for linking the opportunities in a sequential manner which will provide efficient and effective learning opportunities for employees.

Curriculum Integration. Curriculum integration is a curriculum planning process that ensures the inclusion and development of the critical job competencies, each at their appropriate levels of subject-matter content depth and breadth across all elements or strata of an organization's performance improvement curriculum. "Appropriate" in this case means that the subject-matter content is developed at the precise level that is required in order to enhance the probability of the employees' achievement of the job outputs within expected levels of quality.

Customized Generic Model Method. The Customized Generic Model Method for developing a competency model relies on the researcher's identification of a universe of candidate generic competencies that are believed to fully characterize the attributes of the exemplary performers for a job in the organization. The universal list of competencies is then researched and interpreted within the job and the larger organization context. As a result, the specific competencies that characterize the successful employee are verified or denied by the research. Other attributes for the competency model are also researched. The job competencies and the other attributes are then used to develop a customized job competency model.

Delivery. Delivery is the act of providing or otherwise making available one or more learning opportunities for employees.

Development. Development is learning that is not focused or referenced to any particular job (Nadler & Nadler, 1989).

Disinvestment Strategy. When an organization, due to economic or financial losses, decreases or dissolves its operation in order to minimize losses to its stakeholders or constituents, it is using a "Disinvestment Strategy." This strategy could include retrenchment, turnaround, divestiture, or liquidation (Pearce & Robinson, 1985).

Education. Education is learning focused on a future job for the learner (Nadler & Nadler, 1989).

Elective Intervention. An elective learning intervention is one that includes subject-matter content that supports or enhances the acquisition of one or more core competencies.

External-Growth Strategy. When an organization uses an "External-Growth Strategy," it expands its existing resources or strengthens its market position or constituency base through the acquisition or creation of new businesses or constituencies. The emphases are on horizontal or vertical integration. Diversification could include concentric or conglomerate diversification. The overall strategy is to focus existing resources on the development of new or different resources (Pearce & Robinson, 1985).

Flexible Job Competency Model Method. As a competency model development method, the Flexible Job Competency Model Method relies upon having a wide variety of comprehensive information sources for inclusion in its research base. A feature of this method is the identification and use of future assumptions about the organization and the job. Depending upon the organization's preferences, internal and external sources of information can be used. The use of this method results in the availability of job roles, job outputs, quality standards for the outputs, and behavioral indicators for each job competency.

Flexible Job Design. Flexible job design is a job design technique that leads an organization through a series of steps to specify precisely what outcomes it wants to produce and the kinds of jobs and job holders that will be required to produce those outcomes. The emphasis on using participative methods and a very specific and concrete language to facilitate the precise descriptions of what an organization wants to do are features of this job design technique (McLagan, 1990).

Generic Model Overlay Method. When an organization uses the Generic Model Overlay Method to acquire a competency model, it selects or obtains a prepared competency model and then overlays or superimposes it on a job within the organization. Little or no internal resources are invested in developing the competency model internal to the organization.

Human Resource Development. Human resource development (HRD) is an organized set of learning experiences provided by an employer within a specified period of time to bring about the possibility of performance improvement and/or personal growth (Nadler & Nadler, 1989).

Input (I) Evaluation. Input (I) evaluation, from the CIPP Evaluation Model, serves structuring decisions by projecting and analyzing alternative procedural designs (Stufflebeam, 1974).

Intellectual Skills. This includes learning how to do something of an intellectual nature. When an intellectual skill is being demonstrated, the learner shows how an intellectual operation is carried out (Gagne & Briggs, 1979).

Internal-Growth Umbrella Strategy. When an organization uses an "Internal-Growth Umbrella Strategy," it encourages innovation, expands its markets, develops new or related products or services, or establishes joint ventures or coalitions with other organizations to strengthen its own position. The overall strategy is to build upon existing strengths. Emphases are on market development, product development, innovation, and joint venture (Pearce & Robinson, 1985).

Job Competence. Job competence is an employee's capacity to meet (or exceed) a job's requirements and produce the job outputs at an expected level of quality within the constraints of the organization's internal and external environments.

Job Competence Assessment Method. The Job Competence Assessment Method for developing a competency model relies on the use of a rigorous, empirical research procedure, called Job Competence Assessment, to determine job competencies that differentiate exemplary from average job performance. Exemplary and average performers are interviewed about the dimensions of their job performance. Once the competencies have been determined, they—in conjunction with other job elements—are used to construct a job competency model (adapted from Klemp, 1982).

Job Competency. A job competency is an underlying characteristic of an employee (i.e., motive, trait, skill, aspects of one's self-image, social role, or a body of knowledge) which results in effective and/or superior performance in a job (Boyatzis, 1982).

Job Competency Menu. A job competency menu lists all the competencies that are important for the successful production and delivery of the entire range of an organization's job outputs (McLagan, 1990).

Job Outputs Menu. A job outputs menu consists of a list of all the products or services that an individual or group delivers to others, especially to its customers, clients, or colleagues (McLagan, 1989, p. 77).

Learning Intervention. A learning intervention is any planned or structured event that provides an employee with an opportunity to acquire competence.

Learning Level Evaluation. Learning level evaluation, from the Kirkpatrick Evaluation Model, measures the learning achievement that was realized by the participants (Kirkpatrick, 1975).

Learning Strategy. A learning strategy consists of the methods, techniques, approaches, or media that are used to encourage or facilitate learning.

Lower Boundary Competency. A lower boundary competency is a competency that is prerequisite to a job or is a principal competency for the next lower order job in the job hierarchy.

Modified Job Competence Assessment Method. The Modified Job Competence Assessment Method is a competency model development method. It uses the Job Competence Assessment research procedure, with the modification of having the exemplary and average performers, who would normally be interviewed face to face, write or otherwise record their critical behavior stories for use by the researcher.

Motor Skills. Motor skills require a learner to carry out motor activities in a variety of contexts (Gagne & Briggs, 1979).

Pilot Test. A pilot test is a trial or live tryout of an instructional event (or series of events) with a subset of the target population for which the event or events were envisioned.

Principal Competency. A principal competency is any competency whose acquisition by an employee is essential or critical for successful job performance.

Proactive. A proactive action is one that is taken by an organization that acknowledges or addresses future or forecasted employee job performance or requirements.

Process (P) Evaluation. Process (P) evaluation, from the CIPP Evaluation Model, serves implementing decisions by monitoring project operations (Stufflebeam, 1974).

Product (P) Evaluation. Product (P) evaluation, from the CIPP Evaluation Model, serves recycling decisions by identifying and assessing project results (Stufflebeam, 1974).

Psychomotor Domain. The psychomotor domain of learning outcomes includes learning objectives that emphasize some muscular or motor skill, some manipulation of material and objects, or some act which requires neuromuscular coordination (Krathwohl et al., 1964).

Reaction Level Evaluation. Reaction level evaluation, from the Kirkpatrick Evaluation Model, assesses the reactions of the participants to a program or intervention, including such items as its content, instructional design, the media used, the instructor's performance, and so forth (Kirkpatrick, 1975).

Reactive. A reactive action is one that acknowledges or addresses the results or consequences of some circumstance or event in the organization's internal or external environments that impavts the job performance needs or requirements of its employees.

Results Level Evaluation. Results level evaluation, from the Kirkpatrick Evaluation Model, assesses the strategic impacts of the program or learning intervention on the total organization and seeks findings that illustrate how the acquired competencies worked, either singularly or in combination, to achieve the organization's strategic goals (Kirkpatrick, 1975).

Simulation. A simulation is a cross between a role-play and a case study. Participants are asked to act out a long-term process or take part in a dramatic event simulating real life (Rothwell & Sredl, 1992, p. 530).

Strategic Analysis. A strategic analysis is a process (or set of processes) an organization uses to methodically examine its goals and objectives relative to its present and forecasted strengths, weaknesses, opportunities, and threats.

Subordinate Competency. A subordinate competency is one that is of lower order or lower rank relative to another competency.

System. A system is a collection of interdependent, organized parts that work together in an environment to achieve the purpose of the whole (McLagan in Gradous, 1989).

Training. Training results in learning that is focused on the present job of the learner (Nadler & Nadler, 1989).

Upper Boundary Competency. An upper boundary competency is one that is a principal competency for a higher order job in a hierarchy of jobs. Upper boundary competencies share strong relationships with one or more of the principal or critical competencies for the job where the upper boundary designation was given.

Verbal Information. This is verbal knowledge. Verbal information is learned in both formal and incidental ways. The learner states or otherwise communicates information (Gagne & Briggs, 1979).

INDEX

A

M